Public Knowledge and
Environmental Politics
in Japan and the United States

Public Knowledge and Environmental Politics in Japan and the United States

John C. Pierce, Nicholas P. Lovrich,
Taketsugu Tsurutani, and Takematsu Abe

Westview Press
BOULDER, SAN FRANCISCO, & LONDON

Westview Special Studies in Public Policy and Public Systems Management

This Westview softcover edition is printed on acid-free paper and bound in library-quality, coated covers that carry the highest rating of the National Association of State Textbook Administrators, in consultation with the Association of American Publishers and the Book Manufacturers' Institute.

Published in 1989 in the United States of America by Westview Press, Inc., 5500 Central Avenue, Boulder, Colorado 80301, and in the United Kingdom by Westview Press, Inc., 13 Brunswick Centre, London WC1N 1AF, England

Library of Congress Cataloging-in-Publication Data
Public knowledge and environmental politics in Japan and the United
   States / by John C. Pierce . . . [et al.].
      p.   cm.—(Westview special studies in public policy and
public systems management)
   ISBN 0-8133-7662-9
   1. Environmental policy—Japan—Citizen participation—Case
studies. 2. Environmental policy—United States—Citizen
participation—Case studies. I. Pierce, John C., 1943–   .
II. Series.
HC465.E5P83 1989
363.7'057'0952—dc20
                                                    89-22528
                                                        CIP

Printed and bound in the United States of America

The paper used in this publication meets the requirements of the American National Standard for Permanence of Paper for Printed Library Materials Z39.48-1984.

10   9   8   7   6   5   4   3   2   1

Contents

Tables and Figures

xviii

Figures

Preface

This book grows out of the authors' conviction that as public policy issues become increasingly suffused with scientific and technical content, they correspondingly become more difficult for the citizens of democratic polities to understand. We see a fundamental irony in this development. The postindustrial age giving rise to the profusion of technically and scientifically complex policy issues also has generated increased demands on the part of citizens in democratic nations for public involvement in the formulation of policy in those same issue areas. To us, a critical issue for political scientists is determining the degree to which mass publics have the capacity and the motivation to respond to the challenges posed by the heightened need for policy-relevant knowledge in complex issue domains. This book is an attempt to confront that issue and some of its derivative concerns.

We have chosen a cross-national context for the examination of the importance of policy-relevant information in contemporary postindustrial democracies. Such a comparative analysis, in our view, is imperative. It is clear that political cultures differ in how they conceptualize public involvement in the policy process, in how science and technology are treated in politics, and in their norms for access to and the dissemination of policy-relevant information in the political process. We reach a number of conclusions about what aspects of the high complexity/high involvement irony are common to postindustrial democracies and what aspects are nation-specific. The results of the study reported here underscore the importance of cross-national research; our findings indicate clearly that the role of information in citizen responses to environmental policy does depend on whether it occurs in Japan or in the United States. The character of this interaction is, in most respects, consistent with what generally are considered to be the distinctive features of the Japanese and American political cultures.

The first chapter offers several reasons for our decision to examine the issue of public involvement in complex policy areas in the realm of environmental politics. Contemporary environmental issues are both complex and highly sensitive to public demands for citizen participation in policy decisions. Moreover, environmental politics is prototypical of the cross-stratal issues common to the postindustrial age and thus is particularly amenable to cross-national analysis. Of course, other policy areas require similar examination as well. The nature of the policy domain investigated (e.g., science-based as opposed to ideological or class-based concerns) likely structures the way democratic citizenries respond to the need for information facing them as they seek to participate in political decisions. It is our hope that the critical issues raised in this book on the environmental policy domain will also be examined in other policy areas. Such comparative public policy research will add importantly to our knowledge about how the high complexity/high participation irony of postindustrial politics is likely to play itself out in contemporary democratic polities.

Reflecting a desire to write for a somewhat broad audience, we have in many cases avoided the use of the more unfamiliar statistical analyses and omitted the often detailed account of measurement validation, survey documentation and similar important--though exceedingly tedious--technical material. For the particularly curious reader most of this type of analysis and detailed background information is available in one or more of the several primary articles published in professional journals. In particular, the following would be of special interest in this regard: "'Knowledge Gap' Phenomena..." *Communications Research* (1984); "Water Pollution Control in Democratic Societies..." *Policy Studies Review* (1985); "Policy-Relevant Information and Public Attitudes..." *Water Resources Bulletin* (1986); "Vanguards and Rearguards in Environmental Politics..." *Comparative Political Studies* (1986); and "Culture, Politics and Mass Publics..." *Journal of Politics* (1986).

John C. Pierce
Nicholas P. Lovrich
Taketsugu Tsurutani
Takematsu Abe

Acknowledgments

The authors of any book such as this incur numerous debts. We are no exception in this regard, for we owe much to an extraordinary number of people and institutions. Limitations of space preclude a complete listing of acknowledgments, but the following parties were particularly crucial to the completion of this work.

Funds for the research reported here were provided by the Japan/U.S. Friendship Commission in the form of a grant to Lovrich and Abe administered by the Institute for International Education. The Ohta Foundation (Tokyo) provided extensive support to the entire project, including a visiting professorship to Pierce at Nihon University. Nihon University and Washington State University both provided facilities and staff assistance to all members of the research team. While these institutions made it possible for us to conduct our research (for which we are enormously grateful), they bear no responsibility for the contents of the book and should not be blamed for errors of omission or commission.

A number of individuals assisted us in both our Washington and Japanese settings. At this point, the most we can do is list their names, but they should know that our gratitude goes much deeper than that simple enumeration. In Washington State Morey Haggin, Steve Hasson, Margaret Portman and Bill Gray were all essential to the success of our research in Spokane. At Nihon University and in Shizuoka Prefecture Kenji Yamamoto, Masayuki Akiyama, Tsukasa Nishida and Katherine Lovrich were essential to making our research project possible.

There is one person to whom we wish to give particular acknowledgment. Ruth Self, who has had the responsibility for preparing the final manuscript for publication, deserves special recognition. It has been a complex and complicated task inherited from Cynthia Avery as part of a new job. She has handled this enormous task with grace and competence. We promise not to put her through the same protracted torture in the near future.

Finally, we wish to acknowledge the citizens, activists and public officials of Spokane County, Washington, and the cities of Mishima, Numazu and Fuji City in Shizuoka Prefecture, Japan. Their willing participation as survey respondents and informants in this study serves to underscore the capacity of Japanese and American citizens for informed participation in democratic government.

1

Knowledge: The Missing Link

Introduction

The complex content of modern public policy poses special challenges to the citizens of democratic polities. Not only must the public monitor and move policy-makers, it also must counter the claim that its members are ignorant of political fundamentals. The critical need for public knowledge has produced a "legitimacy crisis" surrounding democratic policy formation (Dahl, 1985). Elsewhere this crisis has been called democracy's technical information quandary. "How can the democratic ideal of public control be made consistent with the realities of a society dominated by technically complex policy questions?" (Pierce and Lovrich, 1986). A central theme of this book is that this quandary reflects an irony of the present age. In large part, the forces that produce an increased demand for public involvement also account for much of the complexity causing that involvement to be problematic.

The thesis of this book is that the changes produced by advanced technology and high levels of societal education and media dispersion magnify the importance of policy-relevant knowledge among democratic publics. "Policy-relevant knowledge" refers to the information democratic publics have that will help them understand policy disputes and their implications. Policy-relevant knowledge concerns the conditions that produce policy disputes, the rationales for policy alternatives, and the technical elements of policy implementation. This study contends that such knowledge is critical to the public's ability to understand the postindustrial policy agenda, that such knowledge is essential to understanding the implications of policy alternatives for personal values, and that this type of knowledge is a source of power when citizens are moved to political action.

This book reports a study of citizen knowledge in two postindustrial democracies. The study sites in Japan and the United States and the policy contexts are similar, but the two nations are quite different in their social, cultural and political past. Environmental

1

pollution (water pollution more specifically) is the particular policy context for the study. Pollution policy clearly has complex scientific and technical content. Environmental policy stimulates political action; it has been one of the main arenas of the fight for greater citizen involvement (Pierce and Doerksen, 1976); and it strikes directly at the heart of the political and social values most typical of postindustrial societies (Milbrath, 1984). The environmental policy area is thus nearly ideal for testing the crucial role of knowledge in the relationship of individuals to the democratic political process in postindustrial societies.

This book is prompted by the observation that while clearly important, knowledge is a neglected element in attempts to understand public responses to postindustrial politics. Our argument begins with the proposition that postindustrialism has had a profound effect on public value structures. This much is not new (Inglehart, 1977); but postindustrialism has also heightened the need for specialized knowledge to link those values to political choices.

Value structures among citizens have been studied in some detail in Europe, as well as in Japan and the United States. However, the position taken here is that the study of public knowledge and its impact is equally important to the concern with values. Knowledge provides citizens with the means to identify their self-interest in the political environment. Knowledge assists the public in achieving that self-interest through effective action. Knowledge is an instrument for organizing thoughts about the content of public policy. And finally, knowledge links the public's values to their policy preferences. This study assesses empirical evidence germane to these claims. We begin by reconstructing the line of reasoning that led us to this position, starting with a brief overview of "postindustrialism."

Postindustrialism

Many works examine the social, economic and political implications of postindustrialism (Touraine, 1971; Roszak, 1972; Bell, 1973; Huntington, 1974; Heisler, 1974; Lasch, 1972). A few central features of postindustrial society can be identified from this body of work:

> ...the major features of postindustrial society that emerge...include, among others, the majority of labor employment to be found in the so-called service sector, the service sector generating a larger share of the gross-national product (GNP) than the agricultural and manufacturing sectors combined, a high level of affluence and mass

material well-being, the national economy becoming "knowledge-intensive" (Tsurutani, 1977: 6-7).

Instrumental to postindustrial economic changes is a reliance on modern technology (Ladd and Hadley, 1978: 184). Technology reduces the demand for labor in traditional manufacturing and agricultural areas and increases the demand for and opportunities in the service sector. Technological development itself stimulates the need for special expertise; as technology becomes more specialized and developed, so does the knowledge required to operate it become more differentiated and segmented.

The development of postindustrial systems thus affects who has power and influence (Freudenberg and Rosa, 1984: 339). Postindustrialism both increases the political claims and enhances the favored locations of those with specialized knowledge, thereby creating an "expert elite" (Dahl, 1985). Somewhat ironically, it also expands the size of this elite. As Ladd and Hadley note,

A technologically advanced society requires a mammoth intellectual stratum to direct its sundry operations, but at the same time only a technologically advanced system can generate enough wealth to afford such a stratum. The relationship between a civilization technicienne of mass prosperity and the intelligentsia, then, is symbiotic. Science, technology, knowledge generally, are obviously creations of intellectuals and their client groups. But the intelligentsia depends upon the largess of advanced industrialism (1978: 184).

Thus, power is rooted in knowledge for those portions of society particularly intertwined with the technology. The technological experts are central to and dependent on this newly developed "iron triangle" of postindustrialism--knowledge, affluence, and technology--the inter-connection among which produces power and influence.

The symbiotic relationships among knowledge, technology, and affluence--and the elevation and expansion of the "intelligentsia" and its political power--have been widely noted (Moore, 1979; Benveniste, 1972). The other side of this symbiotic coin is the implication of these interlocking developments for other participants in postindustrial political processes. If postindustrial politics enhances the influence of those with expert status, then others must lose power in relative terms. Of special importance is the consequence of this change for the influence of mass publics. One central political question becomes this--"Are citizens the big losers in postindustrialism?" When the issues confronting the policy process require specialized knowledge, the status of democratic publics clearly becomes threatened (DeSario and Langton, 1984). This threat is especially ironic. The forces leading to the increased power of experts also produce increased demands for public participation. The consequence of these forces for citizen demands on government will be discussed shortly. At this point, we summarize briefly the importance of technical and scientific policy issues.

Ideology and Technical and Scientific Issues

The postindustrial era changed the nature of political conflict and the character of the political agenda. Few trends in western democracies were more widely predicted than the "end of ideology" (Bell, 1962). Traditional divisions between the "haves" and the "have-nots" were defined in terms of the struggle between liberals and conservatives--or between socialism and capitalism. Political discussion revolved around the appropriate role of the state in economic redistribution.

Should government intervene to redistribute wealth and assure some degree of social equity? The widespread economic dislocation of the 1930s and 1940s heightened the intensity of the struggle between those arguing for social welfare democracies and those defending a substantially less intrusive role for government. Because this issue was fought on the territory of political economy, politics became organized along economic dimensions. To a significantly lesser degree, divisions within mass publics were also based on these economic dimensions (Alford, 1963). The fundamental criterion for the comparison of party systems was the extent to which partisan allegiances were based in social and economic classes (Lipset and Rokkan, 1967). Even in those systems in which the mass public failed to hold consistent social welfare beliefs and partisan attachments, such as the United States (Converse, 1964), political elites fit the dominant social welfare model of western politics. Democratic and Republican party elites, for example, differed widely in their beliefs about social and economic policy questions (McClosky, 1964).

By the 1960s, though, the end of ideological politics began to be predicted with increased frequency. Thus,

> ...the wealth of the society has been enlarged to a point where the majority of the population is beyond subsistence concerns. Because of affluence thus construed, a mass public can partake of values previously limited to only a few...(Ladd and Hadley, 1978: 184).

On what basis, then, would ideological conflicts be fought? For many, the answer seemed to be that the traditional ideological contests would cease to be held, for if they were, nobody would show up.

The history of the 1960s and 1970s is well-known; in spite of many predictions to the contrary, ideology failed to disappear. Ideological conflict in fact mushroomed to a breadth and height few had envisioned. By most accounts, the ideological issues and the reasons people divided on them were quite different from those of earlier years. The affluence of the postindustrial society created a fundamental change in public value structures, leading to novel issue demands such as civil rights, environmentalism and women's rights (Inglehart, 1971). The impact of postindustrialism on public values, and through those values on the public issue agenda, is described in subsequent sections. The important point here is that ideological politics persisted.

The scientific and technological basis of postindustrial society also had a substantial impact on the public policy agenda, adding new elements to old policy problems and the role of science and technology itself has become a source of conflict. Nelkin has written:

> Indeed controversy seems to erupt over nearly every aspect of science and technology as decisions once defined as technical (within the province of experts) have become intensely political (Nelkin, 1984: 9-10).

This process links science and technology to politics as a consequence of a *redefinition of their role*--"once the source of safety, science and technology have become the source of risk..." (Douglas and Wildavsky, 1982: 10).

One consequence of these changes is that more public policy issues are scientific and technological in their content. Another result is a new skepticism toward science and technology. A high technology and an advanced science create new possibilities for individuals and for societies. New scientific achievements, whether they are actual or contemplated (e.g., recombinant DNA, organ transplantation technology, Strategic Defense Initiative), also raise new issues about what *ought* to be done and about their anticipated practical and normative consequences.

Thus, from the citizen's perspective, the technological policy agenda has several faces. For the public, scientific issues pose difficult new tasks in linking policy alternatives to fundamental values. Citizens are on unfamiliar ground, and their past political cues seem inappropriate or irrelevant. How is the citizen to become informed about Star-Wars defense technology, the "Greenhouse Effect," ozone depletion, hazardous waste disposal, or acid rain deposition? Moreover, a heightened sense of risk and threat accompanies many of these newly placed issues. Individuals often fear that the costs of making the wrong decision are much higher and potentially more destructive than ever before (Short, 1984).

The risk perceived, the uncertainty, and the absence of guidance by traditional political values combine to raise significant questions about the public's role. On the one hand, these new dimensions to public policy may only serve to highlight the need for the public to become more involved in the policy process. The idea that stakes are just too great to be left in the hands of the experts is a sentiment increasingly heard (Barber, 1984). On the other hand, the presence of numerous scientific and technical issues bolsters the long-held argument that the public should be cordoned off from the policymaking process. Thus,

> ...when technology-intensive public policy is brought to the public forum in relationship to arms limitation, to energy management, to environmental conservancy, to costs of health care, and to the more subtle threats to freedom, there is almost complete lack of public understanding. Rather, there is massive focus on instant gratification, via governmental intervention (Wenk, 1979: 32-33).

Ophuls echoes this view with his comment: "...the average man has neither the time to inform himself nor the requisite background for understanding such complex technical problems" (1977: 159-160).

These technical and scientific policy issues thus raise basic questions about the level of public knowledge, about the criteria by which the public will judge policy alternatives, and about the extent to which the public should be involved in resolving those issues (Van Til, 1984). The purpose of this book is to address some of those questions in two countries that share many traits of postindustrialism, but differ profoundly in historical and cultural context.

Postindustrialism and Value Change

Not only has postindustrialism changed the policy agenda, it is widely argued that it has also changed the foundations of the public's responses to public policy issues (Vickers, 1972). The currently dominant interpretation of postindustrial value change is found in the work of Ronald Inglehart (1971; 1977; 1981), which in turn grows out of Abraham Maslow's research on "the hierarchy of human needs"

(1970; 1971). The fundamental assumption in Maslow's work is that for the individual, some personal needs are more important and more basic than are other needs. As Inglehart notes, "the fact that unmet physiological needs take priority over social, intellectual or aesthetic needs has been demonstrated all too often in human history; starving people will go to almost any lengths to obtain food" (1981: 881). Thus, physiological needs are more fundamental, more basic than are the social, intellectual or aesthetic needs.

If the basic physiological needs are perceived to be in jeopardy, the individual will sacrifice the achievement of the less basic needs in order to achieve those more fundamental states. Inglehart argues that it is not the presence of an actual threat to these needs that generates the individual's values [or, as Rokeach would say, "preferred end-states" (1968)]; instead, it is the individual's *perception* of the threat that is crucial. Thus, individuals may have values designed to satisfy basic needs because they perceive them to be threatened, even if no "realistic" threat obtains. Inglehart refers to this general phenomenon in specifying his "scarcity hypothesis":

> An individual's priorities reflect the socioeconomic environment: one places the greatest subjective value on those things that are in short supply (1981: 881).

Yet, it does not follow that individuals will automatically revert to more fundamental values when times are bad, then relinquish those same lower order values when economic conditions later improve. Personal value preferences are less elastic than such a short-term interpretation would suggest. Individuals are said to acquire and *hold* on to the values that reflect the conditions prevailing during the period of their initial acquisition. Research in political socialization would suggest that it is during adolescence that individuals first acquire the ability to conceptualize politics in the relatively abstract terms suggested by Inglehart's theory (Sigel and Hoskin, 1981).

The relevance of this theory for postindustrial societies is apparent. Postindustrial countries are characterized by, among other things, widespread affluence (Gappert, 1979). This affluence has been accompanied by a relative absence of large scale military conflict. Individuals reared during the postindustrial era--with its high expectations for continued peace and prosperity--would then be likely to emphasize values reflecting the satisfaction of higher order needs. In stark contrast, individuals raised during the Depression and during the era of World Wars should be expected to hold political values which reflect the basic needs of security, safety, and sustenance.

Inglehart has characterized these two fundamental value orientations as "post-materialist" and "materialist," and he suggests that the post-materialist value orientation will be prevalent among postindustrial generations. In Inglehart's initial research, which focused on six European countries (1971), he found substantial cohort differences in value orientations. Younger generational cohorts raised during the era of affluence were more likely than older cohorts to manifest value orientations reflecting higher order needs. In a later study, Inglehart reports that many of the 1960s postmaterialists carried with them into and through the 1970s their focus on "higher level" values (1981).

Inglehart's work stimulated specific country studies which sought either to apply his framework, or to call it into question. In most cases there is agreement that some kind of value change occurred in response to the affluence and security of the postindustrial era. At the same time, some scholars suggest that value dimensions different from those reflected in post-materialism more adequately capture that value change. In some cases, the theory and the measures of political values were said to fail in particular social settings. Most of the critical response to the Inglehart value research is developed either in the context of studies of single European countries (Van Deth, 1983; Marsh, 1978; Lafferty and Knutsen, 1985) or in studies of politics in Japan (Ike, 1973).

Inglehart (1981: 331) has shown the relative proportion of materialists and post-materialists in a number of countries, including the United States and Japan. Using 1972 data, he found that the ratio of materialists (31%) to postmaterialists (12%) in the United States is only 2.65, one of the lowest of 13 countries. In contrast, in Japan the ratio is 9.20 (46.5% to 5%), the highest of the 13 countries studied. This evidence suggests that up to the early 1970s Japanese values had not yet come to reflect the impact of postindustrialism.

Nabutaka Ike (1973) has argued that value change in Japan is less a shift from materialism to post-materialism than a change from a collectivity orientation to one of "individuation." Ike accepts the notion of significant value change in Japan, and he is even open to its roots being planted in affluence and security. He suggests, though, that it is value change per se, rather than its particular direction, that is common to postindustrial countries. According to Ike, one must first understand the character of the pre-change values. In Japan, for example, where collectivism has been emphasized, the youth of the privileged postindustrial age may yearn for privatization. In the West, however, quite the opposite may well be the case. While the fortunate youth of postindustrial Japan and America both reject traditional values, the consequences of that rejection would be expected to differ greatly.

By far the most broadranging attack on the applicability of the Inglehart analysis to Japan has been formulated by Scott Flanagan (1979, 1980, 1982). Flanagan argues that the fundamental value change in Japan has not been from materialism to post-materialism, but rather from a traditional to a libertarian orientation. According to Flanagan, the affluence of the postindustrial era frees many Japanese from their traditional value orientations such as pietism, conformity, and deference to authority (1979: 274).

To recapitulate, largely because of the affluence of the post-war decades, postindustrial society is believed to have induced fundamental value changes. In turn, these value transformations have altered the character of public opinion on many political issues. It is to this impact on public policy preferences that many scholars attribute fundamental shifts in the nature of the politics of Western democracies, the concern of the following section.

The Consequences of Value Change

We have suggested that value change in postindustrial societies has produced changes in many basic political beliefs. As Flanagan notes:

> ...in such issues as pollution, the quality of life, participatory democracy, and general socio-political reform, progressive parties in both Japan and Western Europe have seized upon some potentially powerful political issues that are very much in consonance with the value reorientations presently taking place within these advanced industrial societies (Flanagan, 1980: 205).

Many of the "new politics" issues (Miller and Levitin, 1976) and much of the demand for governmental openness derive from the new values attendant to postindustrial society.

Two particular value-induced changes are especially striking--the shift in the political issue agenda, and the demand for greater popular involvement in the resolution of public issues on that agenda (Heidenheimer et al., 1975). In the first case, individuals with postmaterialist value structures are likely to advocate a political agenda reflecting concerns for "higher" level needs. The items on this agenda include environmentalism, social and political equality, participative forms of economic and political institutions, and an opposition to the use of military force for the advancement of national interests. Peace, protection of the environment, democratization, and collective economic security have become hallmarks of the postindustrial political agenda (Buchanan and Wagner, 1978: 1-8).

Frequently linked to this policy agenda has been an increased demand for public involvement in government (Inglehart, 1979: 314). Along with the heightened concern for the natural environment, for example, came a clear demand for widening the scope of citizen participation in determining environmental policy. This new public involvement created problems for those decision makers previously shielded from public influence by their special knowledge and expertise (Mazmanian and Nienaber, 1979: 167-179). This heightened claim for public involvement also increased the importance of citizen knowledge levels. With what competence will individuals enter the policy arena? The importance of citizen knowledge levels is elaborated in the next section.

The Information Link

To this point we have described some fundamental changes associated with postindustrialism. Postindustrialism created value change, and that value change resulted in increased demands for public involvement in policy formation. The combination of heightened claims for citizen involvement and more complex policy issues places a premium on public policy-relevant knowledge. Thus, this study focuses on policy-relevant information holding among the publics of Japan and the United States. Public knowledge has received considerable scholarly attention, but rarely in a cross-national context. Even though the centrality of public knowledge in postindustrial politics is particularly clear, it has received surprisingly little notice. This linkage role of policy-relevant knowledge seems especially important in scientific and technical issues, and in the novel scientific and technological solutions proposed for traditional issues. Given the likely differences in the way different cultures affect citizen behavior, moreover, the comparison of the dynamics of knowledge to political action linkage would seem particularly instructive to the student of contemporary postindustrial politics.

The importance of policy-relevant knowledge clearly extends to political action. Postmaterial values stimulate a greater desire for political involvement (Barnes and Kaase, 1979). The dictum that "knowledge is power" thus takes on a special relevance. Individuals with more knowledge will have more resources at their disposal when attempting to influence policy makers. Similarly, the knowledgeable will be able to better judge which strategies and which policy alternatives most advance their cause. The empowering effects of knowledge should be highlighted in policy areas with scientific and technical content. Indeed, in these areas experts and officials may use the public's apparent lack of technical expertise to justify excluding them from involvement in the policy process.

Critical Questions

The preceding discussions raise many critical questions for the proper understanding of contemporary politics in postindustrial democracies. This section provides an overview of some of those questions, and how this study attempts to address them.

The Concentration of Knowledge

Knowledge is said to be a major source of power, especially in those policy areas with significant technical and scientific content. The distribution of knowledge across the public will thus structure the distribution of power and influence in the policy process. If knowledge is evenly dispersed, a society may enjoy a more egalitarian distribution of power. Knowledge may reinforce the exercise of independent judgment among a wider spectrum of citizens, reducing their reliance on others. But, as Chapter two notes, knowledge may not be undimensional; there are different kinds of knowledge (e.g., scientific, technical, political, agenda), and different people may hold different types of policy-relevant knowledge.

Chapter two also suggests that individuals may be either information generalists or information specialists. That is, one may know a great deal about how policy is made but very little about the scientific and technical elements of the policy field. In contrast, some people may know a good deal about a wide range of public issues, but not know how to participate effectively. Whether one is a generalist or specialist may affect the kind of influence one exercises in the policy process. The citizen who is highly informed about the scientific and technological aspects of a policy area may be effectively disenfranchised if little is known about the issues on the policy agenda or the procedures through which these issues will be resolved (Davies, 1985). Similarly, individuals informed about the policy agenda will know when their interests are being challenged, but may be disenfranchised if the scientific and technical aspects of the issues are beyond their comprehension.

12

The Social Concentration of Knowledge

If knowledge is a foundation of power, then those who possess knowledge have the potential for exercising power. The question here is whether individuals with different social and demographic characteristics differ in the information they command. If so, individuals in the less knowledge-laden social and demographic locations are likely to be at a distinct disadvantage in influencing policy.

The distribution of knowledge across social strata is also significant in the context of what have been called "transsituational" sources of knowledge (Ettema and Kline, 1977). Those sources are relatively fixed individual traits, such as education. Transsituational traits suggest a permanent lack of knowledge for people with those attributes, regardless of how much they may wish otherwise. To the degree that knowledge is "transsituational," unknowledgeable individuals are unlikely to be able to increase their levels of information. If only transsituational forces are at work, it follows that it would be a waste of effort to seek to enhance the general public's level of policy-relevant information. Moreover, to the extent that transsituational sources of knowledge predominate, individuals may be unable to act wisely in defense of their own interests. If *only* transsituational sources of information are important, attempts to increase the level of informed participation are likely doomed to marginal success at best. Thus, the social bases of information holding are examined in some detail in Chapter three.

The Political Concentration of Knowledge

In contrast to transsituational sources of knowledge are "situation-specific" factors. Situation-specific influences reflect an individual's *motivation* to acquire information about a specific policy area (Lovrich and Pierce, 1984). Knowledge expands or contracts depending on the *motivation* of the individual to acquire the information. If citizens are aware of their stakes in a policy question, that perception then can serve as the incentive to acquire more information.

If information seeking stems from individual incentives, efforts to enhance public knowledge will more likely be successful than if knowledge grows solely out of unchanging background attributes. The path to higher levels of public knowledge would then involve two steps--the first task being to demonstrate the relevance of particular policy questions to the citizenry, and the second being the dissemination of appropriate information to citizens now motivated to

which relate to heightened demands for public involvement in policy formation. This involvement increases the public's need for information. The environmental policy process has been opened up to public involvement over the last three decades in virtually all highly industrialized nations (Milbrath, 1984). In challenges to political elites, citizen movements in Japan, Europe and the United States have pressed their claims for greater influence over the policymaking process.

Cross-National Relevance. Conflict over environmental policy appears in all industrial nations and is a common context within which to do comparative analysis. This is not to suggest that environmental *politics* is the same across all countries, for clearly it is not. However, even as environmental problems become increasingly international in scope, those that are seen as being country-specific reflect many common features of the environmental policy arena.

Cultural Variations. In some cultures, the natural environment may be seen as a resource to be exploited, to be used and manipulated to achieve the ends of humans. In other cultures, in contrast, the natural environment may be regarded as something of inherent value in and of itself. Similarly, environmental movements and their participants may be motivated by unique conceptions of the proper place of nature, and they may respond quite differently to postindustrialism.

An Existing Literature. Another reason to use the environmental policy arena is that a substantial body of literature already exists. The boom in the environmental movements of the 1960s and 1970s brought along with it a large amount of scholarly and governmental research. This research provides a foundation upon which to build our analysis. Much of this literature also focuses on public involvement in policy formation, and discusses the distribution of knowledge about environmental affairs.

These several reasons combine to suggest that the environmental policy area is a particularly good laboratory for assessing the dynamics of citizen knowledge holding in two postindustrial societies differing considerably in their culture and history.

Why Japan and the United States?

This study compares general publics in two selected locations, one in Japan and the other in the United States. Generally, these two countries share important similarities that provide a common context for the research, but they also manifest enough differences to raise the possibility of distinctive patterns of political behavior.

Similarities. Japan and the United States share postindustrial status (Benjamin and Ori, 1981). Both have experienced a high level of economic development and have developed technology extensively in recent decades. Widespread affluence and high levels of education have created postindustrial social revolutions in the two countries. Japan and the United States also have had powerful citizen movements over the past three decades (McKean, 1974; 1981). Many of these movements have been occasioned by important environmental issues. In the United States public involvement in the environmental policy process has become institutionalized in law. In Japan, environmental pollution issues have been given credit for stimulating the formation of citizen movements which, while referred to by this general term, have primarily concerned themselves with environmental issues (Lewis, 1980). The citizen movement/public involvement content to environmental politics in the two countries is especially important to our concern with the role of public information levels. Intensive public involvement in the environmental policy area insures that the general public in both Japan and the United States will have been exposed to a fair amount of discussion of environmental issues.

Japan and the United States share environmental issues involving highly scientific and technical content, which makes the level of public information holding especially important. In Japan environmental issues primarily concern industrial pollution of air and water supplies. Several rather notorious cases of industrial wastes appearing in saltwater fisheries served as crystallizing factors in the environmental movement in Japan (Krauss and Simcock, 1980). Scientific discoveries in Japan not only are part of some environmental issues, but they are often involved in the search to alleviate pollution. Similarly, in the United States questions of the disposal of hazardous wastes, of the appropriate allocation of instream flows to competing uses, of the construction of low-head and/or high dam hydroelectric facilities, of the need to combat acid rain represent just a few environmental issues involving a high level of scientific and technical content. Thus, citizens of both Japan and the United States clearly share similar kinds of public policy concerns about which they form and articulate opinions.

Equally important, Japan and the United States also share similarities with respect to their form of government, which is generally "democratic." Public officials at the municipal, regional (state and prefecture) and national levels are elected through popular participation in periodic elections. Political parties and formal interest groups employ the full range of constitutional protections for freedom of speech and association to campaign among the public. These democratic processes allow citizens of Japan and the United States to take part in formulating general guidelines for environmental policy.

Differences. The two countries also differ in significant ways that may create distinct patterns among their citizens. One of those differences relates to the meaning of environmentalism in the two countries. Simply put, American environmentalists are more preservation-oriented than are their Japanese counterparts (McKean, 1981). American environmentalists certainly argue the need for preventing pollution, but environmentalism in the United States has another dimension. That dimension focuses on the *preservation* of natural resources regardless of their potential economic benefits. Thus, American environmental issues include *both* toxic waste dumpsites *and* the designation of wilderness areas. In Japan, in contrast, the focus of environmentalists has been more on pollution-- not because it alters the natural enviroment, but because it poses significant health hazards to individuals, or to the resources on which their livelihood is based (Matsushita, 1975).

There also are differences in the political mobilization of environmental interests in the two countries. In Japan there is a local cast to environmental activity, with most environmental issues being regional or local. The political response to these issues seems to be structured along local lines as well. Political activity is directed primarily toward the prefectural or local authorities, or at representatives of the national government at the prefectural level. Japanese environmental organizations are not as likely as their American opposites to have peak organizations, or to be national in scope. Moreover, recruitment into environmental organizations in Japan is largely a function of traditional allegiances to local political structures which have been captured by environmentalists (Pierce *et al.*, 1986a). A belief in the environmentalists' cause often is secondary to these other concerns. To be sure, committed environmentalists are present. Yet, many nominal members of the Japanese environmental movement are there only because of their attachment to a co-opted local organization.

Environmental organizations in the United States, on the other hand, are more likely to be populated by members committed to the goal of environmental preservation--although such persons are frequently drawn into the movement by specific, immediate issues (Milbrath, 1984). Environmentalism in the United States is also a more national issue, both in content and in organization. The major environmental organizations span the country, participate in peak organizations, and are represented most strongly at the national political level in Washington, D.C.

These comparisons provide a context for examining differences in the role of knowledge in structuring public reactions to environmental issues. Knowledge may play a more powerful role in linking values to policy preferences in the United States, largely because of the broader scope of environmental issues. In contrast, knowledge may be less central in Japan because of the local, issue-based focus of activism.

Finally, the value structures in the two countries may be quite different. On the one hand, as noted earlier, a number of scholars reject the post-materialist value construct for Japan, since it is derived from the study of Western democracies. On the other hand, most comparative analyses place support for *environmentalism* within just that postmaterialist value structure (Milbrath, 1984). If the Japanese possess distinct value dimensions, knowledge may be less critical for them in linking those *Western* postmaterialist values to policy choices.

The Specifics of the Study

As noted above, this monograph reports the results of a study of citizens in Shizuoka Prefecture in Japan and in Spokane County in Washington State. These particular results reflect one element of a larger study of the two locations. The larger study included surveys and interviews of elected and administrative policy makers, policymaking experts, and organizational activists in environmental, civic and economic interest groups.[1] In both Japan and the United States we sought to identify comparable cases where complex questions of public policy hinged upon the command of scientific and technical information. Moreover, we wanted to find cases where citizens traditionally enjoy and exercise the right of participation in the policy making process. In the American setting an appropriate case was found in the area of Spokane, Washington. In Spokane, the issue of the protection of the sole-source drinking water supply for the region--the Spokane-Rathdrum Prairie Aquifer--had given rise to active citizen involvement and dramatic governmental action.

Central to the Spokane situation was the dissemination of technical and scientific information. Questions such as the following were at the core of policy decisions. Is there an "interchange" between the Spokane River and the aquifer? Do suburban septic tanks and package treatment plants pose a threat to the safety of the underground drinking water of metropolitan Spokane residents? Are the substrata in the area under the City of Spokane and its surrounding communities as porous as the local environmentalists claim? Are newer types of package treatment plants (in use at apartment complexes) environmentally sound over the aquifer? These questions--and many more like them--made the Spokane case prototypical in its scientific and technical content. Moreover, the issue was salient before the local public and area interest groups, and it produced a relatively high level of activism and information dissemination.

Many parties have a direct stake in the Spokane aquifer issue, hence broad-based motivation exists for gathering policy- relevant information. For environmentalists, the issue is clear--limits on growth must be established in order to prevent further damage to the aquifer. In their view, the present dangers of pollution should be removed immediately. To the developer, the home builder, the member of building trades unions, the banker, the financier, or the real estate agent, the issue is equally clear. Environmentalists are "crying wolf" once more and exaggerating the nature of the danger. For the elected officials of local government the question is one of a need for immediate action in the context of perceived public dissensus and apparent general public ignorance. Action is necessary because of federally enacted pure water standards that apply to sole-source aquifers. In contrast to other participants, the policy area expert can serve as educator to all parties.

In Japan, Mishima and the surrounding communities of Numazu and Fuji City (at the foot of the Mt. Fuji watershed) were similarly involved in a long-term dispute. The issue concerned environmental preservation in the Suruga Bay area. The awakening of environmental concern in Japan came with Minamata disease (Reich, 1983). As byproducts of local manufacturing, mercury deposits in Minamata Bay killed fish, birds, pets and even humans. When the national government announced plans to locate a huge petrochemical complex on Suruga Bay, area citizens organized in opposition. When PCB-laced *hedoro* (a dangerous sludge) was discovered in Suruga Bay, area citizens expanded their efforts to include demands for cleaning up Fuji harbor. As in Spokane, the national, regional and local levels of government were all engaged in the policy process. As in the Spokane case, there was a great deal of scientific and technical content in the discussions and in the proposed policy alternatives. This complexity surfaced in the identification of pollution dangers, in estimating risks to the public health, and in devising appropriate remedies for pollution. Finally, as in the Spokane case, a wide range of interests were involved in working out provisions for protecting the area's ecology. Financial interests (in Mishima), paper product manufacturers (in Fuji) and shipping interests (in Numazu) contested area environmentalists at every turn. The Japanese case, like the American, embraced the full range of elements inherent in postindustrial polities.

In both locations survey data were obtained via mail questionnaires distributed to a random sample of residents listed in city directories. Reminder postcards and two sets of follow-up letters and replacement questionnaires were distributed (see Dillman, 1978). In Spokane, an initial sample of 1,200 was drawn, but 186 were excluded because of incorrect listing, or of individuals having moved, died, or otherwise being incapacitated and unable to respond. Of the remaining 1,014 sample size, 524 usable returns were obtained. This response rate of 52 percent seems surprisingly high given both the length and the difficulty of the questionnaire employed. In the case of the Mishima/Numazu/Fuji area study, 500 names were randomly drawn in each of the three cities for the composition of the primary sample of 1,500. Of this number, 45 individuals could not be contacted, leaving a base sample of 1,455. Of the latter number, 694 citizens returned sufficiently completed questionnaires producing a survey response rate of 47.7 percent.

The questionnaires were similar in the two countries, with changes made in some items to accomodate local differences in policy context. The questionnaire was over ten pages long, and contained attitudinal, perceptual, informational and background items. A special problem exists, of course, with regard to cross-national equivalence. A double-back translation method was employed in an attempt to minimize this problem. The American questionnaire was translated back from the Japanese to the English by a bilingual American scholar. Discontinuities were adjusted into a mutually acceptable form.

The Plan of the Book

The organization of the remaining chapters generally follows the set of research questions presented above. Chapter two investigates whether knowledge is evenly distributed through the public, or whether it is held by only a few. Chapter three examines the concentration of knowledge within locations of the social and economic structures of the two countries. Chapter four examines whether knowledge levels are related to differences in the need for motivation to acquire information. Chapter five places policy-relevant information holding within the context of public attitudes about the future. Chapter six assesses the impact of knowledge on public attitudes. It examines whether individuals with more information have uncharacteristic attitudes about public policy questions. Chapter seven confronts the issue of whether policy-relevant knowledge translates into power. That chapter tries to determine whether more knowledgeable individuals are more likely to have their views reflected in the policy preferences of activists and elites. Finally, Chapter eight draws together the patterns and implications of the first seven chapters.

Conclusion

Postindustrial politics poses new and demanding problems for the citizens of democratic nations. The combination of increasingly complex political issues and demands for public involvement places a premium on policy-relevant knowledge (Yankelovich, 1984). Does such knowledge lead to greater influence in the complex public policy issues of postindustrial society? Are individual differences in knowledge holding linked to personal attributes? Does knowledge holding create consistency in public belief systems? Does the role of such knowledge differ in countries which share democratic institutions and postindustrial status, but which differ sharply in their culture and history? The analysis of the surveys presented in the following chapters is intended to answer these questions, and thereby to enhance our understanding of political influence, political change and the public policy processes of postindustrial societies.

Notes

1. The project was funded primarily by a grant to Abe and Lovrich from the Japan-U.S. Faculty Pairing Program of the Japan-U.S. Friendship Commission, administered by the Institute for International Education. The title of the grant was "Citizen Participation in Scientific and Technical Policy Issues: A Japan-U.S. Comparative Study." Additional research funds were provided by the Washington State University Graduate School and the College of Arts and Sciences, as well as by the Ohta Foundation of Japan through a research grant to Abe and Lovrich and a Visiting Professor grant to Pierce.

2

The Distribution of Knowledge

Introduction

This chapter details the study's measures of knowledge, and then compares the distribution of knowledge in the publics of Shizuoka and Spokane. We look at such questions as whether citizens differ widely in their knowledge levels, and whether variability in knowledge occurs by country and by type of information. These questions emerge for two reasons. First, knowledge is central to the citizen's ability to link policy alternatives to fundamental values. Individuals with greater knowledge should be advantaged in their ability to make policy choices instrumental to achieving their personal interests. The second reason for looking at the distribution of knowledge is its presumed contribution to the citizen's political power. Information will make individuals more effective in political argumentation, and better able to formulate views on policy alternatives that serve their self-interest. Having such information will empower the individual to communicate effectively with others possessing similar interests, or to arouse individuals not yet aware of their shared stakes in the policy outcome (Kuklinski et al., 1982).

The Measurement of Knowledge

Five measures of knowledge are employed in this study. The use of multiple measures reflects the fact that several *kinds* of information are relevant to the policy process. In addition, a multi-measure approach mitigates some of the more obvious methodological problems involved in the study of knowledge, especially in a cross-cultural policy context.

First, this study employed mail surveys. Respondents indicated the "right" answer to information questions or indicated the level of their familiarity with particular terms and concepts. With a mail questionnaire, of course, there is no way to control the setting under which responses are recorded. Individuals could "cheat" by looking up the answers to factual questions; they could intentionally over-estimate their knowledge or familiarity with particular items, or they might obtain assistance from other individuals who are more knowledgeable. Fortunately, information is available from an earlier study of similar design in which respondents who had indicated their familiarity with technical terms in a mail questionnaire were contacted by phone and asked to define those same terms (Pierce and Lovrich, 1982). High correlations obtained between the ranking of individuals by their statement of familiarity and the coders' evaluations of the accuracy of the definitions offered over the phone. Moreover, in that earlier study a bogus term was included in a mail survey measure of expressed familiarity with technical concepts. Only 8 percent of the public said they knew that bogus term, and that percentage was the same as found in samples of technical experts and policy area elites. Finally, one of the measures employed in the study reported here also employs a bogus term, and comparable results were once again obtained with American survey subjects.

A *cross-national* attempt to assess policy-relevant knowledge also requires multiple measures. The problem of meaning equivalence, as well as concern for the extent to which the information items are of similar relevance in the two countries, are troubling. Multiple measures, however, provide a partial check on such problems, as does the inclusion of several items designed to tap the idiosyncratic nature of policy conflict in the two local study sites.

Environmental Science Information

This measure assesses the individual's understanding of the fundamental scientific bases of environmental policy questions. Participation in public debate over environmental policy commonly presupposes at least a minimal level of understanding of the ecology science underlying the issue(s) under discussion. Moreover, *effective* participation in that debate may require an elevated level of familiarity with the scientific aspects of ecological phenomena. The four questions employed in this particular measure were adapted from a more lengthy, previously published scale (Maloney et al., 1975). The original scale contained twelve items; the four items employed here were related to the water pollution and environmental protection policy issues of the two study sites. The following four survey items were used:

"In the following questions, enter the number of what you think is the BEST answer in the space provided next to the statement." (If uncertain, leave blank.)

1. Soil pollution is generally due to: 1-sparce rains 2-improper farming 3-poisonous metals 4-poor crop rotation 5-over fertilization **(#3 correct)**

2. The most common pollutants of water are:
1-arsenic and silver nitrates 2-hydrocarbons 3-carbon monoxide 4-sulphur and calcium 5-nitrates and phosphates **(#5 correct)**

3. All but ONE of the following decompose in ocean water:
1-sewage 2-garbage 3-tin cans 4-plastic bags 5-chemical fertilizer **(#4 correct)**

4. What is the harmful effect of phosphate pollution on marine life?
1-causes cancer 2-renders fish sterile 3-destroys the nervous system of fish 4-makes water cloudy 5-promotes growth of algae which suffocate fish **(#5 correct)**

The percentage choosing the correct response to each item among the general public, activists and elite groups in Japan and the United States is shown in Table 2.1. Among Japanese respondents the public registers the lowest percentage of correct answers on each knowledge item. On several of the items the gulf between the public's knowledge and that of other samples is quite great. On the other hand, in most cases there is general knowledge parity among the activists, officials and experts. The one exception is question four. In this case only the experts and the economic interests have a high proportion with the correct answer (64 percent and 75 percent, respectively).

Among the American samples the results generally mirror those in Japan. The first question, on the source of soil pollution, is the only case where there is little difference among the samples. All samples have a high proportion with the "wrong" answer (a point to which we will return). On the other items more than half of each American sample chooses the correct response. In those three other instances, the patterns are what one would expect--the public exhibits less knowledge than do the activists and the elites. Unlike Japan, however, the economic interests fare much worse in the United States, closely following the general public results.[1]

There also are some interesting cross-national contrasts. Generally, the Japanese are much more likely to give the "correct"

Table 2.1

Percentage Correct on Knowledge of Ecology Science Items Among the General Public, Activist and Elite Samples in Japan and the United States

Item[a]

	Soil Pollution Source	Water Pollution Source	Biodegradable Matter in Oceans	Phosphate Pollution	N
Japan					
Public	78%[b]	38%	63%	23%	(694)
Civic Groups	94%	56%	89%	40%	(158)
Environmentalists	91%	64%	90%	35%	(238)
Economic Interests	91%	71%	85%	75%	(192)
Officials	83%	58%	79%	29%	(48)
Experts	89%	66%	84%	64%	(388)
United States					
Public	30%	62%	51%	51%	(522)
Civic Groups	25%	73%	71%	64%	(77)
Environmentalists	32%	73%	70%	62%	(66)
Economic Interests	23%	70%	53%	54%	(92)
Officials	21%	81%	66%	72%	(67)
Experts	35%	96%	90%	93%	(72)

[a]For a complete description of each item, see the accompanying text.

[b]The entry in each cell is the percentage giving the correct response.

answer on the first question, the one about the general source of soil pollution. On the other hand, the American samples generally do better on the question of the harmful effect of phosphate pollution on marine life. These differences may be found as much in the character of the local environmental policy context--and the communication signals they provide--as in any real knowledge difference. That is, Spokane is surrounded by agricultural lands. Questions of proper farm techniques and the content and amount of chemical fertilizers have thus been salient issues. On the other hand, the Shizuoka vicinity has experienced significant pollution by chemical industry byproducts. Many of those pollutants clearly can be construed as "poisonous metals." The differing salience of the two sources of pollution may thus account for the difference in the percentage choosing the answer that is "generally" correct. While the "bias" in the first item worked against elevating the estimate of the Americans' knowledge, the reverse is true of the fourth question concerning phosphates. The growth of algae as a serious water pollution problem has been a significant concern in the Spokane area, with several of the most important recreational lakes requiring major efforts to eliminate the problem.

Using the four individual items, an overall index of science knowledge was created. The index reflects the absolute number of correct answers across the four items, thus having a range from zero to four. The distribution of scores on the index for each of the samples, and the mean index score for each sample, is shown in Table 2.2. As one would expect, in both countries the lowest mean knowledge score is held by the general publics, and the two publics differ very little from one another. In both the Shizuoka and Spokane settings the highest average is shown by the policy area experts. The greater knowledge of experts in the United States, where the original questions were developed, is much more pronounced than is the case in Japan. In the American samples there is a general increase in knowledge as one moves to the more rarefied positions in the political hierarchy; the public is the least well informed, followed by the activists and the public officials, and then capped off by the experts.

Technical Term Familiarity

A second indicator of knowledge was based in respondents' self-assessment of their familiarity with a series of policy-relevant technical terms. Technical terms constitute much of the crucial content of policy-relevant communications. Policy goals are defined, alternatives are identified and evaluated, and policies are implemented via the use of appropriate technologies and the concepts needed to describe them.

Table 2.2

Distribution on Environmental Knowledge Index Among Public, Activist and Elite Samples in Japan and the United States

| | *Environmental Knowledge Index Position*[a] | | | | | | | |
| | *Low* | | | | *High* | | | |
	0	1	2	3	4	Total	N	Mean
Japan								
Public	12	21	32	22	12	100%	(694)	2.0
Civic Groups	2	6	27	44	22	101%	(150)	2.8
Environmentalists	1	8	26	42	24	99%	(238)	2.8
Economic Interests	1	4	13	38	45	101%	(192)	3.2
Officials	8	8	23	46	15	100%	(48)	2.5
Experts	4	9	16	24	48	101%	(388)	3.0
United States								
Public	14	23	28	26	9	100%	(524)	1.9
Civic Groups	13	12	18	44	13	100%	(77)	2.3
Environmentalists	8	18	24	30	20	100%	(66)	2.4
Economic Interests	14	17	30	30	8	99%	(92)	2.0
Officials	12	8	21	49	10	100%	(67)	2.4
Experts	0	4	6	64	27	101%	(72)	3.1

[a]Number of correct answers

In order for citizens, activists and policymakers to understand policy alternatives and to evaluate them in terms of their own goals and interests, they must be able to employ those technical terms with some degree of confidence (Rankin and Nealey, 1978).

In both countries the respondents were asked to indicate their familiarity with nine terms used with varying frequency in policy discussions. In the Spokane area setting survey respondents were queried about one bogus term. Four of the nine terms employed are the same in the two countries, while five items are locale-specific. The use of both common and site-specific items reflects an attempt to collect comparable evidence in both Spokane and Shizuoka Prefecture.

Questions can be raised, of course, about the extent to which self-assessed familiarity with terms reflects variation in respondent's "real" knowledge. There are several responses to such potential criticism. First, as noted earlier, a previous study used some of these same technical terms. Follow-up telephone calls were made to a subsample of the survey asking them to define the terms in question (Pierce and Lovrich, 1982). A high correlation obtained between self-assessed familiarity and actual knowledge of the terms. Second, as in prior studies, a bogus term was included in the American list. Extremely small percentages of the respondents indicated that they knew the meaning of the bogus term. In the Spokane area sample, the percentage claiming knowledge of the bogus term ranged from 3 percent (among the civic organization members) to a high of eighteen percent (among the public officials). Even the experts were more likely (10 percent) than the general public (5 percent) to claim knowledge of the bogus term.

The terms employed in the measure of the level of technical term familiarity were as follows:

Japan/ United States	Japan Only	U.S. Only
Herbicide	Recycling	Hydroelectric
Flouridation	PCB	Riverine Ecosystem
Oxidation	Ground Subsidence	Turbidity
Eutrophication	COD	Effluent
	Hedoro	Resident Fishery

The percentage indicating that they know the meaning of each term is shown in Table 2.3.

In both countries the general public's familiarity with technical terms is lower than that of the activists and the elites. The Spokane public expresses greater familiarity than does the Shizuoka citizenry

Table 2.3

Percentage Saying "Know Meaning" of Policy-Relevant Technical Terms Among Public, Activist and Elite Samples in Japan and the United States

Japan

	COMMON TERMS IN U.S. AND JAPAN					COUNTRY-SPECIFIC TERMS						GRAND
	Herbi-cide	Flouri-dation	Oxi-dation	Eutrophi-cation	MEAN	Re-cycling	PCB	Sub-sidence	COD	Hedoro	MEAN	MEAN
Public	86%	42%	71%	30%	(57)	80%	69%	89%	27%	94%	(72)	65
Civic Groups	95	56	81	47	(70)	91	82	96	46	98	(83)	77
Environmentalists	93	57	84	49	(71)	91	82	95	49	98	(83)	78
Economic Interests	99	72	97	77	(86)	99	98	100	92	99	(98)	93
Elected Officials	96	75	85	79	(84)	94	92	94	86	96	(93)	89
Experts	97	60	90	71	(80)	96	91	98	85	99	(94)	87

United States

	COMMON TERMS IN U.S. AND JAPAN					COUNTRY-SPECIFIC TERMS						GRAND
	Herbi-cide	Flouri-dation	Oxi-dation	Eutrophi-cation	MEAN	Hydro-electric	Riverine Eco-system	Tur-bidity	Ef-fluent	Resident Fishery	MEAN	MEAN
Public	84%	88%	70%	9%	(63)	91%	26%	31%	59%	56%	(53)	57%
Civic Groups	96	96	86	22	(75)	97	62	51	86	52	(70)	72
Environmentalists	92	91	56	41	(70)	97	38	62	71	53	(64)	67
Economic Interests	90	96	84	13	(71)	97	36	46	82	55	(63)	67
Elected Officials	88	88	82	40	(75)	90	45	58	88	64	(69)	71
Experts	99	97	96	92	(96)	99	74	96	97	75	(88)	92

with those terms common to both surveys. However, the Japanese respondents appear to be the better informed on those terms unique to the particular sample. This pattern has several possible roots. It may be the case that the Japanese public is more attuned to their local policy-specific terms--or that they have been used more frequently in the latter's communication channels. On the other hand, it also is possible that the relative "difficulty" of the terms differs in the two countries. That is, the Shizuoka-specific terms may have been "easier" in some absolute sense than the Spokane terms. Likewise, the reverse may be true of the common terms. Those terms were developed originally in studies of information holding among residents of the American Pacific Northwest. While the terms have a common international currency, they still may reflect the particular salience of specific issues in the United States. Given a slight preponderance of the situation-specific terms (five to four) and the better Japanese performance on such terms, the overall familiarity across all nine items is greater for the Shizuoka citizens than for their American counterparts.

The Japanese and American general publics express less familiarity with the technical terms than do their respective activists and elites. Both publics show considerable variability across the terms as well, a variability that is not shared by the activists and elites. One other distinction between the two sets of data is produced by the positions of the policy area experts in the two countries. The experts in Spokane have a substantial margin of familiarity over the other subsamples; on the other hand, such expert dominance is not the case in Shizuoka. This wider knowledge gap may give the Spokane area experts greater relative influence than is enjoyed by their counterparts in Shizuoka Prefecture.

A technical term familiarity index was constructed; it ranges from 9 to 27.[2] All nine terms are included in this index. Each respondent was given one point for knowing a term, two points for having heard of it, and three points for never having heard of it. Thus, a score of nine on the scale represents the highest possible level of knowledge.

Table 2.4 shows how each of the twelve subsamples in the larger study is distributed among three levels of technical term information--those levels being termed high, medium and low. The cutting points for the categories were established by merging the distributions of the two public samples. The top 28 percent in the

Table 2.4

Distribution of Publics, Activists and Elites on Trichotomized Technical Term Index in Japan and the United States

Technical Term Familiarity[a]

Japan	High	Medium	Low	Total	N	Mean[b]
Public	33%	47%	20%	100%	(673)	13.2
Civic Groups	54%	38%	8%	100%	(151)	11.6
Environmentalists	60%	33%	8%	101%	(223)	11.5
Economic Interests	90%	10%	0%	100%	(189)	9.8
Public Officials	89%	7%	4%	100%	(47)	10.0
Experts	80%	18%	2%	100%	(386)	10.4

United States						
Public	20%	39%	41%	100%	(464)	14.9
Civic Groups	40%	50%	10%	100%	(73)	12.4
Environmentalists	33%	52%	15%	100%	(54)	12.9
Economic Interests	29%	46%	25%	100%	(87)	13.5
Public Officials	62%	27%	11%	100%	(55)	11.8
Experts	91%	18%	2%	100%	(68)	9.8

[a]The "high" category includes scores of 9-11 on the 9-27 index, the "medium" category includes scores 12-15, and "low" category contains scores 16-27. This division is based on the merged distribution of scores in the two public samples.

[b]The mean is for the overall index before it is trichotomized.

merged distribution was grouped into the "high" category, this group having index scores of 9, 10, or 11. Thus, to be in the top group the individual had to claim knowledge of more than two-thirds of the nine terms included in the index. The middle group contains the 44 percent of the sample with index scores of twelve through fifteen. The bottom group includes individuals with index scores of 16 or greater, and contains 28 percent of the sample.

In both countries, when compared to the activists and the elites, the general public is the least familiar with the technical terms. Moreover, in both countries the activist portions of the public (civic, environmental and economic group members) are more knowledgeable than are their respective general publics.[3] In Spokane the activists are less knowledgeable than either the public officials or the experts. Thus, in the American samples there is a rather consistent increase in knowledge as one moves "up" the policy hierarchy. Both the activists and the public officials, though, are significantly less well informed than are the policy area experts. In Japan, the pattern is a little different. The gap between the activists and the elites is not as great, and the policy area experts are *less* knowledgeable--or at least claim to be no more informed--than the public officials and the representatives of the economic interests.

In both countries, then, it is clear that there exist wide variations among citizens with respect to familiarity with technical terms. Moreover, the general public has a lower overall level of knowledge compared to that of activists and elites. Even so, the Japanese public is more familiar with these terms than is the American public.

Local Knowledge

The third measure of knowledge taps the individual's familiarity with local environmental conditions and/or regulations. Because the measure is so site-specific, these are the least comparable measures across the two samples. In the Spokane area the respondents were asked about their knowledge of sources of area drinking water. This information is crucial to understanding the policy debates over the proper course to follow in protecting the Spokane region's sole-source aquifer. In Japan the respondents were queried about their knowledge of Japanese environmental law. The questions used were taken directly from a national public opinion poll conducted by the Japanese Prime Minister's Office in November of 1981 (Environment Agency of Japan, 1982). The items employed in the two indices are shown below.

| | U.S. Version | Japan Version |

U.S. Version

Three possible sources of drinking water are available in the Spokane area--water pumped from the Spokane River, water held in dams in the mountains, and water pumped from the Spokane-Rathrum Prairie Aquifer. Please indicate how much of the Spokane area's drinking water is taken from each of these sources.

	Primary Source Now	Secondary Source Now	Not a Source
Spokane River	1	2	3
Mountain Dams	1	2	3
Spokane Aquifer	1	2	3

NOTE: Correct responses underlined.

Japan Version

#1 Do you know of the Basic Law for Environmental Pollution Control?
Yes___ No___

#2 Do you know that environmental quality standards for protecting human health and the living environment are established under the Basic Law for Environmental Pollution Control?
Yes___ No___

#3 Do you know of the Law concerning the settlement of Environmental Pollution Disputes?
Yes___ No___

#4 Do you know whether police handle complaints relating to pollution?
Yes___ No___

Table 2.5 shows the distribution of local knowledge for the publics, activists and elites in Japan and the United States. The index is constructed just a little differently for the two countries (over and above the different content of the questions) because one more question was asked in Japan. The criterion for inclusion in one of the index categories is the number of incorrect (in the American case) or "no" (in the Japanese case) responses. The "high" category contains individuals with none or only one incorrect answer or "no" responses among the Japanese respondents; the moderate grouping missed two; and members of the low group missed all three in the American case and gave three or four "no" answers in the Japanese instance.

The patterns of local knowledge are remarkably similar to the distributions observed earlier with knowledge of ecology science and familiarity with policy-relevant technical terms. While the public distributions are quite similar, both samples also exhibit less local knowledge than do the activists and the elites. The odd exception is the case of the Spokane environmentalists. The environmentalists

Table 2.5

Distribution of Publics, Activists and Elites on Index of Locale-Specific Environmental Knowledge in Japan and the United States

Index of Local Knowledge*

Japan	Low	Low Mod.	High Mod.	High	Total	N	PDI**
Public	33%	26%	24%	18%	100%	(694)	-17
Civic Groups	20%	25%	29%	27%	101%	(158)	+11
Environmentalists	14%	21%	31%	33%	99%	(238)	+29
Economic Interests	4%	8%	26%	63%	101%	(192)	+77
Public Officials	4%	4%	40%	52%	100%	(48)	+84
Experts	6%	14%	27%	54%	101%	(388)	+61

United States							
Public	30%	23%	27%	20%	100%	(524)	- 6
Civic Groups	9%	31%	18%	42%	100%	(77)	+20
Environmentalists	15%	42%	14%	29%	100%	(66)	-14
Economic Interests	17%	20%	19%	45%	100%	(92)	+27
Public Officials	10%	21%	16%	52%	99%	(67)	+29
Experts	4%	7%	29%	60%	100%	(72)	+78

*See the text for a description of the index construction.

**The PDI (percentage difference index) refers to the percentage in the two top knowledge categories minus the percentage in the bottom two categories.

seem out of character from their earlier, more informed positions. On this set of questions they emerge little different from the general public as a whole. To be sure, the environmentalists have been active in some local policy issues, including those having to do with proper provisions for the protection of the sole-source aquifer. But, their general focus may be more regional or national (especially since the organizations to which they belong are the nationally organized Sierra Club and the Audubon Society). Again, in the American sample the experts are the best informed, and the public officials differ little from the civic and economic interest members. In Japan the economic representatives and the public officials appear as well informed as do the policy area experts. Japanese public officials, who on a frequent basis must deal with the content and enforcement of their environmental laws, are the most informed. Substantial differences emerge between the knowledge level of the public officials and that of the general public.

Knowledge as Agenda Articulation

The fourth knowledge measure assumes that the ability to articulate policy problems rests on some information (either correct or incorrect) about those issues (Kessel, 1980; Miller et al., 1980). It also is presumed that the greater the number of problems identified by an individual the greater the information base possessed by that person.

Respondents were asked to identify the problem they saw facing area water resources (in the United States) or the regional environment (in Japan). This measure of information is a simple count of the number of problems mentioned by the respondent. A minimal standard was imposed by coders in determining whether or not the stated problem reflected an identifiable policy question. Table 2.6 presents the distribution of the number of policy problems articulated by the respondents in the study subsamples.

The patterns in agenda problem articulation generally mirror those produced in the other knowledge measures. The general publics proffer fewer policy area problems than do the activists and the elites, and very little difference obtains between the mean scores of the two publics. In Japan the greatest number of policy problems is mentioned by the environmental group members and by the representatives of economic interests. The civic group members, the public officials and the experts exhibit an average number of articulated policy problems that is only slightly greater than that for the public. In the U.S., though, there is a clear preponderance of the expert sample in the number of articulated policy problems. It is ironic, perhaps, that the "nonpolitical" expert elite actually identifies more policy problems than

Table 2.6

Distribution of Knowledge as Agenda Articulation Among Citizens, Activists and Elites in Japan and the United States

Number of Problems Articulated

Japan	0	1	2	3	4+	Total	N	Mean*
Public	33%	33%	18%	7%	9%	100%	(694)	1.27
Civic Groups	34%	30%	13%	8%	15%	100%	(158)	1.38
Environmentalists	21%	30%	24%	13%	12%	100%	(238)	1.63
Economic Interests	27%	26%	23%	8%	16%	100%	(192)	1.60
Public Officials	29%	31%	21%	10%	8%	99%	(48)	1.40
Experts	33%	26%	25%	8%	9%	101%	(388)	1.37

United States								
Public	25%	37%	26%	9%	3%	100%	(522)	1.29
Civic Groups	4%	25%	33%	26%	13%	101%	(77)	2.20
Environmentalists	11%	52%	21%	15%	2%	101%	(66)	1.46
Economic Interests	15%	48%	27%	8%	2%	100%	(92)	1.34
Public Officials	15%	24%	30%	15%	16%	100%	(67)	1.97
Experts	3%	21%	33%	26%	17%	100%	(72)	2.42

*The mean is based on total distribution of actual number of problems without grouping those greater than four into the 4+ category.

do the more politicized public officials. Perhaps even more surprising, though, is the elevated status of the members of Spokane civic organizations on this measure. This finding may stem from the preponderance of League of Women Voters (LWV) members in this group. The LWV is widely known for its study group concentration on particular issues; local water resources issues were the subject of such study groups in recent years.

Self-Assessed Information Levels

Self-assessed knowledge levels are important for several reasons. The *feeling* of being informed may be more important than actual information levels in effecting behavior. *Believing* that one is informed (without that necessarily being the case) may be the significant force in moving that individual to monitor the policy area and to hold preferences about specific policy issues.

In both countries, respondents were asked to respond on a seven-point scale to this question: "How well informed would you say you are at present concerning water resource issues in the Spokane (Mishima, Fuji, Numazu) area?" Respondents were given this response format:

1	2	3	4	5	6	7
Not Informed			Somewhat Informed			Very well Informed

The distributions of responses to this measure are shown in Table 2.7. In that table the two extreme categories on either end (1, 2 and 6, 7) are grouped together, although the original scale values are preserved for the calculation of means.

In both countries, the general public respondents perceive themselves to be less well-informed than do the activists and the policy elites. Thus, self-perception tends to follow the pattern (at least at the aggregate level) of the distributions produced in the other measures of knowledge. In both countries the public officials see themselves at the highest levels of knowledge, even marginally more so than do the policy area experts. Finally, at each level (citizen, activist and elite) the American respondents see themselves as better informed than do the Japanese participants in the survey.

One rationale for examining multiple knowledge measures is the possibility that the relative positioning of citizens may depend in part on the type of information examined. Overall, however, there is substantial aggregate agreement among the rankings of the subsamples on the five measures in both countries, although that agreement is somewhat higher in the American case than in the

Table 2.7

Self-Assessed Information Levels Among Citizens, Activists and Elites in Shizuoka Prefecture and Spokane County*

Level of Self-Assessed Information

Japan	Low 1,2	3	Middle 4	5	High 6,7	Total	N	Mean*
Public	13%	22%	51%	10%	5%	101%	(671)	3.71
Civic Groups	8%	15%	50%	14%	13%	100%	(158)	4.07
Environmentalists	3%	12%	50%	18%	17%	100%	(236)	4.39
Economic Interests	1%	9%	33%	24%	34%	101%	(191)	4.92
Public Officials	0%	4%	38%	23%	34%	99%	(47)	5.00
Experts	3%	12%	40%	24%	22%	101%	(386)	4.55

United States								
Public	13%	11%	41%	19%	16%	100%	(512)	4.11
Civic Groups	1%	1%	24%	28%	47%	101%	(76)	5.26
Environmentalists	8%	14%	31%	9%	38%	101%	(65)	4.68
Economic Interests	4%	10%	35%	21%	29%	99%	(89)	4.71
Public Officials	2%	7%	11%	15%	66%	101%	(62)	5.61
Experts	3%	4%	21%	14%	58%	100%	(72)	5.51

*Responses to a question asking individuals to assess their own knowledge levels were given on a seven-point scale. The two extreme categories on either end (1,2 and 6,7) are grouped together here, although they are kept distinct in calculating the means.

Japanese set (mean rank order correlation of .84 as opposed to .71). These are ranks of aggregates rather than individuals. It is possible that within the particular subsamples (especially in the public) the knowledge levels may not go together quite as consistently, an issue to which we now turn.

The Concentration of Knowledge

The general publics in Spokane and Shizuoka are less well informed than are the activists and the elites with which they interact in the policy process. This suggests the potential for serious information barriers confronting citizens in their involvement in policy processes. It is also the case, however, that substantial variation exists among the measures of information. This variation suggests at the very least that some members of the public have the knowledge for participation in the policy process. A portion of the public appears quite capable of articulating policy preferences and pursuing them with the same knowledge resources possessed by elites.

At this point we examine the extent to which variations in knowledge go together across the different measures. If the knowledge measures are highly correlated, information would be concentrated among a relatively small group of individuals. Those informed across multiple measures may be seen as "knowledge generalists." On the other hand, if the measures are not highly related, this would suggest the presence of "knowledge specialists." In some ways unrelated information measures could reflect a broadened but segmented base of influence in the public. As a consequence of this diversity, the overall public impact upon policy could be increased. On the other hand, with little overlap among types of information, narrowly knowledgeable individuals may possess insufficient incentive and ability to monitor and influence the entire range of the policy process.

Table 2.8 presents the correlations (Pearson r) among the knowledge measures. The upper right-hand portion of that table contains the results for the Japanese public sample, while the lower left-hand section contains the American findings.

Several significant patterns emerge in Table 2.8. First, the two correlation matrices are remarkably similar. The structure of knowledge would appear to be quite similar in Japan and the United States. Second, it is clear that little is to be gained by keeping separate the three measures of technical term familiarity. In both countries the correlations among the overall index, country-specific and country-common measures are quite high. Consequently, in the subsequent chapters reliance will be placed on the composite scale index. Third,

Table 2.8

Correlations (r) Among Information Measures for the General Publics of Japan and the United States

Japan

United States	Locale-Specific Knowledge	Ecology Science	Country-Specific Technical Terms	Common Technical Terms	Total Technical Terms	Self-Assessed Information Level	Problem Articulation
Locale-Specific Knowledge	X	.24	.26	.27	.30	.27	.21
Knowledge of Ecology Science	.32	X	.37	.35	.40	.21	.25
Country-Specific Technical Terms	.32	.34	X	.63	.90	.25	.15
Common Technical Terms	.28	.30	.66	X	.90	.24	.16
Total Technical Terms	.34	.36	.96	.85	X	.27	.17
Self-Assessed Information Level	.35	.23	.38	.26	.37	X	.15
Problem Articulation	.27	.22	.23	.19	.24	.14	X

Table Notes:

1. All negative signs have been reversed because of reverse in direction of familiarity with technical terms measures.
2. Pairwise deletion for missing data.
3. All correlations significant at a probability of $p \leq .001$.

the correlations among the remaining knowledge measures are all statistically significant (p $\leq$ .001), but none surpasses a level of r=.40. These moderate correlations suggest that some common dimension may underlie the several measures; however, these separate indicators of information holding are sufficiently independent that they should not be taken as simple surrogates for one another.

The extent to which knowledge accumulates *across* measures at the individual level would reflect the presence of "information generalists." Table 2.8 shows the number of measures on which respondents in the two countries surfaced as "highly informed." On the measure of technical term familiarity, the "informed" category includes positions 9, 10, 11 on the 9-27 range index. This cutting point segregates 20 percent of the American public and 33 percent of the Japanese public.

In order to qualify as "informed" on the science index, respondents could have no more than one incorrect answer. This classification includes 34 percent of the Japanese public and 35 percent of the American public. The measure of locale-specific knowledge is more problematic. It has three questions in Spokane and four in Shizuoka--and the substance of the particular questions used in the two settings differ somewhat. Based on the distributions shown earlier in Table 2.4, the informed respondents are defined as those at position 4 in Japan and position 3 in the United States. This group contains 18 percent of the Shizuoka cases and 20 percent in Spokane. On the articulation measure the same dividing point was used in both samples. Individuals identifying two or more problems are labeled "informed"; this cutting point includes 34 percent in the Japan and 38 percent in the United States. The "informed" respondents on the self-assessed measure are at positions 5, 6, and 7 on the seven-point scale. This classification contains only 15 percent of the Japanese, but includes 35 percent of the Americans.

The findings in Table 2.9 show only small differences between the Japanese and the Americans in the accumulation of knowledge across measures. In both countries well over one fifth of the public fails to be included among the most informed on any of the five measures.[4] Similarly, among both Japanese and American respondents another 30 percent is among the highly informed on only one of the five knowledge measures. These individuals might be called "information specialists." In both countries about a fifth of the respondents can be called "information generalists" as a result of having been placed in the top group on three or more of the five information measures. Finally, in both samples only one to two percent of the general public received high marks on all five of the knowledge measures.

Table 2.9

Number of Measures on Which Respondents are Highly Informed

Number of Measures on Which Informed*	Japan	U.S.
None	28%	23%
One	33%	30%
Two	21%	25%
Three	12%	14%
Four	5%	7%
Five	1%	2%
Total	100%	101%
N	(694)	(522)

*See the text for operational definitions of "highly informed" on each measure.

Table 2.10

**Patterns of Information Specialization Among Japanese and
American Public Respondents**

Knowledge Pattern*	Japan	U.S.
No Measures	28%**	23%
Technical Terms Only	9%	6%
Locale-Specific Knowledge Only	4%	3%
Ecology Science Only	8%	6%
Problem Articulation Only	9%	10%
Level of Self-Assessed Knowledge Only	3%	5%
More Than One	39%	47%
Total	100%	100%
N	(694)	(522)

*See the text for operational definitions of knowledge patterns.

**Percent "high" on knowledge measure.

44

A more complete view of information specialization is provided in Table 2.10. Once more the results for the Japanese and American respondents are quite similar. No more than 10 percent of the public in either the American or Japanese context is an information specialist on any one of the measures. Five percent of the Spokane public and three percent of the Shizuoka public consider themselves highly informed, even though they score high marks on no other measure. On both locations about ten percent are able to identify important problems without other information that would enhance political effectiveness in trying to solve those problems. Seventeen percent of the Spokane public and twelve percent of the Shizuoka public are informed solely on either the technical or the science measures.

Conclusion

Substantial variation in knowledge occurs among citizens in both the United States and Japan. Within the general publics the distributions on the knowledge measures are generally the same in the two countries. Moreover, in both the U.S. and Japan the relative position of the public compared to activists and elites is similar. This relative disadvantage of the public underscores the significance of the question of how knowledge is used by the public to influence the direction of public policy. In part, at least, our subsequent analysis must identify those informed subpublics that might be able to compete on a level relatively equal to that of the activists and the elites. Chapter three begins this process by assessing the relationship between policy-relevant knowledge and individual social and demographic characteristics.

Notes

1. The economic interests surveyed in the American and Japanese settings were necessarily somewhat different in nature. In the Spokane area a sample of leaders of organizations (e.g., Chambers of Commerce, builders' associations, real estate groups, and building trades unions) possessing an economic stake in further growth in the Spokane Valley area was selected in order to see what effect a clear, predominant economic interest would have on information holding. The same goal was established for the selection of a comparable sample in Shizuoka Prefecture, but certain features of the Japanese socio-political setting made the accomplishment of full comparability very difficult. First, a sampling of economic interests entailed groups very much like those in the Spokane area, with the exception that all economic concerns which have a significant impact upon the area's water, air,

noise or smells are required to employ an "environmental specialist" whose task it is to work with the municipal and prefectural environmental monitoring units to guarantee that the region's environment is not adversely affected by actions of the economic concern involved. Since the area's economy depends very heavily upon the paper products firms of Fuji City, a disproportionate number of economic interests surveyed come from the paper products producers, and a substantial number of surveys were completed by the *environmental specialists* employed by the firms rather than the firm leaders. Consequently, in the Japanese case all persons in the economic interest subsample are indeed tied to organizations which have a predominant stake in economic growth in the area. A goodly proportion of the Japanese subsample, however, is made up of persons with *particularly thorough training* and highly relevant work experience in the area of environmental protection. If the Japanese economic interests do particularly well, then, in contrast to their American counterparts with respect to policy relevant knowledge, it should be no wonder.

2. As a subsequent section of this chapter will show, there is ample empirical foundation for this combination.

3. The "policy area expert" samples in Spokane County setting and the Shizuoka Prefecture are quite comparable in most respects, with the exception that the Japanese setting offered a unique opportunity to collect a greater number of expert person surveys. In both the American and Japanese contexts persons were designated as policy area experts if they had either of two types of official professional positions: 1) worked for the municipal or regional government (city or Prefecture in Japan, and city, county or state in the United States) in the area (Shizuoka region or greater Spokane area) in the capacity of "technical specialist" or "administrative officer" in an agency responsible for monitoring the environment or policing potential polluters of the environment; or 2) university faculty residing in the relevant region whose academic specialization falls in the area of ecology science. In the Japanese setting a particularly fortunate circumstance arose, in that the Prefectural Institute for Environmental and Product Safety Research was located within the study region. Consequently, a high proportion of the Japanese "experts" subsample is composed of some very highly trained and experienced environmental scientists found at the Institute.

4. Interestingly, this distribution mirrors rather closely the percentage of the American public classified as having "no issue content" in their conceptualization of political parties and presidential candidates (Hagner and Pierce, 1982).

3

Background Sources
of Knowledge

Introduction

This chapter examines the social and demographic correlates of public knowledge. Chapter four follows with a focus on the role of motivation in knowledge holding.

Background Sources of Knowledge[1]

Research on the distribution of public knowledge identifies a "knowledge gap" separating persons of higher and lower SES--socioeconomic status (Tichenor et al., 1970). Lower SES persons typically exhibit lower levels of knowledge; they also tend to respond more slowly to mass-mediated attempts to increase the public's knowledge--at least until higher SES individuals encounter the "ceiling effect" (Donohue et al., 1975; Chaffee and McLeod, 1973; Genova and Greenberg, 1979). The ceiling effect refers to conditions under which higher status individuals reach a knowledge level beyond which subsequent information is redundant. In those conditions, lower SES individuals may be able to close the information gap when relevant information is both plentiful and easily accessed.

Ettema and Kline (1977) identify two types of explanations for the knowledge gap separating higher and lower socioeconomic strata. One explanation is rooted in "transsituational" conditions associated with lower SES levels. One of these conditions is a hypothesized "lack of communication skills on the part of lower SES persons" (Ettema and Kline, 1977:188). Ettema and Kline summarize this argument as follows:

> That is, if lack of communication skills on the part of lower SES persons is a cause of gap phenomena, then, because this lack holds under all circumstances, all gaps will always widen and never narrow unless, of course, ceiling effects intervene to allow the less skilled to catch up (1977:188).

In contrast to transsituational explanations, some scholars advance a "situation-specific" account. According to this explanation,

> gaps widen in those circumstances in which lower SES persons are less *motivated* to acquire the information or in which the information is less functional for them, while gaps may narrow (and perhaps even fail to materialize in the first place) when the motivation to acquire the information is increased among the lower SES persons or when the information is functional for them (Ettema and Kline, 1977:188).

These accounts focus attention on the respective roles of SES and motivation in explaining individual level variation in knowledge. The transsituational explanation leads to the prediction that SES variables will explain much more variation in knowledge holding than will motivational attributes, and that motivational effects will largely disappear when controlling for SES. In contrast, the situation-specific hypothesis suggests that even when controlling for SES characteristics motivational indicators will exhibit independent effects on knowledge.

One goal of this chapter is to expand somewhat the scope of transsituational influences. Transsituational factors are typically confined to individual socioeconomic characteristics. This chapter expands this focus to include the contribution of *demographic* traits to knowledge holding. We add age (or cohort), gender, length of residence in the local area, and population density of hometown to the list of transsituational influences. These indicators are included because they are indeed transsituational and a theoretical case can be made for their being related to knowledge. The rationale for including each will be introduced in more detail below. At this point, though, it is important to underscore the implications of the relationship of these variables to knowledge.

First, knowledge is important to the ability of individuals to recognize and act on their self-interest. If knowledge is rooted substantially in transsituational attributes, there will be significant differences in the ability of citizens to recognize their self-interest. This difference would be attached to relatively unchanging characteristics--ultimately resulting in a restriction of the ability of certain segments of the public to perceive their stakes in complex areas of public policy.

Second, knowledge may produce differences in the ability of individuals to influence public policy. The extent to which various transsituational variables are linked to knowledge, then, has significant political implications for the individuals who populate the less advantaged social positions. If socioeconomic classes do indeed differ markedly in knowledge, individuals in the knowledge-deficient classes may be less able to protect and promote their interests. Political advantage historically has accompanied those same characteristics also linked to higher levels of knowledge. The less familiar the policy alternatives and their implications, as in many postindustrial issues, the greater will be the difficulty for the disadvantaged to overcome any knowledge deficit.

A cross-national inquiry into the effects of transsituational sources of knowledge is especially revealing in a comparison of Japan and the United States. Many of the differences in the two countries relate directly to the significance and structure of transsituational variables. Social stratification, class standing, gender, urbanization, generational placement--these and other social and demographic attributes are expected to be related to information levels; they certainly are central to differences between Japan and the United States. It is quite possible, then, that the effects of transsituational factors on knowledge holding will differ in Japan and the United States.

Socioeconomic Correlates of Information

This section examines the relationship of four socioeconomic indicators to knowledge holding. The four indicators are level of education, income, occupation and class self-identification.

Education

The role of formal schooling in knowledge building is widely recognized (Kessel, 1980; Jennings, 1981; Hagner and Pierce, 1984). Education instructs in the use of concepts, abstractions and facts in an analytical context. Educational attainment reduces the costs of acquiring and processing information, and, specific courses of instruction can sometimes convey policy- relevant information.

In a discussion of the relationship of education level and political action levels in a cross-national context, Marsh and Kaase have argued:

> The consensual explanation for this phenomenon is that education provides the cognitive skills necessary to find one's way around the confused miasma that surrounds politics, if not actually teaching such skills directly. Moreover, the experience of higher forms of education will tend to break down people's natural tendencies to oversimplify their view of the world (1979:112).

The uniformity of the expected relationship of education and knowledge across different political systems was underscored in Almond and Verba's classic five-nation study (*The Civic Culture*). That "the more educated individual has more political information..." is one of the cross-national uniformities discovered in Germany, Italy, Great Britain, Mexico and the United States (1965:380).

The impact of education on knowledge obtains across nations. But, there is a vast difference between Japan and the United States in educational systems and process. In a general sense, the educational system in Japan contributes directly to the society's stratified nature (Nakane, 1970:25-39). High status occupants of prestigious political and governmental and industrial positions come directly from the top universities (Johnson, 1975). Entrance to the top universities is therefore highly prized, and competition for admission is fervently pursued from an early age. High schools are ranked in their ability to prepare their students for entrance into the top universities. Elementary and even the equivalent of kindergarten and nursery schools are prized for their ability to "teach to" the nationally standardized admission examinations, ensuring the continual upward mobility of the student.

Elements of elitism and preferential entry also attach to the American educational system. But, the major rationale for its expansion in the twentieth century has been its democratizing consequences for American society (Thomas, 1975; Jencks, 1971). Recent contrasts between Japanese and American educational practices tend to focus on the greater intensity, rigidity and regimentation in the Japanese system. On the other hand, American schools are chastised for their inability to produce students who can effectively compete with the Japanese, especially in the areas of science and mathematics. Conformity and uniformity, along with deference to educational authority, have been the hallmarks of Japanese education. But, those who laud the American educational system underscore its greater encouragement and reward of creativity, individualized analysis, and critical thinking (Gibney, 1979:325; Reischauer, 1977:170-78). In either case, though, it is clear that while Japan and the United States differ substantially in educational focus, they also share the rare status of having among the most highly educated citizenries in the world. The question then becomes: Do differences in the Japanese and American education systems in some measure account for variations in the public's level of policy-relevant knowledge?

Table 3.1

Relationship of Education and Knowledge:
The Percentage with "High" Information Level[a]

Information Measure	JAPAN Educational Level				UNITED STATES Education Level			
	Low[b]	Medium	High	γ[c]	Low	Medium	High	γ
Term Familiarity	27%	32%	44%	.22	10%	17%	32%	.47
Local Knowledge	19%	19%	19%	.07	18%	17%	26%	.22
Ecology Science	25%	36%	45%	.17	23%	33%	49%	.30
Problem Articulation	31%	31%	44%	.19	31%	44%	41%	.15
Self-Assessed Informedness	15%	17%	12%	-.05	26%	30%	46%	.24
Cumulative Index	14%	18%	24%	.17	11%	19%	34%	.32
N	(131-135)	(363-367)	(161)		(128-151)	(158-176)	(168-172)	

[a]The operational measure of high information is contained in the text to this chapter.

[b]In the United States, low education is defined as having completed high school or less; medium education is defined as "some college" or other post-secondary, but not B.A. schooling; high education is "completed college" or more education. In Japan, the cutting points are: low--none through intermediate school; middle--through high school; high--at least some college.

[c]The figure represents Gamma, an ordinal measure of association between education and the particular information measure within each country.

Table 3.1 displays the relationship between education level and knowledge in Japan and the United States. In the United States, low education is defined as "having completed high school or less," medium education is defined as "some college" or other post-secondary schooling, and high education is "completed college" or more education. In Japan the cutting points are slightly different, reflecting both the differing structures of the two educational systems as well as the need to provide some balance in the distribution of respondents among the analytical categories. In Japan the low category includes those individuals who have completed no more than intermediate school, the medium education category contains those whose highest level of schooling is the completion of high school, and the high level of education contains respondents who have at least some exposure to college education.

The operational definition of "high" information for Table 3.1 varies somewhat among the measures. For the index of technical term familiarity, the high level includes those individuals with a score of eleven or less on an index ranging from 9 (high) to 27 (lowest). On the measure of knowledge of local conditions, the high category includes individuals with a three on a scale of zero to three in the American setting, and a score of four on a scale of zero to four in the Japanese case; in both countries, those individuals with no errors are included in the highest level, even though the Japan case has one more item in the scale. On the measure of knowledge of ecology science, the scales ranged from zero correct to four correct answers; the high category contains individuals with a score of three or four. On the articulation measure of information holding (the ability or willingness to identify problems), individuals who identify two or more environmental or water resource problems are included in the high category. On the self-estimate of knowledge, with a range from one (completely uninformed) to seven (very informed), individuals placing themselves at positions 5, 6, and 7 are in the high group. The final measure sums the number of separate measures on which an individual is placed in the highest grouping. Individuals with three or more measures in the top category are classified as belonging in the high group on general knowledge.

Education level generally is a better predictor of knowledge in the United States than in Japan. The one exception has to do with the articulation of public policy problems. In no case among the Japanese respondents does the correlation between knowledge and education surpass .22 (for technical term familiarity). Among the Americans surveyed, five of the six relationships are of that magnitude or higher, and the strongest correlation is Gamma = .47.

The American educational process thus makes a bigger difference in the knowledge of its citizens than is the case in Japan. Recall that some have argued that the more open, less-disciplined American system focuses attention more on conceptualization and critical thinking than on the specific fundamentals of language and mathematics. The latter, of course, are central to educational advancement in Japan. It is the development of abstractions that provides the conceptual structure for acquiring and storing new information (Rosch, 1977).

One of the most significant sources of knowledge--education level--is more important in the United States than in Japan. At first blush, this might suggest that knowledge levels are less changeable in the United States, at least in the short run. If knowledge is limited by education, then the acquisition of information on new issues would be more difficult for Americans than for Japanese citizens. Is, then, the American public more likely to remain permanently cemented by education levels to low knowledge levels?

Three responses would seem appropriate. First, as we shall see shortly, additional sources of information may be more important in Japan than in the United States. Those other sources may produce the same *apparent* inflexibility in knowledge levels. Second, the importance of education suggests that there exists a long-term vehicle for improving overall knowledge levels. To the extent that policy-relevant knowledge can be effectively transmitted, the educational process serves as a potent vehicle. A relatively open educational system may provide a good deal of opportunity for *long-term* knowledge mobility among the citizenry. Third, further analyses may show that citizens can overcome the limitations imposed by education. It is even possible that one's level of education is simply a surrogate for motivational variables present most often among the more highly educated. If so, the short run task of elevating knowledge would be best accomplished by striking at individual motivation rather than addressing long-term considerations of curriculum.

Income

A second indicator of social location that may influence knowledge holding is family income. Individuals with higher income levels may have more resources required for gaining access to information. They may be more inclined to perceive stakes in policy outcomes than those with fewer economic resources. They also may be more likely than less fortunate persons to work and reside in information-rich environments

Table 3.2

Relationship of Income and Knowledge:
The Percentage with "High" Information Level[a]

Information Measure	JAPAN Income Level				UNITED STATES Income Level			
	Low[b]	Medium	High	γ[c]	Low	Medium	High	γ
Term Familiarity	29%	36%	37%	.14	17%	16%	27%	.19
Local Knowledge	16%	18%	24%	.17	10%	22%	25%	.23
Ecology Science	25%	41%	41%	.20	29%	35%	42%	.14
Problem Articulation	31%	37%	38%	.13	34%	38%	43%	.15
Self-Assessed Informedness	12%	16%	19%	.19	29%	33%	39%	.16
Cumulative Index	11%	21%	25%	.17	16%	23%	26%	.22
N	(251-221)	(290-292)	(142-143)		(91-109)	(159-176)	(175-186)	

[a]See the text for definitions of high information level on the several information measures.

[b]The income groupings include: Low: Japan, less than 4,000,000 yen; U.S., less than $15,000; middle: Japan, between 4 million and 7 million yen; U.S., $15,000 to $30,000; High; Japan greater than $7,000,000 yen and U.S., greater than $30,000.

[c]An ordinal measure of association.

54

(Gans, 1973). For these reasons, the relationship between income and information holding is shown in Table 3.2.

In both Japan and the United States, and across all six knowledge measures, there is a weak but consistent relationship between family income level and knowledge level. The differences in the two countries are sufficiently small to suggest that income has the same effects in both Japan and the United States. In several cases (terminology, knowledge of ecology science, and overall) these relationships are quite a bit weaker than those for education. Given the links between income and education, it is possible that income's impact on information will differ when assessed simultaneously with other variables (including education). In the meantime, the most one can say is that income has a marginal independent impact on knowledge.

Occupation

A third indicator of socioeconomic location is the individual's occupation. Japan and the United States both have experienced significant changes in occupational structure during the present century, although such changes were certainly greater in Japan (Vogel, 1979:3-26). Not only did Japanese society industrialize rapidly, it also was transformed from a feudal society into a modern society (Fukutake, 1967). Even though Japan experienced much more rapid change during the move to postindustrialism than did the United States, many deeply rooted elements of traditional Japanese society remain largely intact. One might thus suspect that occupational differences will be more significant in predicting information levels in Japan than in the United States.

Table 3.3 presents the proportion of Japanese and American respondents with "high" information levels within four occupational groupings. The categories are ordered from left to right in a roughly ascending order of occupational status. The U.S. Census ranking order was employed in the American setting, and the Japanese census ranking order was used in the Japanese. Nonetheless, the exact positioning of the occupational strata lacks some rigor since status rankings tend to be rather variable over time.

Two major patterns appear in Table 3.3. The first is that, surprisingly, the strongest relationships between occupation and knowledge are found in the American sample (although the difference is not startling). The second noteworthy pattern is that the relationship between occupation and information holding is more consistent *across* measures of information in Japan than in the United States. In both countries, though, the overall link between

Table 3.3

Relationship of Occupation and Knowledge: The Percentage with "High" Information Level

JAPAN

Occupation Grouping[a]

Information Measure	Not Employed Student (1)	Farm Work Labor (2, 3)	Office Worker (4)	Self Employed (5)	White Collar (6, 7)	γ
Term Familiarity	27%	28%	28%	51%	43%	.19
Local Knowledge	14%	16%	16%	27%	22%	.13
Ecology Science	33%	34%	33%	39%	43%	.10
Problem Articulation	32%	34%	28%	37%	44%	.11
Self-Assessed Informedness	9%	14%	18%	24%	20%	.16
Cumulative Index	14%	15%	18%	29%	25%	.18
N	(53)	(16)	(61)	(91)	(130)	

UNITED STATES

Occupation Grouping[b]

Information Measure	Laborer (1)	Operative Service (2, 3, 4)	Sales Clerical (5)	Prof./Managers White Collar (6, 7)	γ
Term Familiarity	13%	16%	22%	27%	.20
Local Knowledge	16%	20%	21%	24%	.08
Ecology Science	16%	28%	34%	50%	.23
Problem Articulation	16%	44%	39%	42%	.05
Self-Assessed Informedness	37%	32%	39%	38%	.08
Cumulative Index	16%	20%	21%	27%	.17
N	(73)	(199)	(74)	(57)	

[a]Categories based upon Japanese Census enumeration groupings.

[b]Categories based upon U.S. Census enumeration groupings.

occupation and information is relatively weak, and in neither case does it approach the impact of education found in the United States.

Class Identification

The analysis has focused on relatively "objective" measures of status. It may be that individuals who *think of themselves* as occupying higher status positions in society will sense a particular desire to acquire and hold policy-relevant information. Table 3.4 presents the relationship between subjective class identification and information holding. All survey participants were asked to classify themselves as either "working class" or "middle class." A slight difference obtains between the two countries in the relative proportion in the two categories; in the U.S. a little less than half (45%) of the respondents classify themselves as working class, while in Japan a little more than half (57%) of the respondents place themselves in the working class category.

The findings in Table 3.4 suggest that while class self-identification makes very little knowledge difference in Japan, it has some impact on the knowledge levels of the American respondents. The strongest association is found between class self-identification and familiarity with technical terms (Gamma = .36). In Spokane, other positive correlations are found between class and knowledge of environmental science facts, awareness of local conditions and the cumulative knowledge index.

Cumulative Impact of SES Variables

The relationships between socioeconomic variables and knowledge are not particularly strong. Yet, it remains possible that *taken in combination* they will produce a significant effect on citizen knowledge. Two important issues can be addressed. The first concerns the cumulative impact of the SES indicators on knowledge. The second issue is the relative impact of the separate indicators. Does subjective class identification retain its impact on technical term familiarity in the American sample when education, occupation and income are considered at the same time? The tool used here is multiple regression analysis. The results are shown in Table 3.5.

Even when taken as a group, the SES variables are not particularly powerful predictors of knowledge levels in either sample. In only one case is more than 10 percent of the variance in a particular knowledge measure explained in either Japan or the United States ($R^2 = .14$ for technical term familiarity among American respondents). A number of the other results are statistically significant, but they

Table 3.4

Relationship Between Class Self-Identification and Knowledge:
The Percentage with "High" Information Level[a]

Class Self-Identification[b]

Information Measure	JAPAN			UNITED STATES		
	Working Class	Middle Class	γ[c]	Working Class	Middle Class	γ
Term Familiarity	36%	32%	-.06	15%	25%	.36
Local Knowledge	20%	16%	-.14	16%	26%	.20
Ecology Science	36%	38%	.02	29%	43%	.22
Problem Articulation	34%	38%	.08	39%	40%	.03
Self-Assessed Informedness	16%	16%	-.04	33%	35%	.12
Cumulative Index	19%	19%	-.01	15%	27%	.19
N	(348-346)	(252-253)		(191-218)	(243-262)	

[a]For the definition of "high" information, the reader is referred to the text.

[b]The question used was the following: "There's been quite a lot of talk recently about different social classes in our country. Most people say they belong to the middle class or to the working class. If you had to make a choice, would you call yourself middle class or working class?

[c]Gamma is an ordinal measure of association between class and information levels.

Table 3.5

Regression Analysis of Socioeconomic Variables and Knowledge

	Term Familiarity		Local Knowledge		Ecology Science		Problem Articulation		Self-Assessed Informedness		Cumulative Index	
	Japan	U.S.	Japan	U.S.	Japan	U.S.	Japan	U.S.	Japan	U.S.	Japan	U.S.
R^2	.07	.14	.03	.04	.03	.04	.02	.01	.04	.06	.08	.07
F	10.86	12.2	4.23	3.51	4.45	3.00	3.05	.78	5.92	4.82	11.2	6.03
Class	X	X	X	X	X	X	X	X	X	X	X	X
Education	.10	.30	X	X	X	X	.08	X	.10	.18	.08	.20
Income	.15	X	.13	X	.12	X	X	X	.12	X	.15	X
Occupation	.17	X	.10	.10	.10	X	X	X	.15	X	.19	X
N	(553)	(302)	(553)	(302)	(553)	(302)	(553)	(302)	(553)	(302)	(553)	(302)

Entries in the cells are the standardized regression coefficients. Only those significant at the $p \leq .05$ level are entered in the table.

contribute relatively small amounts to the ability to explain knowledge differences among individuals.

Some distinct differences do emerge between the two countries in the relative impact of the socioeconomic indicators. While class self-identification is eliminated in both samples, *education* clearly remains the most pervasive factor in the Spokane sample, and both income and occupation dominate in the Shizuoka sample. In Japan, occupation is significant on five of the six measures (excluding problem articulation) while it appears in the table only once for the Americans (on the knowledge of local factors measure). Similarly, income in Japan is significant on five of the six measures (again with the exception of problem articulation), but evaporates entirely in the analysis of the Americans. In the United States, education falls out on the local information, ecology science and problem articulation measures. While education is singled out in Spokane, it also influences three of the Japanese knowledge measures. However, the impact of none of the Japanese coefficients approaches the strength of those for the Spokane respondents.

Demographic Correlates of Information Holding

The analysis turns now to the evaluation of the impact of several demographic variables on information holding. These attributes include gender, generational cohort, and the population of the area where the individual was reared. As in the previous section, each of these factors will be examined individually, then their cumulative and independent effects will be assessed. Finally, the demographic variables will be integrated into an analysis containing the socioeconomic indicators as well. The analysis turns first to gender.

Gender Differences[2]

In recent years, gender differences in personal political resources have become a frequent research topic (Campbell et al., 1960; Lansing, 1974; Jennings and Farah, 1980; Welch and Secret, 1981). Early research found women to be less likely than men to have the characteristics that lead to political influence. Indeed, compared to men, American women had lower levels of political efficacy, lower rates of political participation, and less abstract levels of political conceptualization. Some later findings, though, show that the gender gap in political participation is decreasing, at least in the United States, even while overall voting turnout rates have declined and gender-based differences have grown in some areas of support for public policy (Wassenberg, 1983).

An important, yet frequently overlooked, question pertains to the matter of gender differences in knowledge. Policy-relevant knowledge, as reiterated throughout this book, is particularly important as a political resource. Even in policy areas that do not *directly* relate to women's issues--as may be the case in environmental affairs--gender-based deficits in knowledge can place significant limits on the gender-based representativeness of the policy process.

Increasing attention has focused on cross-national differences in these gender-based political inequalities (Hottel, 1968; Verba et al., 1978; Seward and Williamson, 1970; Jennings and Farah, 1980). Cross-national analyses provide for the identification of possible culture-specific constraints on gender differences. In that context, comparison of gender differences in knowledge in the United States and Japan seems especially appropriate. Japan and the United States clearly differ in some significant ways, including the relative integration of women into male-dominated social, economic and political structures, the development of egalitarian sex role orientations, and the size and activity of the women's movement (Pharr, 1981). The presence of these dissimilarities provides the rationale for investigating Japanese and American gender differences in knowledge (Lebra, 1984).

A summary of the relationship of gender and knowledge is presented in Table 3.6. That table shows the percentage with "high" levels of policy-relevant knowledge among men and women in Japan and the United States. On five of the six measures in Table 3.6, men are better informed than are women; this pattern occurs in both Japan and the United States. In both countries the only measure that fails to generate gender differences is policy problem articulation. While American women have been said to be among the most liberated in the world and Japanese gender relationships are the more traditional (Pharr, 1981), the gender differences in knowledge holding are consistently greater in Spokane than in Shizuoka.

What might account for the greater knowledge impact of gender in the United States than in Japan? One possibility may be the areas from which the samples are drawn. Politically and socially, the Spokane area is relatively traditional. Recent changes in gender norms may not have penetrated as deeply in Spokane as in other places in the United States, especially in less accessible policy areas. However, a similar analysis of the Shizuoka Prefecture area would be equally tenable. While deeply affected by the modern demands for citizen involvement, the Shizuoka area remains less modern than the more urban areas of Tokyo and Kyoto, for example. Consequently, compared to other locations within the same nations the two areas

Table 3.6

Relationship of Gender and Knowledge:
The Percentage with "High" Information Level[a]

	JAPAN			UNITED STATES		
Information Measure	Male	Female	γ	Male	Female	γ
Term Familiarity	37%	31%	.15	27%	12%	.33
Local Knowledge	22%	14%	.16	27%	12%	.32
Ecology Science	38%	31%	.16	40%	31%	.20
Problem Articulation	36%	32%	.03	38%	40%	.08
Self-Assessed Informedness	19%	11%	.21	44%	23%	.38
Cumulative Index	22%	15%	.19	27%	16%	.30
N	(346)	(339)		(281)	(223)	

[a]For definitions of "high" information, see the text.

62

would not seem to differ in the relative traditionalism in gender-based norms.

Another possibility is that not all political attributes would respond equally to changes in social and political norms. Achieving gender equality in rates of political participation may be "easier" than eliminating gender differences in policy-relevant knowledge. The question arises, however, as to why such differences would show greater persistence in Spokane than in Shizuoka. The answer might be in the length of the environmental policy conflicts in the two areas. The Shizuoka dispute has lasted for more than two decades, has involved a wide range of interests and citizens, and has been a frequent and often dominant subject of local communication networks (Lewis, 1980). In contrast, the aquifer pollution issue in Spokane is more recent, involved a somewhat more limited segment of the general public, and has been less dominant in the local information channels. The Shizuoka information surfeit may have reduced gender-based information disparities arising out of more traditional sources.

Generational Cohort

Individual responses to sociopolitical changes vary by social location and by personal characteristics (Inglehart, 1971). One of the more telling of these personal factors is the nature of the individual's cognitive development. People have been shown to be more affected by changes in their environment at some stages of life than at others. A "window" period exists for the influence of the environment upon the personal development of a person's thinking. People are thought to be most responsive to the environment in adolescence and early adulthood, the time during which they are said to reach "political maturity" (Sigel and Hoskin, 1981).

If this account is at least partially correct, persons socialized during unusual periods of history would have distinctive political attributes. If so, members of generational cohorts may share characteristics that distinguish them from persons attached to other generational cohorts. Individuals socialized during periods of heightened sensitivity to environmental issues might thus be expected to be more concerned and likely better informed about those issues than persons coming into maturity at other times. The cohorts socialized primarily during the height of the environmental movement would be expected to be the better informed.

True cohort analysis requires comparable data for the same age groups of individuals at different points of time. With such evidence it is possible to determine the degree to which particular age cohorts change through time. Thus, for example, individuals who are 21-24 years of age in 1960 would be compared to a group that is 41-44 in 1980 to determine if they differed from persons of another age cohort in some hypothesized manner (Nie et al., 1976). In our data, appropriate longitudinal data are unavailable to test the generational hypotheses. With a single data point, cohort differences must be inferred from comparisons of age groups. Thus, the potentially confounding effects of life cycle or maturation changes cannot be obviated. With data collected at a single point in time, it is not possible to determine whether the youngest age group will become like the oldest one with the passage of time (aging), or whether its unique character exhibited early in life will persist relatively unchanged.

The interaction of age and generation is especially important to our concern with knowledge. One might expect to find life-cycle effects in knowledge. A life-cycle pattern would argue for an increasing store of knowledge with advancing age. An age-related knowledge curve would result from the length of the individual's exposure to information, general involvement in politics, and the increasing economic and personal stakes in public policy associated with the middle years.

The relationship of age groupings to knowledge is shown in Table 3.7. Three cohorts are identified. These three are: 1) age less than forty--individuals reaching maturity in the 1960s or later, the time of the awakening of the "new politics" social and cultural revolutions, as well as the major periods of post-industrial development; 2) individuals between the age of forty and sixty--coming of age in the period during and immediately after World War II; and 3) individuals sixty and over--coming into political maturity prior to the Second World War.

No consistent pattern obtains in the relationship of cohort to knowledge. The general pattern in Japan is a weak curvilinear relationship; in four of the six cases the middle cohort/age group is the most knowledgeable. There is some variation among the measures as to whether the oldest or the youngest group is the least knowledgeable, but in no case is the difference especially great between the most and least knowledgeable.

The Japanese findings would seem to fit a life-cycle interpretation of knowledge holding better than a generational explanation. Consistent with McKean (1981), in no case is the youngest generation--the one presumably socialized during the period of greatest environmental content--the most informed; indeed, in several cases it is the least informed. The age group with the greatest personal stakes in policy outcomes, those in the middle years, are generally the most highly informed.

Table 3.7

Relationship of Generational Cohort (Age) and Knowledge: Percentage with "High" Information Level[a]

| | Generational Cohort[b] | | | | | | | |
| | JAPAN | | | | UNITED STATES | | | |
Information Measure	Young	Middle	Old	γ	Young	Middle	Old	γ
Term Familiarity	32%	36%	22%	.02	20%	21%	20%	.20
Local Knowledge	12%	23%	19%	.23	18%	25%	22%	-.19
Ecology Science Problem	33%	38%	25%	.07	43%	46%	30%	-.16
Articulation	32%	34%	42%	.02	53%	42%	28%	-.26
Self-Assessed Informedness	14%	16%	21%	.26	33%	31%	39%	.20
Cumulative Index	15%	21%	19%	.08	31%	25%	19%	-.12
N	(44)	(93)	(100)		(15)	(36)	(100)	

[a]For definitions of "high" information, see the text.

[b]Cohort boundaries are described in the text.

The findings are even less clear in the American data. On the measure of technical term familiarity, virtually no difference is apparent among the three age groups. On one measure (self-assessed information levels) the oldest cohort is slightly more well informed than are the other groupings, but on three others that age group is the least well informed. The youngest age group stands out on the problem articulation measure, and it also is more likely to have persons with multiple kinds of knowledge.

Urban-Rural Origins

Considerable research has been reported comparing individuals in rural, less densely populated areas to those in urbanized, more densely settled locations (Honadle, 1985). In general, the literature suggests that urban areas provide the "cradle" for social, economic and political modernization and democratic practice (Goodman and Goodman, 1960:218-226). Not only are individuals from urban areas more likely to participate in the political process, they have often been shown to be more tolerant and more open to social, economic and political change (Campbell et al., 1960). While at one point the picture of the agrarian sage toiling in the fields as the backbone of democratic government may have held sway, empirical research in the postwar era usually has run in counter directions. Richardson has summarized this literature in these words:

> According to this view of political behavior, some individuals are more integrated than others into political communications, especially those which provide links with important decision-making centers. Variations in social location and communication involvement are in turn related to differences in overall political involvement and participation. People near the center of public life, in terms of social location, are thus expected to participate more than those closer to the periphery. Among the various factors defining social location is place of residence. Urban dwellers are considered to be closer to the center of society than their country counterparts, and as a result are expected to be more involved in politics (1974:129).

Then, in application to Japan, Richardson continues: "Ike and Kyogoku saw urban dwellers as politically more conscious than rural residents while Ward felt that the typical city dweller had a more developed awareness of what government could do for him" (Richardson, 1974:131).[3]

In an early review of political behavior in the United States, Robert Lane reached a similar conclusion:

> Perhaps because of the greater politicalization of the urbanites, their exposure to more political news and comment, their more salient class and ethnic cleavages, and their higher educational level, they are led to make politics a more significant part of their lives (1959:152).

Within both the American and Japanese samples there *is* variation in the size of the place in which respondents were reared. The availability of this information, however, only approximates the information required to test adequately the hypothesis that knowledge levels are higher in urban areas than in rural regions. The ideal test would use survey data collected simultaneously in many locations of differing size.

Table 3.8 displays findings reporting the relationship between the size of place and knowledge. The three categories employed in the Japanese setting are: under 50,000, between 50,000 and 100,000 residents, and over 100,000. the three categories in Spokane are: under 2,500, between 2,500 and 100,000 and over 100,000 souls. In both countries individuals raised in large urban areas are no better informed than those raised in other places. In Japan, the only differences of any magnitude is on problem articulation; here, respondents raised in the least populated areas named the fewest environmental policy problems. In the American sample in two cases the middle category respondents appear to be marginally less well informed than others. Such small differences do not represent any systematic underlying "place of upbringing" effects.

Cumulative Impact of Demographic Variables

The next question concerns the cumulative impact of the three demographic variables. The results are shown in Table 3.9.

Overall, the demographic variables are not as potent as the socio-economic variables in explaining variations in knowledge. Together, the three demographic indicators explain no more than seven percent of the variation in any of the knowledge measures. That level of explained variation is met or exceeded in four cases with the socioeconomic variables.

At this point comes the question of the relative impact of demographic indicators. Cohort/age is significant in two cases (both in Japan), where the older cohorts are the better informed (the measure

Table 3.8

Relationship of Size of Place Raised and Knowledge: Percentage with "High" Information Level[a]

Information Measure	JAPAN				UNITED STATES			
	Small[b]	Medium	Large	γ	Small	Medium	Large	γ
Term Familiarity	33%	34%	34%	.05	18%	19%	23%	.07
Local Knowledge	21%	16%	19%	.06	23%	12%	23%	.12
Ecology Science	41%	35%	34%	.06	34%	36%	39%	.05
Problem Articulation	18%	40%	36%	.10	37%	42%	38%	.03
Self-Assessed Informedness	18%	17%	15%	.01	39%	30%	33%	-.04
Cumulative Index	13%	20%	19%	.01	25%	16%	23%	.03
N	(342)	(286)	(66)		(195)	(131)	(198)	

[a]For definitions of "high" information, see the text.

[b]For cutoff points on size of place, see the text.

Table 3.9

Regression Analysis of Demographic Variables and Knowledge

	Term Familiarity		Local Knowledge		Ecology Science		Problem Articulation		Self-Assessed Informedness		Cumulative Index	
	Japan	U.S.	Japan	U.S.	Japan	U.S.	Japan	U.S.	Japan	U.S.	Japan	U.S.
R^2	.01	.04	.02	.06	.01	.00	.01	.00	.04	.07	.03	.04
F	1.21	3.95	4.43	6.36	2.24	.18	2.46	.49	8.06	7.54	4.93	3.91
Cohort	X	X	.11	X	X	X	X	X	.16	X	X	X
Gender	X	.19	.10	.24	.10	X	X	X	.11	.23	.14	.19
Size of Home Town	X	X	X	X	X	X	X	X	X	X	X	X
N	(553)	(302)	(553)	(302)	(553)	(302)	(553)	(302)	(553)	(302)	(553)	(302)

Only significant ($p \leq .05$) coefficients included. Entries in the cells corresponding to each independent variable are standardized regression coefficients.

of knowledge of local conditions and the self-assessed information measure); the size of one's hometown is significant (b=.09, p≤.05) in only one case--that being in Japan on the problem articulation measure (a point noted above).

Among the demographic variables, gender is by far the most consistent and the most powerful predictor of knowledge levels. In both Japan and the United States men are better informed than women on four of the six knowledge measures when controlling for age cohort and size of hometown. It is possible, of course, that the impact of gender on knowledge may disappear when controlling for the several social variables.

Social and Demographic Influences Considered Together

The final issue of this chapter is the cumulative impact of social and demographic attributes on knowledge. A series of multiple regression analyses was performed, the results of which are shown in Table 3.10.

In no case does the full set of variables explain as much as 20 percent of the variation in knowledge holding. The highest R^2 is .17 for technical term familiarity in the United States. In only two other cases does the proportion of explained variation reach or surpass .10--that being self-assessed information levels and the summary index in the American sample. These findings suggest that considerable variation in knowledge cannot be attributed to social and demographic variables.

In contrast to the pronounced role of education in both countries, but especially in the Spokane sample, the broad effects of occupation and income are evident in Shizuoka. Income level has a significant effect on five of the six knowledge measures, and occupation affects four of the six. That the wealth-based status variables are more important than education in Japan may reflect the continuing presence of a traditional, hierarchical social structure (Nakane, 1970).

Contrasting cross-national patterns appear as well in the relative impact of age cohort and gender. When considered with the other six variables, cohort has a significant impact (standardized regression coefficients) on four of the six knowledge measures in Japan only--but none in the American sample. The reverse is true, however, for the role of gender; statistically significant (p≤.05) coefficients appear on four of six cases in Spokane, but in none of the six in Shizuoka. Older people are better informed than younger persons in Japan, when controlling for their other social and demographical attributes; men are better informed than women in the American setting when controlling

Table 3.10

Regression Analysis of Impact of Social and Demographic Variables on Knowledge

	Term Familiarity		Local Knowledge		Ecology Science		Problem Articulation		Self-Assessed Informedness		Cumulative Index	
	Japan	U.S.	Japan	U.S.	Japan	U.S.	Japan	U.S.	Japan	U.S.	Japan	U.S.
R^2	.08	.17	.04	.09	.04	.04	.04	.02	.06	.13	.09	.10
F	6.60	8.50	3.55	4.25	3.02	1.81[a]	3.36	.67[a]	5.05	6.30	7.53	4.77
Class	X	X	X	X	X	X	X	X	X	X	X	X
Education	.09	.28	X	X	X	X	.13	X	X	.17	.14	.19
Income	.16	X	.11	X	.11	X	X	X	.09	X	.13	X
Occupation	.20	X	X	X	X	X	.11	X	.12	X	.16	X
Generational Cohort	X	X	.11	X	X	X	.12	X	.15	X	.12	X
Gender	X	.17	X	.21	X	X	X	X	X	.21	X	.17
Size of Home Town	X	X	X	X	X	X	X	X	X	X	X	X
N	(553)	(302)	(553)	(302)	(553)	(302)	(553)	(302)	(553)	(302)	(553)	(302)

Only significant ($p \leq .05$) coefficients included. Entries in the cells corresponding to each independent variable are standardized regression coefficients.

[a] F - ratios of $p \leq .05$ level of significance.

for their other characteristics.

Across knowledge measures, the cumulative impact of social and demographic attributes on information levels varies from $R^2 = .02$ on problem articulation in the American sample to $R^2 = .17$ on knowledge of policy-relevant terminology, also in Spokane. These characteristics are most important on measures that focus on the individual's self-perception of knowledge. Especially in the Spokane sample, education and male gender lead one to rate self knowledge level as high, and to claim considerable knowledge of technical terms. In Japan, such confidence is more a consequence of age, income and occupational status--all of which constitute traditional bases of power and influence in that country.

Conclusion

This chapter has assessed the impact of social and demographic attributes on knowledge levels. The effects of these variables have wide-ranging implications. Since knowledge links interest and policy, the degree to which knowledge is held by persons of differing social and demographic attributes is an important question. In this context, the results of this chapter suggest several preliminary conclusions.

First, in both Japan and the United States the social/demographic variables exert significant effects on knowledge. However, a substantial portion of the variance in knowledge remains unexplained by those variables. Second, some rather consistent cross-national differences obtain in the impact of specific variables. In the American sample the most important sources of knowledge are education and gender. In Japan, the most significant influences on knowledge holding are income, occupation and generational cohort. These differences once again underscore the importance of studying cross-national differences in response to the commonally experienced forces of post-industrialism.

Notes

1. This section is drawn largely from Lovrich and Pierce, 1984:415-418.
2. This discussion is based in part on Lovrich et al., 1985.
3. The references are to Jun'ichi Kyogoku and Nabutaka Ike (1960).

4

Motivation and Knowledge

Introduction

This chapter continues the examination of why some individuals have more knowledge than do others. The preceding chapter focused on the individual background correlates of knowledge. This chapter turns to "situational" correlates of knowledge holding. Situational explanations reflect an individual's ties to the specific policy area, ties which may vary from one policy "situation" to another. These situational factors are "motivational." In this context, motivation reflects the presence of a situation-specific *incentive* to acquire information. The proposition in question is that knowledge holding will reflect variations in the motivation to acquire such information. Recall that knowledge is argued to link the citizen's personal values and substantive interests to policy alternatives. Thus, one would expect greater knowledge among individuals who see a particular stake in policy outcomes, who are more strongly committed to their policy views, who see government as likely to be responsive to their efforts to influence public policy, and who have actually attempted to influence policy. This chapter thus examines these four particular indicators of a citizen's motivation to acquire knowledge.

Policy Salience. Simply put, the proposition here is that the more importance an individual attaches to a particular policy area, the greater will be the incentive to acquire information (Jennings and Zeigler, 1970). Individuals who perceive the policy area as important should be more likely to attend to information about that area, and more likely to focus on the specific issues and policy options being discussed (Zimbardo and Ebbesen, 1970:20-23).

Policy Issue Urgency. Individuals with a greater sense of policy urgency should be more knowledgeable. Individuals with a greater sense of urgency may see themselves as having more at stake in policy disputes and they may be more likely to care about the policy direction taken. Such persons thus have a disproportionate incentive to acquire policy-relevant information. This sense of urgency is indexed by the *extremity* of policy opinions expressed (Pierce and Lovrich, 1980).

Perception of System Responsiveness. If one views a policy area as important and/or holds extreme or strong views, perceptions of an unresponsive political system may still intervene to inhibit information gathering. Feeling that a political system is unresponsive may dampen the incentive to acquire policy-relevant information. The hypothesis, then, is that the level of knowledge holding will be greater among individuals who expect government to be responsive than among those who lack such expectations (House, 1981:2-6).

Policy Area Participation. Perhaps the most telling indicator of one's stake in a policy area is an attempt to influence particular policy outcomes. Unlike voting, which may be highly ritualistic (Milbrath, 1965), policy area activism is much more clearly definable as goal-directed behavior (Dutton, 1984). In one sense, the act of participation may be a culmination of perceptions of policy salience, commitment to policy views, and perception of political system responsiveness. Participation, then, may well be a strong predictor of knowledge holding. Information may make participation more effective, and participation itself should have substantial educative consequences (Tait et al., 1980).

Policy Area Salience

Policy area salience refers to the subjective importance attached by individuals to the substantive content of a particular policy area. The more salient the policy area to the individual, the more likely one will see a self-interest in policy area outcomes. Thus, respondents with high policy area salience also should be motivated to acquire knowledge. That knowledge will aid participation, help identification of self-interest in policy alternatives, and promote the pursuit of strongly held policy views.

Policy salience is used here as a rather general construct. Three specific indicators of salience are employed in the subsequent analysis--policy area seriousness, satisfaction with current policy and the status of environmental conditions to which the substance of policy is directed. The *policy seriousness* question used asked respondents to consider the relative importance of natural resource problems vis-a-vis other concerns by posing the following query (Spokane form):

Compared to other problems in the Spokane area (for example, crime, unemployment, air pollution, etc.), how would you rate the seriousness of water resource problems?
1. Not a serious problem
2.
3.
4. A somewhat serious problem
5.
6.
7.One of the most serious problems facing the Spokane area

The closer one's response is to the "one of the most serious" end of the scale, the greater should be the incentive to acquire water resource policy-relevant information.

The question used to assess *policy satisfaction* (Spokane version) took the following form:

Generally speaking, how satisfied are you with the management of water resources in the Spokane area?
1. Very dissatisfied
2.
3.
4. Not sure
5.
6.
7. Very satisfied

Our expectation is that individuals who are relatively dissatisfied with the current management of water resources will have the greater incentive to acquire information. Policy dissatisfaction implies a critical view, often based at least in part on some information as to how the present situation differs from that which is desired (Arnstein, 1969). Policy dissatisfaction also is connected to higher rates of participation in the water resource policy area (Pierce et al., 1976), and such participation in turn is linked to greater knowledge (Pierce and Lovrich, 1980).

The third salience measure reflects the respondent's perceptions of the *quality* of the current policy domain. The question used (Spokane version) follows:

Considering all aspects of the situation of water resources in the Spokane area--that is, adequacy of supply, quality of drinking water, availability of sewer services, environmental quality of surface waters (rivers and lakes), etc.--how would you locate your position on this seven-point scale ranging from 'Spokane represents a terrible situation to Spokane represents a wonderful situation'?

1. Terrible situation
2.
3.
4. Adequate situation
5.
6.
7. Wonderful situation

Respondents evaluating the 'situation' less favorably should be more knowledgeable than others by virtue of their heightened incentive to acquire information. This is not because the "objective" or "knowledgeable" view of the situation is necessarily unfavorable. Rather, an incentive to acquire policy-relevant information would adhere to a *perception* that one's environment is at some risk.

What the expectation should be in comparing Japan and the United States may not be clear. Policy area salience may be higher in the Shizuoka public than in Spokane. The Shizuoka focus on pollution has spanned more than two decades compared to a relatively recent history of public conflict in Spokane. Moreover, in some ways the Shizuoka context seems to have posed a more immediate danger to the public. As described in the first chapter, the Japanese citizens movement was born in the Suruga Bay region of Shizuoka Prefecture. The movement arose in response to an attempt by the national government to locate a large petro-chemical plant complex when awareness was spreading quickly over the presence of the infamous Minimata disease in Suruga Bay. This central nervous system disease is caused by ingestion of fish and shellfish contaminated by mercury contained in industrial waste. Thus, at least at the public level there may have been a higher level of salience in Shizuoka than in Spokane (Lewis, 1975). In Spokane there is less consensus since a division exists between Spokane City residents--whose water supply is under threat of contamination by suburban septic tanks--and the residents of Spokane Valley who would pay the greatest costs of eliminating the contamination (Lamb and Lovrich, 1987).

Table 4.1 shows the distributions on the three policy salience measures--satisfaction, quality and seriousness. Salience *is* greater in

76

Table 4.1
Distribution of Policy Area Salience in Shizuoka and Spokane

Satisfaction With Current Water Resource Management Policy	Japan	U.S.	*Quality of Situation Local Environment*	Japan	U.S.	*Perceived Seriousness*	Japan	U.S.
Very Dissatisfied 1.	7%	5%	Terrible 1.	5%	2%	Not Serious 1.	2%	8%
2.	12	8	2.	14	5	2.	3	10
3.	26	12	3.	28	18	3.	14	16
Not Sure 4.	26	27	Adequate 4.	38	28	Somewhat 4.	34	25
5.	21	28	5.	10	21	5.	23	15
6.	7	14	6.	4	20	6.	14	12
Very Satisfied 7.	1	6	Wonderful 7.	1	6	One of Most Serious 7.	11	14
Total	100%	100%		100%	100%		101%	100%
N	(672)	(502)	N	(672)	(511)	N	(672)	(511)
PDI*	-16	+23	PDI	-32	+22	PDI	+29	+7

*Percentage Difference Index equals percent in positions 5, 6 and 7 minus percent in positions 1, 2 and 3.

Japan. The policy area is viewed as worth more serious attention and the environment is considered to be of lesser quality in Shizuoka than in Spokane. Moreover, Shizuoka citizens are less satisfied with current water resource/environmental policy than are their American counterparts. Important for our concern with explaining knowledge holding, though, is the presence of substantial variation in salience among both the Japanese and the Americans. There remains ample opportunity for differences in knowledge levels to originate in differences in motivation.

The bivariate relationships between the salience measures and knowledge are shown in Table 4.2. Substantial differences occur across the three salience measures. Among both the American and Japanese respondents, perceptions of environmental quality and policy area satisfaction are related only to the articulation of policy area problems (correlations between .16 and .21). Individuals who perceive environmental quality as poor and who are dissatisfied with environmental policies are somewhat more likely than others to articulate policy area problems. Even for these relationships, though, the correlations are not very strong.

By far the most consistent and the strongest predictor of knowledge holding is the perception of the relative seriousness of environmental water resource problems compared to other policy areas. The results are remarkably similar in both the Japanese and American cases. These correlations approach the size of the social and demographic variables investigated in the prior chapter.

In summary, the preliminary evidence suggests that motivation (especially in the form of perceived policy area seriousness) is related to policy knowledge. Moreover, these findings hold across the knowledge measures in both Japan and the United States.

Policy Urgency

This section evaluates the possibility that individuals with more extreme beliefs will have greater incentive to acquire policy-relevant knowledge. More extreme beliefs may reflect more committed beliefs. Extremity and commitment constitute considerable stakes in policy outcomes. To test this expectation, four measures of belief extremity are used. These four measures reflect extremity (as opposed to direction) in preservationist identification, political values, the ranking of preservation as an environmental/water resource priority, and an index of sensitivity to pollution.

The preservationist identification measure is based upon a five-point scale. The respondent places himself/herself on a continuum

Table 4.2

The Relationship of Policy Salience Beliefs to Policy-Relevant Knowledge Levels[a]

Policy Salience Measure

Knowledge Measure	Policy Area Satisfaction Japan	U.S.	Policy Area Seriousness Japan	U.S.	Policy Area Quality Japan	U.S.
Technical Term Familiarity	-.04	.00	.20	.25	-.10	-.04
Local Conditions Knowledge	-.05	.00	.23	.16	-.03	.02
Ecology Science	-.01	.00	.13	.13	-.11	-.01
Problem Articulation	-.16	-.21	.19	.37	-.18	-.18
Self-Assessed Information	.00	.14	.28	.19	.00	.08
Cumulative Index	-.05	-.01	.23	.27	-.09	-.03

[a]The entries in each cell are gamma coefficients

ranging from strong developmentalist to strong preservationist. The responses were "folded," grouping strong preservationists and strong developmentalists, moderate preservationists and moderate developmentalists, and leaving the middle category ungrouped. This folding process results in a 3-point index. The extremity of ranking of preservation is based on seven alternative policy priorities (agriculture, domestic, energy, transportation, recreation, industry and preservation). Each was ranked vis a vis the others as to its relative importance. Each use thus has a distribution of ranks from one to seven, one being most preferred and seven the least preferred. Again, this multi-item summary index was folded, with seven and one being the extreme categories. The third extremity measure is based in the "post-materialist" index developed by Inglehart (1971). This four-item measure classifies respondents into three mutually exclusive categories--materialists, those holding 'mixed' values, and post-materialists. The materialists and the post-materialists inhabit the "extreme" categories. The final extremity measure is grounded in the assessment of ten items (e.g., fireplace smoke, auto emission, loud noises) for the degree to which they constitute environmental "pollution." An overall index of environmental pollution sensitivity was created. That index ranged from those who considered none of the conditions to constitute "pollution" to those labelling them all as "definitely pollution." Again, this multi-item index was folded, with individuals on *either* end on the pollution continuum sharing the "extreme" grouping.

The relationships between extremity and knowledge (Table 4.3) is certainly unimpressive; no correlation coefficient (gamma) exceeds .20. Only the preservationist identification extremity measure among the Spokane area respondents carries some impact across knowledge measures.

Perceived Government Responsiveness

The motivation to acquire knowledge can be tempered by the perception that the political system is unresponsive to citizen petitioning (Cobb and Elder, 1972:151-159). Few benefits would come from one's knowledge if government is in fact unresponsive (Parenti, 1978:63-80). Moreover, if a citizen is of the view that citizen involvement is of little value generally, there then is little reason to acquire the policy-relevant information needed to enhance such political participation (Downs, 1957:260-276).

This section employs two measures to assess (1) the respondents' perceptions of the value of citizen participation, and (2) their judgment

Table 4.3

The Relationship of Opinion Extremity and Policy-Relevant Knowledge Holding[a]

Extremity Measure[b]

Knowledge Measure	Pollution Sensitivity		Preservationist Identification		Postmaterialist Values		Ranking of Preservationist Use of Water	
	Japan	U.S.	Japan	U.S.	Japan	U.S.	Japan	U.S.
Technical Term Familiarity	.10[c]	-.10	-.11	.16	-.07	-.04	-.00	-.01
Local Conditions Knowledge	.13	-.01	.15	.20	-.11	.01	-.02	-.12
Ecology Science	.11	.03	-.04	.04	-.05	.04	-.03	-.02
Problem Articulation	.09	.05	-.02	.16	-.17	.03	.02	-.01
Self-Assessed Information	-.05	-.06	.02	-.02	-.07	.09	.06	-.10
Cumulative Index	.08	.04	-.00	.16	-.13	.05	-.08	-.01

[a]The entries in each cell are gamma coefficients

[b]For descriptions of the extremity measures the reader is referred to the text.

[c]Signs reversed where necessary for consistency in interpretation.

of the openness of government. The survey item employed to assess the value ascribed to legal provisions for citizen participation in environmental policy processes has the following form:

In recent years there has been considerable debate over the value of efforts to increase the amount of citizen participation in government policy making in the environmental policy area. How would you locate yourself on the following scale regarding these efforts?

1. These efforts are of no value
2.
3.
4. Uncertain
5.
6.
7. These efforts are of great value

The distributions of the Japanese and American samples on this measure are shown in Table 4.4. A favorable evaluation of citizen participation exists in both countries, although the Japanese are a little more positive than are their American counterparts.

The measure of perceived impact on government has this form:

According to what you have read, heard of, or know from your own personal experience, how much opportunity does each level of government listed below provide citizens like you to express their views on natural resource and environmental issues?

In the American questionnaire the three levels of government used were the federal, state and city. In Japan these strata of government were labeled national, prefectural and local. Respondents were given the opportunity to rate government openness on a scale ranging from "a great deal" to "none at all." The distribution of responses within the two samples is also shown in Table 4.4. Once more the response patterns in both settings are remarkably similar. In both locations the most frequent view of government is negative, and in both nations the feeling of openness increases as one moves from the national level of government down to the local level.

The magnitude of the relationships in Table 4.5 is not startling. However, individuals perceiving citizen participation to be of greater value are more knowledgeable. These patterns are different from those which pertain to the relationship between knowledge and perceptions of government responsiveness. The relationships generally are quite

Table 4.4

Public Perceptions of the Value of Citizen Participation in Policy Formation

Value of Citizen Participation		JAPAN	UNITED STATES
No Value	1.	1%	4%
	2.	1%	4%
	3.	2%	6%
Uncertain	4.	28%	32%
	5.	19%	21%
	6.	19%	17%
Great Value	7.	29%	16%
Total		99%	100%
(N)		(668)	(496)
PDI*		+63	+40

Perception of Opportunity to Express Views at Different Levels of Government

	JAPAN			UNITED STATES		
	National	Prefectural	Local	National	State	Local
Great Deal	2%	3%	11%	6%	7%	14%
Some	25%	30%	44%	24%	34%	45%
A Little	36%	42%	29%	36%	43%	27%
None	36%	25%	16%	34%	16%	14%
Total	99%	100%	100%	100%	100%	100%
(N)	(627)	(627)	(632)	(484)	(487)	(486)
*PDI	-44	-34	+10	-34	-18	+18

*PDI is percentage at great deal or some **MINUS** the percentage at a little or none.

Table 4.5

Relationship of Perception of Value of Citizen Participation and Policy-Relevant Knowledge[a]

Knowledge Measure	JAPAN	UNITED STATES
Technical Term Familiarity	.22	.24
Local Condition Knowledge	.25	.12
Ecology Science	.17	.20
Problem Articulation	.19	.22
Self-Assessed Information	.16	.07
Cumulative Index	.20	.21

Relationship of Perception of Opportunity to Express Views to Policy-Relevant Knowledge Holding[a]

Knowledge Measure	JAPAN			UNITED STATES		
	National	Prefectural	Local	National	State	Local
Technical Term Familiarity	-.03	-.04	-.04	-.07	-.13	-.05
Local Conditions Knowledge	-.14	-.17	-.18	-.07	-.02	-.07
Ecology Science	-.05	-.06	-.06	-.13	-.19	-.13
Problem Articulation	-.02	-.01	-.04	.01	.02	-.01
Self-Assessed Information	-.14	-.10	-.14	-.07	-.04	-.00
Cumulative Index	-.11	-.08	-.04	-.07	-.08	-.05

[a]Entry in each cell is gamma coefficient.

weak and they are inconsistent across knowledge measures. In addition, there are some differences between the two countries (e.g., the strongest correlations in Shizuoka are with local knowledge, while in Spokane they are with ecology science).

Political Participation

Political activity is the means by which the citizen's knowledge can be translated into power. Participation is the vehicle through which like-minded citizens can maximize the link between their value preferences and possible policy outcomes (McClosky and Zaller, 1984:234-262).

Individuals with more knowledge may be better able to perceive their interests in policy outcomes. They thus may participate more fully in civic affairs than their less well informed peers. At the same time, political involvement may inform one about the substantive content of major political issues. There may thus be a reciprocal relationship between knowledge and participation. But it is our suggestion that the major portion of the linkage moves *from* participation *to* knowledge. Citizens are often drawn into political action by some general policy concern. Upon such direct involvement the experience of participation accelerates the gathering of further information needed to support and protect one's policy position.

Japanese and American respondents were asked to indicate whether they had participated in each of six activities for the purpose of influencing environmental policy. The activities are: letter writing, joining a group, giving time or money to political candidates, going to a public meeting, signing a petition, and campaigning for a candidate for political office. An index was created by summing the number of activities in which the individual participated.

The relationships between knowledge and participation are shown in Table 4.6. First, with few exceptions, participants in every kind of political act are more informed than is the non-participating public. Second, in almost every case the knowledge differences between participants and non-participants are greater in the United States than in Japan. Third, in Spokane participation's effects are strongest on technical term familiarity and self-estimated knowledge. Only 34 percent of the Spokane public places itself in the highly informed group; however, fully 65 percent of those who participated in an electoral campaign call themselves highly informed. The effects of participation are smaller in the Japanese data, and there is also less range across knowledge measures. Fourth, there are few differences among particular types of American participants. The sole exception

Table 4.6

Percent "High" Information Level Among Six Types of Participants

Knowledge Measure	Overall Participation Index		Letter Writing		Joining Groups		Giving Time or Money		Attending Meetings		Signing Petition		Campaigning for Candidate	
	Japan	U.S.	Japan	U.S.	Japan	U.S.	Japan	U.S.	Japan	U.S.	Japan	U.S.	Japan	U.S.
Term Familiarity	33%*	20%	33%	36%	43%	40%	43%	39%	40%	41%	37%	24%	36%	37%
Local Knowledge	18	20	17	25	27	33	23	24	24	19	20	21	25	32
Ecology Science	34	35	33	46	41	51	43	46	44	50	42	40	37	40
Problem Articulation	34	38	33	42	43	41	40	48	39	53	40	43	37	37
Self-Assessed Informedness	15	34	25	57	25	59	24	51	15	60	18	38	21	65
Cumulative Index	18	21	17	35	32	37	25	38	27	36	22	28	24	37
Minimum N	(624)	(464)	(12)	(72)	(44)	(47)	(127)	(93)	(89)	(81)	(324)	(240)	(172)	(63)
Maximum N	(694)	(522)	(14)	(79)	(45)	(51)	(131)	(103)	(93)	(88)	(333)	(262)	(176)	(68)
Difference from Average[a]			+2	+12	+10	+16	+8	+13	+6	+15	+5	+3	+5	+13

*Entry in each cell is the percentage participating in that political activity who also have "high" levels of knowledge on that measure

[a] Average difference from population percentage

pertains to the petition signers who comprise nearly half of the public and whose action is relatively "easy" to perform (Pierce and Lovrich, 1982). In Japan the group joiners are the most distinctive in knowledge levels, and the letter writers stand out the least.

A more general view of the relationship between knowledge and participation is shown in Table 4.7. The participation index is correlated with each measure of knowledge. A consistent, positive association obtains between participation and knowledge. The strongest relationship occurs between participation and familiarity with technical terms (Gamma = .40). In both Japan and the United States political participation contributes to a citizen's knowledge. Knowledge assists the individual in identifying interests, and action provides the means to maximize those interests.

The Cumulative Impact of Motivational Variables

In each set of motivational variables at least one measure has a significant effect on knowledge. This section examines the independent effects of these motivational variables. Only one measure has been selected from each of the four sets of motivational indicators, that being the one measure with the strongest and most consistent relationship to knowledge. The four indicators selected are: 1) perceptions of the seriousness of environmental/water policy issues; 2) perceptions of the value of citizen participation; 3) extremity of preservationist identification; and 4) the overall index of policy area political participation. The multiple regression analysis results are shown in Table 4.8.

First, in most cases the cumulative impact of the motivational variables is greater in the United States than in Japan. This difference is especially striking on the indicators of problem articulation, self-assessed informedness, and the summary index. In Spokane the motivational variables explain fifteen percent of the variance in the problem articulation measure; this figure compares to only four percent in Shizuoka. In contrast, the perception of the value of citizen participation is more important across knowledge measures in Japan than in the American setting. Political participation is important for all knowledge measures in both the United States and Japan. However, the magnitude of the regression coefficients is greater among Americans than among Japanese. Apparently, more knowledge is to be gained from political involvement in the United States than from participation in Japan.

In summary, motivational variables have a significant impact on knowledge. There are some differences between the citizens of Japan

Table 4.7

The Relationship of Knowledge and Political Participation

Knowledge Measure	Japan	U.S.
Technical Term Familiarity	.22[*]	.40
Local Condition Knowledge	.30	.25
Ecology Science	.32	.30
Problem Articulation	.27	.22
Self-Assessed Information	.29	.36
Cumulative Index	.31	.35

*Entry in each cell is the gamma coefficient between the three-category information measures and the seven-category participation index.

Table 4.8

Regression of Policy-Relevant Knowledge Measures with Selected Motivational Variables: Shizuoka Prefecture and Metropolitan Spokane

	Term Familiarity		Local Knowledge		Ecology Science		Problem Articulation		Self-Assessed Informedness		Cumulative Index	
	Japan	U.S.	Japan	U.S.	Japan	U.S.	Japan	U.S.	Japan	U.S.	Japan	U.S.
R^2	.07	.11	.08	.07	.04	.08	.04	.15	.09	.16	.09	.19
F	11.08	13.1	13.9	8.18	6.74	8.6	6.32	17.6	15.04	19.7	15.5	24.7
Perceptions of Issue Area Seriousness	.12[b]	.17[c]	.13[b]	.16[b]	*	*	.09[a]	.30[c]	.19[c]	.19[c]	.16[c]	.31[c]
Political Participation	.09[a]	.24[c]	.18[c]	.18[c]	.14[c]	.21[c]	.12[b]	.12[a]	.18[c]	.33[c]	.17[c]	.25[c]
Value of Citizen Participation	.13[b]	*	.10[a]	*	.10[a]	.10[a]	.08[a]	.11[a]	*	X	.10[a]	*
Preservationist Identification												
Extremity	.13[c]	*	*	*	*	*	*	*	*	.11[a]	*	*

[a] p ≤ .05 (F = 3.84)
[b] p ≤ .01 (F = 6.64)
[c] p ≤ .001 (F = 10.83)

*not significant (p ≤ .05)

and the United States (e.g., the greater role of the perceived value of citizen participation in Japan), but the overwhelming impression is one of similarity. When motivated, citizens in both countries appear able to gather information relevant to significant policy questions.

Background and Motivational Sources of Knowledge

Background factors alone may determine knowledge. If so, the individual is limited both in political power and in the recognition of self-interest by the relative absence of the "right" attributes. On the other hand, if motivation also is an important source of knowledge it becomes possible for even lower SES citizens to respond to changing public policy agendas. The relative impact of the several background and motivational variables on knowledge is shown in Table 4.9.

In every case, the amount of variation (R^2) explained in knowledge is greater in Spokane than in Shizuoka. In several instances the differences are quite substantial (e.g., technical term familiarity, self-assessed familiarity and number of measures on which one is informed). Our preliminary explanation for this is primarily contextual. Variations in knowledge may be less explainable in Shizuoka than in Spokane because of differences in the histories of environmental policy conflict.

While environmental policy conflict is salient in both contexts, there are several important differences. In Shizuoka, pollution and its consequences have been the subject of much discussion for two decades. Even the early conflict over the establishment of major industrial complexes was highly charged and penetrated well into the mass public, furthering citizen movements in Japan (Lewis, 1980). These historical factors, combined with high population density, may have flooded the communication channels over a long period. In this context, position in the social structure and motivation would have less influence on exposure to and retention of policy-relevant knowledge.

In Spokane, in contrast, the public history of the conflict is shorter, and has not permeated as far into the mass public's consciousness (Spokane County Engineers, 1982). With a shorter history and lower overall salience, knowledge becomes "harder" to acquire. Personal attributes--be they background or motivational--may thus become more important in predicting variations in knowledge (Lovrich et al., 1986:231).

The apparently greater leveling of knowledge across social and motivational strata in Shizuoka may come also from different environmental politics in the two countries. Environmental activism in the United States is generally confined to a rather small group

Table 4.9

Multiple Regression of Policy-Relevant Knowledge Measures with Background and Motivational Variables: Shizuoka and Spokane

	Knowledge Measure											
	Term Familiarity		Local Knowledge		Ecology Science		Problem Articulation		Self-Assessed Informedness		Cumulative Index	
	Japan	U.S.	Japan	U.S.	Japan	U.S.	Japan	U.S.	Japan	U.S.	Japan	U.S.
R^2	.11	.24	.10	.13	.07	.10	.06	.12	.12	.23	.14	.25
F	8.8	12.1	8.6	6.0	5.3	4.2	5.2	5.1	10.4	11.6	12.4	13.1
N	(608)	(321)	(608)	(321)	(608)	(321)	(608)	(321)	(608)	(321)	(608)	(321)
Education	.09[a]	.25[c]	*	*	.12[b]	*	.13[b]	*	*	.12[a]	.14[c]	.14[a]
Occupational Status	.18[c]	*	*	*	*	.17[b]	*	*	.11[a]	*	.13[b]	*
Generational Cohort	*	*	.11[b]	.25[c]	*	*	*	*	*	*	*	*
Gender	*	.13[b]	*	*	*	*	*	*	.12[b]	.19[c]	.10[a]	.18[c]
Perceptions of Issue Seriousness	.16[c]	.21[c]	.12[b]	.13[a]	*	*	.10[a]	.27[c]	.19[c]	.18[c]	.18[c]	.26[c]
Political Participation	.08[a]	.18[b]	.17[c]	.15[b]	.12[b]	.16[b]	.11[b]	*	.15[c]	.30[c]	.15[c]	.24[c]
Value of Citizen Participation	.08[a]	*	.09[a]	*	*	*	*	*	*	*	*	*
Pres. Ident.	.10[a]	*	*	*	*	*	*	*	*	*	*	*
Extremity	*	*	*	*	*	*	*	*	*	.13[a]	*	*

[a] $p \leq .05$ [b] $p \leq .01$ [c] $p \leq .001$ *not significant ($p \leq .05$)

actively involved in explicit environmental organizations, or in closely related civic organizations. Rarely are environmentalist groups explicitly tied into long-standing partisan, personal or other political organizations. In sharp contrast, Japanese environmentalism has been part of a broad-based citizens' movement. At the local level, Japanese environmentalism has been tied into long-standing political organizations which themselves help integrate the community (Pierce et al., 1986a). With environmental activism linked to traditional integrating institutions, *individual* variations in background and motivation will have less to do with either group involvement or with knowledge acquisition.

Some differences between the two locations also are present in the relative impact of specific variables. Occupational differences are more prevalent in Japan than in the U.S.; generational cohort is important only in the Japanese sample; and gender is important in both Shizuoka and Spokane, but there are cross-national differences in magnitude and in the particular knowledge measures to which schooling is linked. In both countries, the perception of policy area seriousness affects a range of knowledge measures. The extremity of one's preservationist beliefs (pro *or* anti) is related to only one knowledge measure in each country. Political participation is a significant factor in both locations across the range of measures. However, the *perceived* value of citizen participation exhibits a significant impact on knowledge only in Shizuoka.

These findings show that many motivational variables influence knowledge *even while controlling for the background characteristics to which those motivations themselves are linked.* Moreover, there is greater cross-national similarity in the impact of motivational variables than in that of the background variables. It is to the implications of these findings that the remainder of this chapter now turns.

The Sources of Knowledge and Their Implications

Recall the general argument of this monograph. Knowledge among citizens is especially crucial in postindustrial democracies where policy questions have become increasingly technical and complex. Such complexity threatens to place barriers in the way of informed citizen participation. Knowledge is crucial to the ability to recognize self-interest in policy options, and to influence the policy process. Power and self-interest, then, are at least partially dependent on the citizen's ability to acquire and make use of policy-relevant knowledge. The attributes associated with knowledge holding thus may indicate who has this basis for power and who might exercise it to their own benefit. Similarly, the correlates of knowledge have important implications for the degree to which information levels can be enhanced. Finally, the cross-national pattern illustrates that cultural variations may affect the sources of knowledge and, hence, the exercise of power and self-interest.

Background and motivational attributes alike have an independent impact on citizen knowledge levels. This impact suggests the presence of a reservoir of individuals who, by virtue of their shared characteristics, are likely to have disproportionate influence. If only background is related to knowledge, serious limits would exist on the capacity of demographically unfavored elements of the citizenry to respond to policy challenges. In both Shizuoka and Spokane, however, it is clear that policy-relevant knowledge is *not* limited solely by background factors. Even when controlling for those background factors, motivation factors contribute significantly to knowledge. This observation has at least three important implications.

First, if knowledge is an independent source of influence, power is possible outside of favored positions in the social structure. This ability to exercise power assumes, of course, the presence of an open democratic system. An open system provides citizens with the opportunity to acquire knowledge outside of social status as well as the opportunity to apply that knowledge to the policy process. If a system is open in this sense, the motivational sources of knowledge are especially important in postindustrial policy arenas. It is the postindustrial scientific and technical policy arena that may be especially sensitive to the ability to exercise influence based on knowledge. Ironically, then, while substantively complex and difficult, under some conditions postindustrial policy arenas thus *may* provide *greater* opportunity for egalitarian access to decision points.

Second, if knowledge contributes to the ability to define and act on one's self-interest, such self-interested behavior also seems only partially restricted by one's place in the social structure. Arguments for limiting public involvement often are based on assumptions about the "irrationality" of an uninformed public (Bazelon, 1967; Berger, 1979). Citizens are broadly thought to be imperfectly capable of evaluating the individual costs and benefits in policy options; they are also thought incapable of protecting the "commons" (Hardin, 1968). The findings reported in this chapter suggest, however, that if citizens at any position in the social structure are provided an appropriate incentive, they can be motivated to seek policy-relevant knowledge.

Third, these results have implications for attempts to raise the level of knowledge in the public. The influence of motivation on knowledge means that public education efforts should not be restricted to the higher status elements of society disproportionately represented among the attentive publics (Devine, 1970). Efforts to enhance public awareness must first demonstrate the potential relevance of policy area issues to individuals. That relevance will provide them with a *reason* to expend efforts to acquire, store, process and apply policy-relevant information. Moreover, there must be a credible opportunity for citizens to participate in the policy formation process. That participation itself may enhance knowledge levels, feeding back in a way that increases the quality of the participation.

To be sure, this begs the question of who controls the information disseminated to mass publics. Mass publics' "real" influence will not be enhanced if access to information is strictly controlled (Cirino, 1971). Indeed, tight control over information has been proposed precisely in those issue areas characteristic of the postindustrial age. National security, complexity, danger of disastrous consequences of error, novelty, scope of societal effect and many other characteristics of policy issues are used to withhold or to taint information that might be provided to the public (Wise, 1973:341-354). Some elite observers, who themselves are opposed to government policy and who perceive themselves to be acting on behalf of the public, still argue for restricting public access to information and to involvement in policy processes (Pranger, 1968; Sennett, 1978; Segal, 1985). Those critics (in a way both pro and anti-public) are just as negative in their assumptions about the public as are the elites they typically oppose (see Barber, 1984:261-311); they fear the possibility of easy manipulation of a trusting and naive public (Edelman, 1964; Roelofs, 1976).

There also are some differences between Japan and the United States in the influence of background factors. To be sure, education has a similar effect in both countries. However, this impact is on different knowledge measures in the two countries. In Japan, education is strongly related to scientific knowledge and to the articulation of policy area problems. In the United States, however, education's independent effect is on the individual's self-estimated information level. In the American setting, then, education contributes to the confidence with which the individual approaches the policy process. In Japan, in contrast, education increases the resources for articulating and understanding those problems.

Still other types of knowledge may be produced by other social forces which themselves may differ between Japan and the United States. Thus, the impact of occupation on knowledge also differs in the two samples. In the American context occupation is important only for the ecology science knowledge measure. In the Japanese case, however, occupation affects familiarity with technical terms and self-assessed information level. Thus, occupation would seem to play a role opposite to that shown by education. Among the Japanese respondents occupational status contributes to confidence in one's own knowledge levels, while in the United States it is associated with greater actual knowledge of policy substance.

The contrast between the two countries is even more explicit in the effects of age and gender. Age is more important in Japan than in the United States. On the other hand, gender differences are more persistent in the American sample. Again, these patterns may reflect cultural differences between Japan and the United States. The findings in Japan may reflect the greater social status and position of privilege associated with increasing age. The age variable may reflect the greater political involvement of the older Japanese; in fact, there is a small correlation--$r=.17$--between age and participation among the Japanese respondents. However, no such relationship is present in Spokane. The status ascribed to older Japanese may provide the resources required for gathering and using information.

Finally, the greater gender differences in knowledge among Americans are especially startling in light of contrasting views of sex roles. Japanese society is among the most traditional of the postindustrial democracies with respect to sex role orientations. On the other hand, American society is seen as among the more "liberated." Ironically, it may be precisely this difference that produces the greater impact of gender in the United States. Gender differences are more tightly bound into the social structure in Japan, and those structural differences themselves are linked to knowledge. Thus, the impact of gender may become absorbed by those other forces. As an example, occupational status is related to knowledge in Japan. Gender is much more strongly related to occupational status in the Shizuoka sample ($r=.57$) than in Spokane ($r=.06$). On the other hand, the *relative* openness of the socio-economic structure of the United States may actually provide more room for *independent* effects of gender role differences on knowledge to play themselves out.

How, then, might the conclusions of this chapter be summarized? While background factors are important predictors of policy-relevant knowledge levels, so are motivational variables. This pattern provides the opportunity for self-interested citizens to respond to postindustrial policy questions. At the same time, U.S./Japanese differences, especially in the impact of background forces, suggest that cultural dissimilarities remain central to an understanding of the implications of postindustrial society for contemporary democratic polities.

5

Knowledge and Beliefs About the Future

Introduction

This chapter examines the relationship between knowledge and "beliefs about the future." The specific question is the extent to which knowledge is associated with postmaterialist value structures, support for the "New Environmental Paradigm," and confidence in the role of science and technology.

Several reasons exist for probing the link between knowledge and these beliefs about the future. Postindustrialism, it is often argued, reflects a new developmental stage. That stage has ushered in new complexity and new substance in issues of public policy (Kahn, 1972), providing a direct challenge for citizens in democratic polities. Responding to the challenge from the future would thus seem to require a significant store of information (Dunwoody, 1980).

One could also argue that greater knowledge will produce future-oriented political values (Mazur, 1981). Knowledge, the argument would go, provides one with the intellectual resources to approach the future with confidence. Knowledge may reduce one's anxiety about change, creating openness to changing values. Another linkage may also support a connection between knowledge and these beliefs about the future. Orientations toward the future and knowledge may be common products of the same cause. Expansion of public education, for example, may generate both higher societal knowledge levels and more open attitudes about the future. This chapter will examine these and other possibilities in the linkage between public knowledge holding and mass attitudes about the future.

Beliefs About the Future

This chapter uses the term "beliefs about the future" to characterize measures of three general orientations to politics and

society: 1) the Inglehart measure of support for postmaterialist values
(1977); 2) the Dunlap and Van Liere index of support for "The New
Environmental Paradigm" (1978); and 3) three Resources for the
Future items on support for technology and science (Mitchell, 1980).
Each measure addresses one part of what various desirable versions of
the future would look like. The Inglehart values measure assesses
one's most highly valued political and social goals by which such a
future would be judged. The New Environmental Paradigm (NEP)
focuses on the relationship between people and nature, with particular
attention given to the "spaceship earth" concept of finite resources
(Moore, 1983). The science and technology support index indicates the
degree to which the individual believes confidence can be placed in
those modern means to direct solutions to future problems.

Americans and Japanese may well differ in these orientations
toward the future--in their substantive content, in the way they are
structured, and in the way they are aligned with major social and
political divisions. Recall, first, that Japanese postindustrial value
change may be quite different from that experienced among western
publics (Inglehart, 1979; Flanagan, 1979; Ike, 1973). In some cases it
has been argued that the values of the Japanese public have changed
rather slowly. In other cases it is hypothesized that value change
clearly has occurred--but in a distinctive way reflecting Japan's unique
social and cultural past (Richardson, 1974; Benjamin and Ori, 1981).

Second, Japan's unprecedented economic growth is largely based
on a rapid introduction of advanced technology into a society with
firmly established traditions and customs. As suggested in Chapter
One, Japan owes much of its postwar growth to intense and
concentrated uses of technology. Consequently, the Japanese may link
technology directly with affluence and thus exhibit greater support for
the role of science and technology than might the American public.
Shigeru Kimura goes so far as to argue that the "cult of anti-science
thought" in the United States is a key detriment in the American
attempt to compete with Japan in the world marketplace (Kimura,
1985).

Third, recent studies of environmentalism in Japan and the
United States suggest somewhat different worldviews. Japanese
environmentalism has been described as victim-oriented, focusing on
harm to humans (Matsushita, 1975; McKean, 1981; Lovrich et al.,
1985a, 1985b; Gresser et al., 1981:29-54). In contrast, American
environmentalism has a stronger "preservationist" dimension, valuing
environments in their natural state because of an inherent aesthetic
worth. These divergent environmental worldviews may then lead to

different conceptions as to how the future should be shaped, and the appropriate form of the human-nature relationship in that future.

Postmaterialist Values

At several points we have described a putative link between postindustrialism and value change in mass publics. The importance of value change comes from the extent to which fundamental "needs" are satisfied (Maslow, 1970). The argument goes that things people value reflect the satisfaction of basic needs--especially during early years (Inglehart, 1971). The economic and political safety associated with postindustrial status would free many people from worrying about security and material needs. That freedom permits them to be more concerned with satisfying the need to participate in politics and to express political views. The extent to which one holds postindustrial values is one indicator of the degree to which a society has undergone the fundamental transformations associated with postindustrial economic development.

Personal and political values have been measured with a number of instruments (see especially, Rokeach, 1973, 1979; and Hofstede, 1979). One widely cited index of political values has been developed (in several forms) by Ronald Inglehart (1971, 1977, 1981, 1984, 1985). The present work adopts one version (1971) of the Inglehart scale. Respondents were asked to answer this question:

If you had to choose among the following, which are the *two* that seem most desirable to you?
1. maintaining order in the nation
2. giving the people more say in important decisions
3. fighting rising prices
4. protecting freedom of speech

The particular value type into which each respondent is grouped depends on which *pair* of goals is chosen. Individuals who choose the combination "maintaining order" and "fighting rising prices" are labeled "materialists." Materialist values reflect fundamental needs for security--in this case, economic and physical. The post-materialist value set contains "protecting freedom of speech" and "giving the people more say in important decisions." These priorities are hypothesized to evolve among individuals who are socialized when economic and security needs are being amply met. Other combinations are simply labeled as representing "mixed" priorities.

98

Table 5.1

Percentage of Japanese and American Citizens Choosing Each of Four Materialist/Postmaterialist Values*

Value Statement	Japan	U.S.
1. Maintaining Order	60%	53%
2. Giving People More Say	34%	52%
3. Fighting Rising Prices	57%	42%
4. Protecting Freedom of Speech	36%	40%
No Response	13%	13%
N	(694)	(522)

*Respondents were asked to choose *two* of the four in response to the following: "If you had to choose among the following, which are the *two* that seem most desirable to you?"

Source: The question was taken from Inglehart (1971).

The percentage choosing each value statement is shown in Table 5.1. As expected, the Japanese are more likely than the Americans to select the materialist (Inglehart, 1982) statements. Sixty percent of the Japanese compared to 53 percent of the Americans selected "maintaining order in the nation." There is an even larger difference on "fighting rising prices," where the figures are 57 percent for the Japanese compared to 42 percent for the Americans. The reverse is true, then, for the postmaterialist value statements. A slight margin is present on "protecting freedom of speech" for the Americans--40 percent compared to 36 percent. However, a substantial gap appears between the two publics on the choice of "giving people more say in important decisions"--52 percent in Spokane compared to 34 percent in Shizuoka. In Japan, the materialist value statements were the two most frequently chosen by the respondents. Protecting freedom of speech is least frequently chosen in both countries, while "giving the people more say" is a distinctively American preference.

Table 5.2 shows the distribution of value types--materialist, postmaterialist and mixed. A slightly greater percentage in Spokane are postmaterialist (19 percent compared to 14 percent), and more Americans are in the mixed category (60 percent versus 48 percent). The largest difference is in the number of materialists in the two countries; nearly two-fifths of the Japanese are classified as materialists, compared to only one-fifth of the Americans.

The postmaterialist findings are substantially different from those reported 10 years earlier on the basis of nationwide surveys. In 1972 only 5 percent of the Japanese and 12 percent of the Americans were identified as postmaterialist, and 47 percent of the Japanese and 31 percent of the Americans were materialist. If these locales are typical of the United States and Japan, there has been considerable aggregate value change over this ten-year period. In Japan the ratio changed from 9:2 materialists to postmaterialists to 2:1; in the United States the ratio changed from 2:6.5 to 1:1. To be sure, this interpretation is limited by the character of the two study sites. The strong citizen movement in Shizuoka Prefecture may reflect a greater concentration of postmaterialist values there than in the rest of Japan. Nonetheless, Shizuoka Prefecture--especially in the coastal area--is considered quite traditional (Lewis, 1980). Likewise, Spokane County in Washington State also is considered socially and politically conservative (Swanson and Hart-Nabbrig, 1978:178-180).

Table 5.2

Distribution of Japanese and American Publics on Inglehart Measure of Political Values

Value Type[a]		Japan	United States
Materialist	(1)	38%	21%
Mixed	(2)	48%	60%
Postmaterialist	(3)	<u>14%</u>	<u>19%</u>
Total		100%	100%
N		(557)	(433)
Mean		1.75	1.98
		(.687)	(.634)

[a]Value types reflect respondent choice of value statements listed in Table 5.1. Materialists chose *both* statements one and three; postmaterialists chose *both* statements two and four; mixed types selected some other combination.

The New Environmental Paradigm

The concept of the "New Environmental Paradigm" grew out of observations of environmental politics in the 1960s and 1970s. That period seemed inconsistent with dominant American values. The dominant ethic had assumed unlimited resources, a vast frontier, and a belief in the mastery of humans over nature (Rosenbaum, 1973). The environmental movement flew directly in the face of this ideology. Environmentalism proclaimed different goals for society and advocated a different relationship between people and nature. It also rested on a different set of assumptions about the world (Milbrath, 1984). William Catton and Riley Dunlap have labeled this emergent world view the "New Environmental Paradigm" (1978, 1980).

The New Environmental Paradigm assumes limited resources and challenges the dominance of humans over nature. This "paradigm" elevates the role of nature and affirms the importance of the "ecological balance" found in the natural environment. The new Environmental Paradigm views humans as merely one of many elements of the natural system, and an element with no *a priori* superiority. Finally, the new environmentalist ethic includes the popular concept of "spaceship earth." The earth is seen as a closed system, limited in the amount of resources available, with those resources requiring recycling if the environment is to continue to support human life (Gulowsen, 1976).

The measure of the New Environmental Paradigm (the NEP) beliefs used here was adopted from Dunlap and Van Liere (1978), as given in a report of the Continental Group (1982). The six items in the NEP index are shown in Table 5.3, along with the distributions for both samples. The differences between the Japanese and American publics would seem more a matter of degree than of direction. Americans are slightly more likely to agree that the balance of nature is very delicate (84 percent compared to 71 percent). But Japanese are more likely to agree that the earth is like a spaceship (66 to 34 percent strong agreement). A similar pattern occurs on the other items. When combining the two pro-NEP categories for each item, the cross-national differences between citizens are not great; in some cases the American percentage is even greater than that for the Japanese respondents. On the other hand, when comparing only the terminal categories, Japanese citizens clearly exhibit more extreme positions.

The New Environmental Paradigm index is constructed by summing individual responses across the six items. The index ranges from six (strongly anti-NEP on each item) to thirty (strongly pro-NEP on each item). The resulting index then was trichotomized into low,

Table 5.3

Distribution of Japanese and American Publics on the Items in the New Environmental Paradigm Measure

			Japan (694)	*U.S.* (524)
1.	The balance of nature is very delicate and easily upset by human activities.	Strongly Agree	44%	41%
			27%	43%
		No Opinion	16%	5%
			4%	9%
		Strongly Disagree	10%	2%
		Total	101%	100%
2.	The earth is like a space-ship with only limited room and resources.	Strongly Agree	66%	34%
			17%	43%
		No Opinion	7%	9%
			2%	11%
		Strongly Disagree	9%	4%
		Total	101%	101%
3.	Plants and animals do *not* exist primarily to be used by humans.	Strongly Agree	45%	26%
			20%	41%
		No Opinion	15%	9%
			8%	17%
		Strongly Disagree	12%	7%
		Total	100%	100%
4.	Modifying the environment for human use seldom causes serious problems.	Strongly Agree	5%	3%
			6%	14%
		No Opinion	17%	8%
			23%	49%
		Strongly Disagree	49%	27%
		Total	100%	101%
5.	There are no limits to growth for nations like the United States (Japan).	Strongly Agree	8%	6%
			11%	15%
		No Opinion	16%	7%
			26%	44%
		Strongly Disagree	40%	28%
		Total	101%	100%
6.	Mankind was created to rule over the rest of nature.	Strongly Agree	6%	10%
			8%	20%
		No Opinion	18%	13%
			17%	32%
		Strongly Disagree	51%	25%
		Total	100%	100%

Source: Items from Dunlap and Van Liere (1979)

Table 5.4

Distribution of Japanese and American Publics on the New Environmental Paradigm

		Japan	United States
Low*	(6-21)	27%	35%
Medium	(22-24)	20%	32%
High	(25-30)	<u>53%</u>	<u>32%</u>
	Total	100%	99%
	N	(620)	(479)
	x**	24.3	22.7
		(4.28)	(4.15)

*The categories are based roughly in the thirds of the American public distribution, on the index that ranges from 6 to 30.

**The difference in means is significant at $p \leq .001$.

104

medium and high categories. The cutting points were defined by
dividing the American public distribution into approximate thirds,
since the initial index was developed in the American context. The
distribution of the two publics is shown in Table 5.4. Again, the
Japanese public is more pro-NEP than is the American public--53
percent in the "high" category compared to 32 percent for the
Americans, and a mean score of 24.3 compared to 22.7 (p<.001).

The NEP and postmaterialist values findings raise several issues.
While the Japanese public is somewhat less postmaterialist than the
American public, it exhibits greater support for the New
Environmental Paradigm. These findings may seem somewhat
paradoxical. Yet, some of the fundamental concepts in the New
Environmental Paradigm, which may have been novel for Westerners,
may actually correspond to some long-held fundamental beliefs
comprising Japanese culture (Murota, 1985). Moreover, the notion of
spaceship earth and limited resources may also be especially relevant
to modern Japanese society with its extremely high population density,
its insular geographic status, and its high reliance on external sources
of most raw materials. These factors may provide an apparent merger
of traditional culture and contemporary environmentalism.

Support for Science and Technology

A prominent characteristic of modern society is the widespread
influence of science and technology. By some they are seen as
nefarious sources of evil--environmental and social (Davies, 1985). For
others, science and technology offer the bright promise of hope for a
better future (Naisbitt, 1982). Public attitudes about science and
technology will exercise a strong impact on the future faced by
postindustrial societies. A society that affirms technology will look very
different from the one that is suspicious and views it as a likely source
of evil and danger. At the same time, however, a society which
promotes science and technology must necessarily deal with
unanticipated consequences and with challenges to governance (Dahl,
1985). The greater the role provided for science and technology in the
shaping of public policy, the more important becomes the need for
citizen knowledge (Miller et al., 1980).

This section compares Japanese and American publics' attitudes
about science and technology. Three items are used from a measure
initially employed by the Resources for the Future in their survey of
American environmental attitudes. This survey was conducted for the
Council on Environmental Quality (Mitchell, 1980). The survey items
are shown in Table 5.5. Two of the questions deal with technology,

Table 5.5

Distribution of Japanese and American Citizens on Support for Science and Technology Items

			Japan (694)	U.S. (524)
1.	Technology will find a way of solving the problems of shortages and natural resources.	Strongly Agree	33%	12%
			38%	46%
		No Opinion	13%	12%
			7%	26%
		Strongly Disagree	9%	5%
		Total	100%	101%
2.	People would be better off if they lived a more simple life without so much technology.	Strongly Agree	9%	9%
			17%	26%
		No Opinion	24%	8%
			27%	39%
		Strongly Disagree	24%	18%
		Total	101%	100%
3.	Future scientific research is more likely to cause problems than to find solutions to problems.	Strongly Agree	11%	5%
			23%	13%
		No Opinion	33%	10%
			17%	44%
		Strongly Disagree	17%	28%
		Total	101%	100%

Table 5.6

Distribution of Japanese and American Publics on Index of Support for Science and Technology

		Japan	*United States*
Low	(3-8)	23%	25%
Medium	(9-11)	48%	33%
High	(12-15)	29%	43%
	Total	100%	101%
	N	(620)	(477)
	x*	10.22	10.50
		(2.38)	(2.62)

*Mean difference is significant at p ≤.05.

while the third elicits an attitude about science.

On the two technology questions (the first two in Table 5.5) somewhat different cross-national patterns obtain. Japanese are more likely than Americans to believe that "technology will find a way of solving the problems of shortages and natural resources" (71 percent compared to 58 percent). Americans, however, are more likely to disagree with the statement that "people would be better off if they lived a more simple life without so much technology" (57 percent compared to 51 percent). The largest difference, though, occurs on the third question, the one having to do with whether "future scientific research is more likely to cause problems than to find solutions to problems." Well over two-thirds of the Americans disagree with that statement, compared to only about one-third of the Japanese. Thus, on the technology questions the two items appear to balance out the Japanese and American differences. On the science question, however, the Americans clearly are the more supportive. The overall index for support for science and technology is built by combining the three items. The summative index reflects the same response pattern shown on the individual items.

Table 5.6 displays distributions for the two public samples on the index of support for science and technology. That index was trichotomized into low, medium and high categories. The overall index ranges from 3 (complete opposition) to fifteen (complete support). As the table shows, support for science and technology is a little higher in Spokane than in Shizuoka ($p \leq .05$).

The aggregate picture of the "beliefs about the future" among Japanese and American citizens remains a little out of focus. As expected, the Americans are more likely to be postmaterialist than are the Japanese. On the other hand, the Japanese give more support to the New Environmental Paradigm, and somewhat less support to science and technology than do the Americans. This pattern suggests that perhaps these attitudes are inter-related in different ways in the two countries.

The Structure Among Beliefs About the Future

Analysis of the structure among beliefs assesses the extent to which responses on the future-oriented measures systematically "go together." The interest here is whether beliefs cohere to form a larger integrated constellation--a kind of ideological package.

The coherence among these beliefs will suggest some things about the extent to which postindustrial society has permeated the public's thinking. It often is argued that one consequence of postindustrialism is a disruption of traditional ways of grouping political beliefs (Lasch, 1972). The new kinds of issues, values and beliefs are said to cut across traditional political cleavages--class, ideology, party (Miller and Levitin, 1976). This issue is particularly interesting when comparing Japan and the United States (Flanagan, 1979). Japan is seen as more traditional in its contemporary politics, with the party organizations remaining strong as political institutions and as vehicles for attaining and exercising power. At the same time substantive fractionalization and realignment has occurred in the Japanese party system (Dalton et al., 1984). In the United States, on the other hand, the parties have declined (Burnham, 1975) and in the view of many are no longer effectively used by individuals to organize and interpret their relationship to politics (Nie et al., 1976).

This section, then, will examine the coherence of these future beliefs. The analysis also will look at the extent to which those beliefs are systematically connected to traditional social and political cleavages. Table 5.7 presents the correlation (gamma) among the three indexes--postmaterialist values, New Environmental Paradigm, and beliefs about science and technology in the future--for both Japanese and Americans.

Japanese and Americans differ only marginally in the inter-relationships among the three beliefs. In both countries the highest correlation is between postmaterialist values and support for the New Environmental Paradigm, but the relationship is greater in Japan than in the United States. Thus, even though Americans are somewhat more postmaterialist and the Japanese are somewhat more pro-NEP, support for or opposition to *both* of those is more likely to be found in Shizuoka than in Spokane. On the other hand, the relationship between postmaterialist values and support for science and technology is stronger in Spokane. Postmaterialists are a little more likely to reject science and technology, even though the magnitude of the association is not great.

Even so, the conclusion must be that the three orientations measured in this chapter are not strongly interrelated, either in Japan or in the United States. A separate question, though, is the degree to which these beliefs are connected to traditional political sources of cleavage. Thus, Table 5.8 presents the correlations (r) among the postmaterialist values measure, the individual items in the NEP index, the individual items in the support for science and technology index and party identification, ideological identification and class identification.[1]

Some significant differences appear between Spokane and Shizuoka in the relationship of these beliefs to party, ideology and class

Table 5.7

**Correlations (r) Among Postmaterialist Values,
Support for NEP and Support for Science and Technology
Among Japanese and American Publics**

		United States	
	Post- materialist Values	New Environmental Paradigm	Support for Science and Technology
Postmaterialist Values	x	.21	-.16
Japan New Environmental Paradigm	.36	x	-.08
Support for Science and Technology	-.04	.01	x

Table 5.8

Correlations (r) of Party, Ideology and Class Identification with Postmaterialist Values and Individual Items in the NEP and Support for Science and Technology Indexes

	Japan			United States		
	Party	Ideology	Class	Party	Ideology	Class
Postmaterialist	-.07	.30	.04	.14	.16	.01
Tecsol	.03	-.04	-.07	.13	.07	-.03
Notech	.13	.07	.17	.15	.12	-.27
Futsc	<u>-.04</u>	<u>-.11</u>	<u>.02</u>	<u>.12</u>	<u>.02</u>	<u>-.22</u>
Mean	.07	.07	.09	.13	.07	.17
Dunlap 1	-.03	.11	.01	-.18	-.16	.04
Dunlap 2	.05	.11	.12	-.06	-.13	.02
Dunlap 3	.00	.03	.07	-.11	-.27	.05
Dunlap 4	-.14	.10	.06	.02	-.02	.05
Dunlap 5	-.11	-.16	-.04	-.05	-.17	.05
Dunlap 6	<u>.01</u>	<u>-.06</u>	<u>-.07</u>	<u>-.20</u>	<u>-.25</u>	<u>.05</u>
Mean	.06	.09	.06	.10	.17	.04

identification. The strongest relationship with postmaterialist value orientations is exhibited by ideological identification in Japan (r=.30); liberals are somewhat more likely to be postmaterialist than are conservatives. Among the Americans the direction of the association is the same, but of considerably lesser magnitude (r=.16). Party identification in Spokane also is marginally related to postmaterialist values (r=.14), with Democrats more likely than Republicans to be postmaterialist.

Except for the link between ideology and postmaterial values, very little else in Japan is consistently related to party, ideology or class. On the other hand, in Spokane support for the science and technology items is weakly related to party identification, and two of the three are moderately related to class identification. Republicans are a little more likely than Democrats to support science and technology; self-identified members of the middle class are more likely than self-identified working class respondents to support science and technology. The only consistent pattern on the NEP items is their relationship to ideological identification in Spokane. Again, the self-identified liberals are more likely than the self-identified conservatives to agree to the tenets of the New Environmental Paradigm.

In short, these future-oriented beliefs are not strongly integrated into traditional political and social divisions in either of the two publics. The attitudinal connections that do surface are consistent with expectations--postmaterialists more liberal in Japan, pro-NEP respondents more liberal in the United States, and pro-science and technology individuals more middle class.

The final approach to the structure of these beliefs is shown in Table 5.9. That table contains the results of a factor analysis (varimax rotation) of the postmaterialist value measure, the items in the support for science and technology index and NEP measures, and the party, class and ideological identification items.

There is considerable similarity in the factor structures for Spokane and Shizuoka respondents. First, in both countries party and ideology load strongly on the same factor, accompanied by *none* of the future belief items; in both samples, the first pro-science and technology item loads strongly on none of the factors, but the second and third items are found together on a single factor accompanied by no other items; in both matrices the third and sixth NEP items load on the same factor with no other variable, and in both cases the first and second NEP items load on the same factor, accompanied in Spokane by the fifth NEP item.

The differences between the two factor structures are not as startling as the similarities. In Spokane the postmaterialist value

112

Table 5.9

Varimax Rotated Factor Matrix of Future-Oriented Beliefs and Political Orientations in Japan and the United States

FACTOR	JAPAN					COMMU-NALITY	UNITED STATES					COMMU-NALITY
	1	2	3	4	5		1	2	3	4	5	
TECSOL	-.059	-.007	.242	.245	-.101	.133	.300	-.131	-.268	.007	-.031	.180
NOTECH	-.035	-.078	.800	.058	-.072	.655	.694	-.099	-.005	.097	.047	.502
FUTSC	-.039	-.003	.518	-.106	.105	.292	.726	.062	.056	-.010	-.118	.548
DUNLAP1	.121	.116	-.023	.678	.091	.497	-.070	.534	.122	-.175	.036	.337
DUNLAP2	.093	.142	.011	.514	.188	.328	-.029	.714	.005	-.088	-.034	.519
DUNLAP3	.029	.490	-.158	.190	.038	.304	.024	.226	.553	-.152	.167	.409
DUNLAP4	.197	.345	.086	.273	.378	.383	-.022	.358	.207	.119	.170	.215
DUNLAP5	.083	.202	.045	.144	.610	.443	-.029	.428	.224	-.023	.079	.241
DUNLAP6	.130	.806	.106	.032	.282	.759	-.006	.138	.698	-.217	-.088	.561
INGLE	.351	.203	-.026	.014	.169	.194	-.032	.083	.035	-.137	.560	.341
PARTY	.506	.038	-.096	.049	.148	.291	.173	-.037	-.081	.594	-.069	.396
IDEOLOGY	-.868	-.018	.077	-.123	.130	.791	.054	-.119	-.209	.533	-.122	.359
CLASS	.075	-.015	-.139	-.093	-.052	.037	-.317	.021	.021	-.163	-.013	.128
Eigen value	2.13	1.17	.86	.63	.31		2.04	1.18	.69	.46	.35	
% of Variance	42%	23%	17%	12%	6%		43%	25%	15%	10%	7%	

stands by itself in the weakest of the five factors, but in Japan it meets the arbitrary loading cut-off on *no* factor, although coming quite close on the party/ideology dimension. In Japan the fifth NEP item stands by itself, while in the American setting it loads with the first and second items; and, perhaps most significantly, the relative importance of the substantive content of the five factors is quite different--e.g., the most important factor among the Americans surveyed, explaining 42 percent of the variance, contains two pro-science and technology items, while the first factor in the Japanese setting contains party and ideology, marginally accompanied by values.

In short, the structures of these beliefs are generally the same in the two countries, with dimensions similar in content but varying in their relative importance. The greater centrality of party and ideology in Japan than in the United States suggests less movement away from the dominance of political thinking by traditional partisan and ideological feelings. This may reflect, as well, the much smaller gap in Japan between the content of "new" environmental attitudes and traditional political and cultural values.

Knowledge and Beliefs About the Future

Do people who know more have different attitudes about the proper direction of the future? A first answer can be found in Table 5.10.   Overall, there is a weak to moderate relationship between knowledge and beliefs about future in both countries. In almost every case at least one knowledge measure makes a difference on each of the beliefs. The identification of technical terms, the articulation of policy problems, and the number of measures on which one is knowledgeable all have the strongest impact on support for the New Environmental Paradigm. Technical term familiarity, knowledge of ecology science and the number of measures on which one is knowledgeable are the best predictors of postmaterialist values in Japan.   However, postmaterialist values seem only marginally linked to knowledge in the United States. The best predictor of support for science and technology in Japan is technical term familiarity, while in the United States it is knowledge of local conditions.   In Japan, then, technical term familiarity is the most important of the knowledge measures. Individuals with more knowledge *do* seem to hold somewhat different beliefs about the future. The more informed give greater support to the New Environmental Paradigm, are more likely to be postmaterialist, and are less likely to support science and technology.

Table 5.10

Correlation (Gamma) Between Knowledge Measures and Future Orientations

Future Orientation	Familiarity with Technical Terminology		Knowledge of Local Factors		Knowledge of Ecology Science		Articulation of Problems		Self-Assessed Informedness		Summative Index	
	Japan	U.S.	Japan	U.S.	Japan	U.S.	Japan	U.S.	Japan	U.S.	Japan	U.S.
NEP	.27	.25	.11	.16	.20	.11	.25	.21	.01	.08	.25	.19
INGLE	.20	.12	.10	.06	.18	.04	.15	.12	.09	.09	.21	.11
PROSCI	.22	.16	.05	.24	.12	.12	.03	.09	.10	.12	.15	.16

Table 5.11

Relationship of Participation Levels and Education to Beliefs About the Future in Japanese and American Publics (Gamma)

Participation	Post-materialist Values	New Environmental Paradigm	Support for Science/ Technology
Japan	.06	.02	.06
United States	.18	.20	.12

Education	Post-materialist Values	New Environmental Paradigm	Support for Science/ Technology
Japan	.18	.19	.12
United States	.05	.15	.18

Education, Participation and Knowledge

Table 5.11 shows the relationship between participation, education and beliefs about the future. Some interesting contrasts are present. The impact of participation is greater in Spokane than in Shizuoka. Spokane activists give more support to postmaterialist values and the NEP than do their Shizuoka Prefecture counterparts. In both countries, education has a similar impact on the NEP and support for science and technology measures--namely, a positive but weak association. Education, however, has a greater impact on postmaterial values in Japan than in the United States.

These patterns suggest that a control for education and/or participation may alter the relationship between knowledge and support for postmaterialist values, NEP and science and technology. Table 5.12 shows the correlation between knowledge and those beliefs within categories of education and participation.

Controlling for education and participation fails to erase the link between knowledge and beliefs about the future. In Japan, the more knowledgeable citizens remain more likely to be postmaterialists than do their less well informed peers. The impact of knowledge is greater in the participation levels than in the education groupings. Moreover, the impact of knowledge on values does decline somewhat as the level of participation increases. Knowledge holding among the least active Japanese is more likely to lead them to postmaterialist values than it is among the most active.

In Spokane knowledge is unrelated to the values of low education respondents, but it has a small impact among the two higher education categories. A reverse pattern obtains, though, for the control for participation. Similar to Japan, it is among the high participation Spokanites that knowledge's impact on values fades. Education thus seems to bring out the impact of information on values in the American setting while participation suppresses it somewhat in both countries. The participation effects may occur because more extreme values of either type (materialist or post-materialist) lead citizens to participate, and that participation itself increases knowledge levels.

Among both the Japanese and the Americans, knowledge is related to support for the NEP across education and participation levels. For support of science and technology, however, the pattern appears uneven. Indeed, the impact of knowledge declines as education increases in the American sample. In Japan, then, more so than in the United States, schooling may enhance the citizen's application of knowledge to the effective evaluation of science and technology. In both Japan and the U.S., knowledge is most strongly

Table 5.12

The Relationship (Gamma) of Knowledge[a] and Future Beliefs, Controlling for Level of Education and Participation

A. Education

	Low Japan	U.S.	Medium Japan	U.S.	High Japan	U.S.
Postmaterialist Values	.13	.04	.12	.17	.12	.17
New Environmental Paradigm	.31	.18	.22	.23	.22	.23
Support for Science and Technology	-.08	.18	.23	.06	.23	.06

B. Participation

	Low Japan	U.S.	Medium Japan	U.S.	High Japan	U.S.
Postmaterialist Values	.27	.23	.20	.30	.16	.05
New Environmental Paradigm	.23	.18	.29	.12	.22	.20
Support for Science and Technology	.21	.30	.19	.01	.01	.16

[a]The knowledge measure is the number of information indexes on which the individual is in the top third or "high" category.

related to support for science and technology among the *least* active.

In summary, then, the overall effect of knowledge on the *direction* of beliefs about the future persists under controls for education and participation. Indeed, in some measure the effect of knowledge is *elevated* within categories of education and participation.

Knowledge and Constraint Among Beliefs About the Future

High levels of technical term familiarity make no consistent impact on the correlations among future oriented beliefs (Table 5.13). Indeed, of the six belief pairs across the two countries, in only one case--the pairing of the NEP and pro-science and technology measures--is the correlation even marginally higher among the most knowledgeable. A similar pattern occurs for knowledge of local conditions, with only one case of high knowledge leading to high constraint--the correlation of postmaterialist values and support for science and technology in Japan. Knowledge of ecology science has a little more effect on constraint among beliefs about the future. In Japan, the more knowledgeable are more highly constrained on each belief pair, but this occurs only once in the American setting. Similarly, articulating greater numbers of policy problems elevates constraint only in one case in each country. In other cases agenda knowledge seems to substantially depress the magnitude of the correlations. Finally, no consistent difference in constraint is found among levels of self-assessed information.

Overall, then, it is not possible to say that knowledge uniformly cements together the general views of the future assessed here--postmaterialist values, the New Environmental Paradigm and support for science and technology. It is possible, though, that knowledge does lead to a distinct structuring of beliefs when the several indexes are disaggregated and linked to more general political orientations. That is, it may be that policy-relevant knowledge affects the degree to which the individual items in each index cohere. More knowledgeable individuals, for example, may be better able to visualize the common elements in the index items. It may also be that more informed citizens are better able to structure these beliefs along the same dimensions as those represented in traditional political divisions.

Factor analyses were performed for the most informed and the least informed citizens in both Shizuoka and Spokane. Looking at the extreme knowledge groups provides the opportunity to pose a stark contrast. The summary index of knowledge--which indicates the number of areas in which the respondent is highly informed (highest

Table 5.13

The Effect of Policy-Relevant Knowledge Holding on Constraint Among Beliefs About the Future (Gamma[a])

	Japan			United States		
Knowledge Level:	Low	Medium	High	Low	Medium	High
A. Familiarity with Technical Terminology						
Postmat & NEP	.18	.43	.28	.15	.19	.09
Pro-Sci/Tech & NEP	.11	-.06	-.06	-.07	-.14	-.22
Postmat & Pro-Sci/Tech	.20	-.10	-.16	-.26	-.13	.03
B. Knowledge of Local Factors						
Postmat & NEP	.43	.21	.30	.19	.28	.17
Pro-Sci/Tech & NEP	-.02	.07	-.02	-.05	-.27	-.04
Postmat & Pro-Sci/Tech	.06	-.02	-.32	-.21	-.13	.12
C. Knowledge of Ecology Science						
Postmat & NEP	.25	.34	.42	.27	.26	.14
Pro-Sci/Tech & NEP	.10	.04	-.16	.03	-.11	-.23
Postmat & Pro-Sci/Tech	.13	-.08	-.16	-.23	-.25	-.02
D. Articulation of Policy Areas Problems						
Postmat & NEP	.14	.54	.35	.25	.32	.07
Pro-Sci/Tech & NEP	.00	-.01	.02	-.10	-.05	-.27
Postmat & Pro-Sci/Tech	.01	-.01	-.12	-.32	-.20	-.03
E. Self-Assessed Informedness						
Postmat & NEP	.38	.33	.42	-.01	.23	.28
Pro-Sci/Tech & NEP	-.21	.02	-.10	.06	-.08	-.18
Postmat & Pro-Sci/Tech	-.04	-.10	.07	-.25	-.04	-.26

[a]The entry in each cell is the correlation (Gamma) among the two belief measures, within a particular level of knowledge.

Note:

Postmat = Postmaterialist Values

NEP = New Environmental Paradigm

ProSci/Tech = Pro-Science and Technology Orientation

third)--is used to identify the high and low knowledge groups. This measure ranges from zero to five. The individuals with no measures on which they are highly informed are compared to those highly informed on three or more indexes. When these criteria are applied to those individuals with responses on all relevant items, the following number of cases result: in the Spokane setting, 82 high knowledge individuals and 87 low knowledge respondents; in the Shizuoka sample, 99 high knowledge and 120 low knowledge citizens.

Thirteen variables were entered into the factor analyses: 1) three items in the support for science and technology index; 2) six items in the New Environmental Paradigm index; 3) one item for the postmaterialist values measure; and 4) one item each for the measures of partisan, ideological and class identification. Varimax rotation was employed. The results are shown in Table 5.14.

In both Spokane and Shizuoka knowledge affects how individuals put together their political beliefs. Not only do high and low knowledge groups within each country differ from each other, but some major similarities *and* differences obtain between groups with the same relative knowledge level in Shizuoka and Spokane.

First, one of the most significant patterns is the way party and ideology group together with postmaterial values. Only for the high knowledge respondents--in both the Japanese and the American settings--do the three general orientations fit together. High knowledge in *both* countries contributes to the integration of postmaterial values into traditional partisan and ideological dimensions. This suggests that better informed individuals are better able to identify the traditional implications of postmaterial value dimensions. To the more knowledgeable citizens the postmaterial value orientation may make better sense, even when taken in the context of long-standing partisan and ideological dimensions.

Even with this consistent grouping of party, ideology and values, an important cross-national difference remains. That difference is the *relative* importance of the value/party/ideology factor in the overall factor structure of the most knowledgeable respondents. Among the American sample this factor ranks third in importance, accounting for only 20 percent of the variance. However, this factor is the most important one appearing for the most informed Japanese. Thus, the belief system of the best informed Japanese is dominated by the integration of the traditional political orientations and postmaterialist value orientations. For the least informed, though, postmaterialist values, party identification and ideology are both poorly integrated and in a subordinate position.

Table 5.14

Factor Analysis (Varimax Rotation) of Beliefs About the Future and Political Identification in Spokane and Shizuoka Publics, Controlling for Policy-Relevant Knowledge Levels

SPOKANE AREA

FACTOR	High Knowledge (n=82)					Low Knowledge (n=87)					
	1	2	3	4	h^2	1	2	3	4	5	h^2
TECSOL	-.509	.139	.029	-.144	.30	.238	.033	-.029	.161	.355	.21
NOTECH	-.178	.822	.031	.033	.71	.810	.089	-.034	-.004	-.000	.67
FUTSC	.014	.577	.023	-.213	.38	.684	-.028	.007	-.153	.263	.56
DUNLAP1	.323	-.069	-.182	.425	.32	-.007	.536	.199	-.056	-.075	.34
DUNLAP2	.232	-.199	.045	.707	.60	.051	.736	.107	.002	.277	.63
DUNLAP3	.504	.186	-.280	.161	.39	.032	.152	.652	-.025	-.181	.48
DUNLAP4	.475	.153	.062	.191	.29	-.235	.320	-.075	.101	-.018	.17
DUNLAP5	.769	-.107	.130	.026	.62	.016	.555	.025	-.140	-.092	.34
DUNLAP6	.535	-.024	-.063	.031	.29	.018	.030	.796	-.239	.047	.69
INGLE	-.116	-.020	-.413	.178	.22	.019	.030	.069	.079	-.600	.37
PARTY	-.082	.287	.615	.117	.48	-.043	-.014	-.104	.629	.036	.41
IDEOLOGY	-.141	.006	.701	.020	.51	.036	-.089	-.241	.310	-.028	.16
CLASS	-.106	-.369	-.220	.063	.20	-.498	.178	-.075	-.308	.105	.39
Eigen value	2.26	1.41	1.04	.60		1.70	1.55	1.04	.67	.47	
% of Variance	43%	27%	20%	11%		31%	29%	19%	12%	9%	

(continues)

Table 5.14 (continued)

SHIZUOKA PREFECTURE

FACTOR	High Knowledge (n=99)						Low Knowledge (n=120)				
	1	2	3	4	5	h^2	1	2	3	4	h^2
TECSOL	-.109	.454	-.038	.036	-.117	.23	.281	.416	.034	-.061	.18
NOTECH	-.102	.626	-.022	-.217	.148	.47	-.061	.183	.646	-.142	.47
FUTSC	-.016	.714	-.023	.090	-.012	.52	.031	-.168	.690	.043	.51
DUNLAP1	-.063	-.034	.087	.177	.598	.40	.123	.782	-.300	.130	.73
DUNLAP2	.075	-.010	.143	.868	.312	.88	.067	.499	-.051	.242	.31
DUNLAP3	.017	-.245	.362	.106	.105	.21	.627	.094	-.206	-.039	.45
DUNLAP4	.242	-.022	.324	.071	.503	.42	.623	.226	.061	.158	.47
DUNLAP5	.063	.036	.485	.018	.227	.29	.397	.163	.017	.211	.23
DUNLAP6	.308	.001	.838	.056	-.006	.80	.960	-.101	.044	-.066	.94
INGLE	.473	-.072	.180	.150	.082	.29	.318	-.037	.091	.304	.20
PARTY	.664	.060	.088	-.121	.102	.48	.080	.169	-.038	.605	.40
IDEOLOGY	-.712	.284	.080	-.016	.022	.59	-.023	-.046	.070	-.622	.39
CLASS	.213	-.030	.086	.030	-.027	.05	-.056	-.309	-.152	-.074	.13
Eigen value	2.23	1.29	1.01	.69	.43		2.29	1.42	.96	.76	
% of Variance	40%	23%	18%	12%	8%		42.4%	25.9%	17.7%	14.1%	

Second, differences are present in the New Environmental Paradigm items. In both countries, the NEP items cluster differently in the most knowledgeable group than they do in the least informed group. But, the differences in those two groups are reversed between the two countries. Four of the six NEP items cluster in the first factor in the *most* knowledgeable American group, and the same four cluster in the first factor of the *least* knowledgeable Japanese group. Among the most knowledgeable Shizuoka Prefecture citizens, though, no more than two of the NEP items are found on the same factor. In the *low* knowledge Americans three of the NEP items group together on the second factor, but only one of those three is part of the group in the first factor for the *most* knowledgeable.

Third, perhaps the greatest similarity across the four groups appears in the science and technology support items. In three of the four groups the same two items--relating to reducing dependence on technology and sensing concern for science-caused problems--load on the same factor. In the deviant group (Japan, high knowledge) the science question appears on the same factor as an item dealing with belief in technology's ability to solve problems. Only among the least knowledgeable American group do the science and technology beliefs load on the same dimension as any of the general political orientations--in this case that of class identification.

One cannot argue, of course, that this analysis includes all of the potentially relevant beliefs that should be included in attempting to characterize the impact of knowledge on public orientations to the future. Nonetheless, there is enough information here to raise some significant questions, and to allow some preliminary explanations.

1. Why does the postmaterialism measure load on the same factor as that including party identification and ideological identification only among the most knowledgeable respondents? A fairly straight-forward argument can be suggested. Greater knowledge allows one to identify the implications of fundamental postindustrial values for traditional partisan and ideological views. Knowledge about the environmental policy arena, of course, would not be enough to illuminate all of the partisan and ideological implications of postindustrial value choices. On the other hand, as the "quintessential postindustrial issue," environmental knowledge certainly would both stimulate an engagement of values and political choices, and reflect the individual citizen's more general awareness of the political world and its value implications.

These findings thus underscore a cross-national continuity in the response of knowledgeable publics to the choices presented by postindustrialism. It is important to remember, though, that this chapter focuses on what here are called "beliefs about the future." These beliefs have broad sweeping implications for a preferred direction for politics and society. A later chapter will look at the impact of policy-relevant knowledge on the individual's consistency in linking general orientations to rather specific policy orientations, and on the constraint obtaining among those specific beliefs.

2.   *Why--in both countries and among both the most and least informed citizens--do the beliefs about science and technology seem to cohere together and generally stand apart from other dimensions?*[2] The answer, it seems, lies in the historical role of science and technology in the industrial and postindustrial development of Japan and the United States. Science and technology have been so central to the elite and mass perceptions of the dynamics of social and economic growth that beliefs about their proper role are generally stable and well-integrated.   Science and technology, as major dimensions of contemporary social institutions, may have become part of the "Dominant Social Paradigm."[3]   This centrality provides a constant reference for mass publics. Because of that centrality, attitudes about science and technology--and the integration among them--would be independent of knowledge levels.

3.   *Why, among the Japanese, are the New Environmental Paradigm beliefs more coherent among the* least *knowledgeable Japanese, when the expectation and the American case is the reverse (i.e., more coherence among the most knowledgeable)?* The answer to this question may be based in the interplay of the forces involved in the development from traditional to postindustrial society, and the differential rates of responsiveness to that change by individuals with different levels of knowledge. An outline of this proposed explanation is shown in Figure 5.1.

The possible explanation takes this form.   In traditional society, there would be widespread agreement as to the content of the dominant social paradigm across social sectors and across levels of involvement in the polity. It is not so much that everyone necessarily agrees on the fundamental tenets of that paradigm, but rather that there is widespread consensus as to its meaning and the relationships among its elements.   Substantial coherence would exist on beliefs about that paradigm across all levels of knowledge.

Relatively early in change away from a dominant paradigm, citizens will respond at different rates. One reason for that differential responsiveness is the individual's knowledge level.   A society's most knowledgeable stratum would be the first to become aware of impending large scale changes. It also would become aware that such changes could have major implications for the dominant social

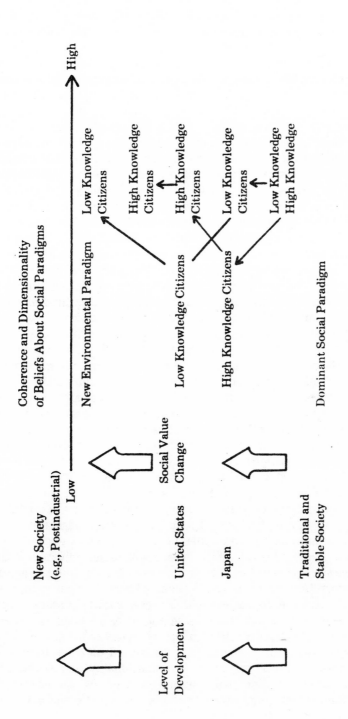

Figure 5.1. The Impact of Knowledge and Development on Coherence of Beliefs About Social Paradigms

paradigm. In the early stages of the change from one kind of society to another, then, the most knowledgeable citizens would have the initial task of sorting out and integrating the new policy dimensions into the old belief structures. Such an integration, of course, would not come immediately. A transition period would obtain during which the evaluation and processing of these issues would take place. Thus, the *least* informed stratum would remain disengaged from the new paradigm, and hence still see as well defined the issue dimensions of the old order. But, the most knowledgeable would find their beliefs about the new order in a state of flux, temporarily less well defined than they had been--and than they will become in time.

The earlier stages of change from one type of society to another (in this case from traditional to postindustrial) will thus present a seemingly anomalous pattern. The more knowledgeable segments of society will have the apparently less well-integrated sets of beliefs *about the kinds of issues that most reflect the central substance of the social change*. As the transition from traditional to postindustrial society continues, though, more changes occur which would alter the relative positions of the more and less knowledgeable. With time, conflicts between old and new ideas and new and old values will filter to the least knowledgeable segments of society. While these conflicts become subject to the social diffusion process, two things happen. First, the least knowledgeable stratum develops the same disintegration of belief systems on these issues as that earlier experienced by the most informed. Second, after processing the policy and value conflicts of postindustrial society and assessing their implications the beliefs of most knowledgeable will again acquire coherence and dimensionality.

An additional stage in this relationship would develop as a final part of the transition to postindustrial society. At some point even a nation's least informed portions may again exhibit the same kinds of dimensionality as that shown by the most knowledgeable. The increased dimensionality and order of the least knowledgeable will come from several sources. First, there will be an adjustment that takes place simply from the need for cognitive economy and the greater ease of interacting with the environment. Through experience, some order and sense will appear even to the least knowledgeable citizens. Second, there will be a kind of packaging of belief systems through which the more knowledgeable segments of society communicate to the least knowledgeable just how sets of beliefs go together (Converse, 1964; Sartori, 1969). Third, the new dimensionality representing the dominant social paradigm will become part of the content of the socialization process, taught to individuals through the major political and social institutions--with more or less success--but without regard for their policy-relevant knowledge levels. Thus, as society enters a subsequent stage of the social change process, the most and the least knowledgeable citizens may again converge in the *dimensionality* of their beliefs as they relate to dominant and new social paradigms.

The relative positions of the most and least knowledgeable Japanese makes even more sense in the context of a recent analysis by Yasuhiro Murota (1985). Murota argues that the Japanese have historically had a much different conception of nature than that held by the Western societies. In the West, nature is something to be subjugated to the will of humans, it is an opposing force with which to contest for control. In contrast, "the Japanese people considered themselves so intimately integrated with nature that they could not identify it objectively as a separate entity" (Murota, 1985:105). If this belief continues to exist, then among the Japanese the least knowledgeable would have reasonably well organized beliefs about the New Environmental Paradigm--not because of the "new" part of it, but because of its similarity to the *traditional* Japanese view.

Conclusion

This chapter has focused on the link between knowledge and "beliefs about the future." These beliefs are postmaterial values, support for the New Environmental Paradigm, and support for science and technology. As major sources of conflict in the movement of societies from traditional to postindustrial status, the shared substance of these beliefs is important in the linkage of the individual to a changing environment. How knowledge affects that linkage has been the concern of this chapter.

Americans are slightly more postmaterialist and substantially less materialist than are the Japanese. On the other hand, the Japanese exhibit greater support for the "New Environmental Paradigm" than do the Americans. The Spokane public gives a little more support for science and technology than does the Shizuoka sample, although there is a different pattern on the science item than on the two technology questions. In both countries the highest intercorrelation among the three future-oriented beliefs is between postmaterialism and the New Environmental Paradigm. In Japan, ideology is linked to postmaterialism, while in Spokane ideology is linked to support for the New Environmental Paradigm. Overall, the structures of these beliefs are generally similar in the two countries--i.e., dimensions are similar in content--but there are differences in the relative importance of that content in the overall structure.

128

In both Shizuoka and Spokane there is a weak tendency for individuals with more knowledge to give more support to postmaterialism and the NEP, and less support to science and technology. The impact of knowledge on these beliefs persists under controls for education and participation. Knowledge also affects the way individuals structure their beliefs, although that effect is somewhat different among the Japanese and the Americans.

Again, then, these findings show that knowledge is important in linking the individual to perceptions of the desirable future. At the same time, the effect of that knowledge is tempered by cultural differences. There is an interaction between the cognitive effects of knowledge, the uniqueness of national culture and history, and the impact of large scale social and political change. It is the theme of this book that this interaction has profound implications for democratic politics, for how citizens define their self-interest, and how they affect policy in a changing and often difficult world.

Notes

1. The item employed for the assessment of partisan identification read as follows: "Generally speaking, which of the following best applies to you when it comes to political parties?" The options provided to respondents were these: strong Democrat; Democrat; Independent; Republican; strong Republican. The comparable item for the Japanese setting entailed a continuum ranging from Communist Party, through Socialist Party, to Liberal Democratic Party. For the measurement of ideology, this item was used: "Generally speaking, which of the following best applied to you when it comes to politics?" The response options provided were these: very liberal; liberal; middle of the road; conservative; and very conservative. Finally, the item on social class read thusly: "There's been quite a bit of talk recently about different social classes in our country. Most people say they belong to the middle class or to the working class. If you had to make a choice, would you call yourself middle class or working class?"

2. To be sure, in three of the four groups only two of the three items load together on the same factor. However, it is the same two items and in the fourth group (the most knowledgeable Japanese) those two beliefs are joined by the third.

3. The "Dominant Social Paradigm" is a term used by Catton and Dunlap (1978, 1980) and Milbrath (1984) to summarize the set of development-oriented beliefs supportive of western industrial/economic growth, and the institutions that underpin it.

6

Knowledge and Policy Preferences

Introduction

This chapter continues the examination of the *effects* of knowledge. This book has argued that knowledge is the "missing link" in understanding the ways in which postindustrial citizens adapt to and influence the policy process. Chapter five suggests that public knowledge levels interact with the stage of postindustrial development to structure general citizen political values. This chapter narrows the focus, examining in some detail the effects of knowledge on the public's more specific policy orientations.

The following questions are addressed in this chapter. First, what role does knowledge play in the direction and consistency of policy area beliefs? One assumption in critiques of mass democracies is that public policy preferences are somehow different from what they would be if only citizens were better informed (Moore, 1979). Such questions concern both the direction of policy preferences and the "quality" of those opinions. Underlying such questions is the presumption that beliefs which are buttressed by information are inherently "better" beliefs. Another view of opinion quality concerns the consistency of preferences. In particular, knowledge of a policy area may provide the resources to create a consistent linkage among specific policy positions (Pierce and Lovrich, 1980). Indeed, earlier research suggests a connection between knowledge and both opinion direction and opinion consistency. Kuklinski et al., for example, show that better informed members of the public are more likely to support nuclear power development (1982:10). Individuals with greater knowledge levels are also more likely to have internally consistent environmental belief systems (Pierce and Lovrich, 1980).

A second central question is the role of knowledge in linking policy preferences to more general political orientations. Of particular interest is the impact of knowledge on the linkage of traditional and postindustrial dimensions to policy area attitudes. Being able to fit one's policy preferences into the dominant dimensions of political conflict would seem crucial to the citizen's ability both to define self-interest, and to promote that self-interest through political action. If knowledge links individuals to a policy area, better informed individuals may be more consistent in their preferences. If knowledge signals an engagement with postindustrial society, better informed citizens would be more likely to use their postindustrial orientations to guide policy preferences. That much is reasonably clear. A further question is less clear, though. That issue has to do with the impact of knowledge on the role of the traditional political dimensions of party, ideology and class. Will knowledge cause the traditional dimensions' organizing power to be replaced by the postindustrial dimensions? Or, are the more knowledgeable simply more likely to link their preferences to the conventional dimensions regardless of their postindustrial values? Yet a third possibility exists, for knowledge may allow one to keep feet in both the traditional and the postindustrial political worlds.

We must again raise the question of the independence of the effect of knowledge. Education and participation levels are strongly associated with variations in knowledge levels. It is possible that any impact of knowledge is simply that of education and participation working through the intervening knowledge measure. Indeed, a comparison of the role of education and participation to that of knowledge holding reveals some significant cross-national differences. These nation-specific findings once more appear related to some distinctive elements of the political cultures of Japan and the United States.

Environmental Policy Preferences

Several methodological considerations somewhat complicate the measurement of environmental policy area preferences. First, the policy preferences must be sufficiently more specific than the broader political and social orientations to which they will be linked. Second, a wide range of beliefs is required to broaden the possibilities for knowledge to have an impact. Third, we need measures of policy beliefs that are strictly comparable between the two countries. Finally, it is necessary to employ at least some preferences that approximate concrete, "real world" choices available to the citizens.

Four measures of policy orientations are available which appear to meet the conditions stated above. The first of these is *preservationist identification*. This measure requires the respondent to choose a position along a five-point continuum ranging from strong developmentalist to strong preservationist. This measure is available in both the Shizuoka and Spokane surveys. Preservationist identification reflects a central dimension in natural resource/environmental policy conflict. That dimension concerns the relative emphasis to be accorded to economic development versus preservationist concerns. Preservationist identification is perhaps particularly appropriate in this context because it reflects the individual's *self-placement* in relationship to the policy area. The following item measured preservationist identification:

> Please indicate which of the following best describes your opinion about the preservation and development of natural resources and the environment. (Please circle the number of your choice)
>
> 1. STRONG DEVELOPMENTALIST. The only consideration in deciding what to do with natural resources and the environment should be what will contribute most to the growth of the economy.
>
> 2. DEVELOPMENTALIST. The growth of the economy should be the most important, but not the only consideration in deciding what to do with the environment and natural resources.
>
> 3. MODERATE. Protection of the environment and the growth of the economy should be given equal consideration in deciding what to do with the environment and natural resources.
>
> 4. PRESERVATIONIST. Protection of the environment is the most important, but not the only consideration in deciding what to do with natural resources.
>
> 5. STRONG PRESERVATIONIST. The only consideration in deciding what to do with natural resources should be the preservation of the environment.

This particular question has been employed successfully in several other studies of mass publics (Pierce and Lovrich, 1980; Soden et al., 1985) and political activists (Pierce, 1977).

Table 6.1 shows the distribution of the Shizuoka and Spokane samples on the preservationist identification measure. The Japanese

Table 6.1

Distribution of Preservationist Identification and Support for Citizen Participation: Shizuoka Prefecture and Spokane County

	Preservationist Identification	
	Shizuoka	*Spokane*
Strong Developmentalist	1%	1%
Developmentalist	6%	10%
Moderate	57%	61%
Preservationist	34%	26%
Strong Preservationist	2%	2%
Total	100%	100%
N	(642)	(483)
Mean	3.3	3.2

		Citizen Participation	
		Shizuoka	*Spokane*
No Value	1.	1%	5%
	2.	1%	5%
	3.	2%	6%
Uncertain	4.	28%	32%
	5.	19%	21%
	6.	19%	17%
Great Value	7.	29%	16%
	Total	99%	102%
	(N)	(668)	(494)
	Mean	5.4	4.7

sample registers a slightly more preservationist orientation than does the Spokane sample. In both sites, though, there is a reluctance to locate outside of the middle of the five-position scale. Among those who are willing to identify either with the preservationist or developmentalist position, the preservationists are much more numerous than are the developmentalists (5:1 in Japan and 2.5:1 in the United States). As in several prior studies, the important distinction seems to be between those willing to call themselves preservationist and all other respondents (Pierce, 1977).

The second measure assesses the level of support for citizen participation in environmental policy formation. This question does not pertain directly to the substance of a policy dispute. However, because citizen participation is central to the history of environmental politics in both Japan and the United States it does seem appropriate to include it. In Japan, environmental protest spawned the "citizens movement" phenomenon which some scholars of Japanese politics claim has changed the face of the political process of postwar Japan (Simcock, 1973; Lewis, 1980; McKean, 1981). In the United States, as well, the question of public involvement has been central to environmental politics over the last two decades (Mazmanian and Nienaber, 1976; Godschalk and Stiftel, 1981; Wenner, 1982). Environmental legislation at federal and state levels has come to contain numerous requirements for the development and use of systematic public involvement mechanisms (Groves and Thompson, 1982). Public hearings, citizen surveys, citizen advisory committees and expanded access to the judicial process are just some of the procedural changes produced in the name of public involvement (Rosenbaum, 1978).

In both the United States and Japan expanded citizen involvement has been associated with anti-development, pro-environmental policy preferences. In both nations the environmental interests successfully pressed claims for additional opportunities for public involvement. Thus, there are further, broader policy implications associated with the issue of citizen involvement (Theobald, 1978). The question used to elicit attitudes about citizen involvement is:

> In recent years there has been considerable debate over the value of efforts to increase the amount of CITIZEN PARTICIPATION in government policy making in the environmental policy area. How would you locate yourself on the following scale regarding these efforts?

These efforts are -- 1 2 3 4 5 6 7 -- These efforts are
of **no value** and   of **great value** even
add needlessly to   Uncertain   if they add to the
the cost of government   cost of government

The distribution of responses to this question is shown in Table 6.1. Support for citizen participation is somewhat higher among the Japanese than among the Americans. Forty-eight percent in Shizuoka compared to 33 percent in Spokane are located at the "great value" positions--scale points six and seven. In both countries, though, the respondents are fairly well dispersed across the upper ranges of the measure. In the Japanese sample only 4 percent are found to the "no value" side of the middle position, and only 16 percent of the Americans reside there.   Just as the preservationist identification patterns indicated little support for self-identification as a developmentalist, these data indicate little willingness to oppose the injection of the public into the policy process. In some ways it appears that these attitudes have become part of consensual politics in recent decades.

As a way of correcting somewhat for the consensual nature of public involvement and preservationism, the third measure assesses the *relative* emphasis the citizen would give to alternative priorities. Actual policy making involves trade-offs among competing uses of natural resources and the environment. In most cultures one would expect certain consensual or widely accepted priorities over which there is little dispute, but policy conflict can be expected to occur over those emphases which are found in the middle. These policy priorities are on those which people tend to disagree and for which such disagreements are rather widely distributed across the public. The publics were asked to rank seven alternative uses of water (Spokane) or natural resources (Shizuoka). The question used to assess this relative emphasis read as follows:

When decisions are made about what to do with water, many uses must be considered. These uses are listed below. Please place a "1" by the use you think is most important, a "2" by the use you think is next most important, and so on until you have a "7" next to the use you think is least important.

  ___AGRICULTURE (irrigation on farms)
  ___DOMESTIC (home use)
  ___ENERGY (power production with dams or cooling for energy
   plants)
  ___INDUSTRY (manufacturing)
  ___PRESERVATION (for beauty, fish and wildlife habitat)
  ___RECREATION (camping, fishing, boating)
  ___TRANSPORTATION (barges and ferries)

The distribution of these rankings is shown in Table 6.2.

  The aggregate rankings by the Japanese and American citizens are quite similar. In both countries domestic and agricultural uses receive consensual support. Similarly, in both samples recreation and transportation receive the lowest rankings. In both Shizuoka and Spokane, middle priorities (and priorities which seem to generate the greatest possibility for conflict) are energy, industry and preservation. Preservation's ranking on the average is higher in Shizuoka than in Spokane. However, a particular problem developed in the Japanese responses to this question. Japanese respondents were reluctant to choose among the competing emphases by ranking one higher than the other. Thus, occasionally multiple emphases would be ranked "1" while none would be ranked "7." In any case, though, in both the Japanese and the American settings, preservation use had a widely distributed band of rankings.

  The fourth measure concerns perceptions of what constitutes pollution. This was chosen for several reasons. First, competing perceptions of what constitutes pollution often rest at the heart of environmental/natural resource conflict. Second, perceptions of what constitutes pollution may differ across cultures, and across subgroups within those cultures. Third, a definition of what constitutes pollution may be related to an individual's knowledge. If the perception of pollution stimulates political action, the role of knowledge in that perception is important. The following question was used to measure citizen perceptions of what things constitute pollution:

  The term POLLUTION is used to label things "whose presence in the environment constitutes a danger to the public health." Below we have listed some things that some people say are definitely pollution while other people say they are definitely *not* pollution. (Please circle the number that best reflects how *you* feel)

	Definitely Not Pollution		Not Sure		Definitely Pollution
Fireplace smoke	1	2	3	4	5
Auto exhaust	1	2	3	4	5
Nuclear waste	1	2	3	4	5
Herbicides	1	2	3	4	5
Residential sewage	1	2	3	4	5
Agricultural runoff	1	2	3	4	5
Neon signs	1	2	3	4	5
Airport noise	1	2	3	4	5
Vulgar language	1	2	3	4	5
Pornography	1	2	3	4	5

Several attributes of the pollution question deserve elaboration. First, note that the question provided a definition of pollution--things "whose presence in the environment constitutes a danger to the public health." This definition was included in order to provide a common context for the respondents. Second, a wide range of specific referents were provided that could be called pollution--perceived as dangerous-- by respondents with different social and political locations in the Japanese and American settings. This provision for diverse elements is particularly important in the context of recent analyses suggesting that perceptions of risk, of when the public is in danger, have a significant cultural component (Enloe, 1975; Douglas and Wildavsky, 1982). The goal was to provide a broad enough range of belief objects for cultural forces to come into play. Third, the hope was to provide a range of potential pollutants. That range might produce one or more items with enough variation to be responsive to other attributes--such as knowledge or general environmental orientations. Fourth, we wanted to include some items that might be at least partially dependent on "knowledge" for their evaluation. The results are shown in Table 6.3, which displays the percentage of each sample responding with a "5" (definitely pollution).

Table 6.3 shows that the ten items elicited a wide range of responses. On some items few of the respondents view it as a pollutant (e.g., neon signs), while on other items nearly everyone did so (e.g., auto exhaust). Moreover, in some cases there is general agreement between the two samples (e.g., nuclear waste) and in a few others there

Table 6.2

Distribution of Ranks of Alternate Environmental/Natural Resource Policy Emphasis

Shizuoka Prefecture

		Agriculture	Domestic	Energy	Industry	Preservation	Recreation	Transportation
Rank	1	22%	76%	19%	9%	17%	3%	4%
	2	41	14	19	12	14	5	4
	3	21	5	19	23	17	6	5
	4	12	3	21	29	14	12	6
	5	3	0	13	18	28	11	13
	6	1	0	5	8	9	26	32
	7	1	1	5	2	1	38	37
	Total	101%	99%	101%	101%	100%	101%	101%
	N	(649)	(655)	(645)	(644)	(644)	(642)	(643)
	Mean	2.4	1.5	3.2	3.7	3.6	5.5	5.6

Spokane County

		Agriculture	Domestic	Energy	Industry	Preservation	Recreation	Transportation
Rank	1	9%	79%	7%	1%	4%	0%	0%
	2	44	11	26	9	9	3	1
	3	23	5	36	17	10	7	3
	4	14	3	14	37	18	9	4
	5	5	1	9	16	24	23	22
	6	4	1	5	18	26	30	16
	7	0	0	3	3	10	28	55
	Total	99%	100%	100%	101%	101%	100%	101%
	N	(491)	(496)	(489)	(490)	(489)	(487)	(488)
	Mean	2.7	1.4	3.2	4.2	4.7	5.5	5.6

138

Table 6.3

Percentage Identifying Various Substances as Pollution: Shizuoka Prefecture and Spokane County

Substance	Shizuoka Prefecture	Spokane County	Difference
Fireplace Smoke	3%	27%	+24
Auto Exhaust	79%	73%	- 6
Nuclear Waste	71%	72%	+ 1
Herbicides	32%	41%	+ 9
Residential Sewage	28%	44%	+16
Agricultural Runoff	15%	17%	+ 2
Neon Signs	8%	5%	- 3
Airport Noise	64%	10%	-54
Vulgar Language	9%	25%	+16
Pornography	24%	35%	+11

is substantial disagreement between Japanese and American respondents. The most substantial cultural gap appears in the perception of the harmful nature of "airport noise." Over three-fifths of the Shizuoka citizens consider airport noise to be a pollutant while less than one-fifth of the Spokanites take that perspective. One possible explanation for that difference may have to do with the prominent nature of the continuing conflict over the development of Narita airport east of Tokyo (Takabatake, 1975). The airport controversy has been a focal point for some Japanese citizen movements, including some activist environmental organizations. Similarly, fireplace smoke and residential sewage are more likely to be seen as pollutants in the Spokane area than in Shizuoka Prefecture. The Spokane area has a much higher incidence of wood burning for heat than would be the case for Shizuoka Prefecture residents (where fireplaces in private residences are virtually nonexistent).

One potential pollutant in Table 6.3 was included in the subsequent analysis. The term "herbicides" was chosen for several reasons--namely, because of the relatively similar distributions obtaining in the two countries, because of its being in the middle of the distributions of different items being considered as pollutants, because it would seem to have a prima facie sensitivity to variations in policy relevant knowledge, and because preliminary analyses showed it to exhibit at least a marginal relationship to the other indicators of environmental attitudes.

At this point the question arises as to the coherence among these four separate indicators of environmental attitudes. The correlation coefficients among the policy preferences in question are set forth in Table 6.4.

In *both* countries there is some coherence among the four environmental attitudes. However, the correlations are somewhat higher in Spokane than in Shizuoka. In both locations preservationists are more likely than developmentalists to assign preservation uses of natural resources a high priority, to advocate citizen involvement in policy formation, and to identify herbicides as a pollutant. These correlations suggest that some common dimension may link the four different attitudes, but that each measure taps a sufficiently different aspect of that dimension to justify separate consideration. Finally, these findings suggest that there is ample room for knowledge to have an impact on the level of association among these beliefs.

Table 6.4

Correlation (Gamma) Among Environmental Policy Attitudes in Shizuoka Prefecture and the Spokane Area

	SHIZUOKA PREFECTURE (x = 14.3)[a]			
SPOKANE COUNTY (x = 19.6)	Preservationist Identification	Policy Ranking of Preservation	Attitude Toward Citizen Participation	Herbicide as Pollution
Preservationist Identification	x	-.15	.15	.11
Policy Ranking of Preservation	-.40	x	-.09	-.15
Attitude Toward Citizen Participation	.25	-.10	x	.21
Herbicides as Pollution	.26	-.17	.17	x

[a]Mean gamma for the six combinations of environmental policy attitudes.

NOTE: The six gammas above the diagonal pertain to Shizuoka Prefecture residents, and those below the diagonal apply to Spokane County respondents.

Knowledge and Direction of Environmental Attitudes

Do better informed individuals have different policy attitudes than their less knowledgeable fellow citizens? Does knowledge bring a kind of "enlightenment" to individuals that leads them to share policy perspectives? Table 6.5 shows the relationship between the five measures of knowledge and the four environmental policy preferences.

Some rather distinctive patterns appear in Table 6.5. First, knowledge does have some effect on policy orientation. Second, knowledge has the single most consistent effect upon the perception of herbicides as a pollutant in Shizuoka. Regardless of the specific knowledge measure, the more informed citizens of Shizuoka are more likely to perceive herbicides as definitely being pollution. Among the five knowledge measures, though, the impact of technical term familiarity is greater than that of the other four information measures. In Spokane a similar pattern is present in the impact of knowledge on preservationist identification. Four of the five knowledge measures are associated with preservationist identification among Spokane area residents; the sole exception is technical term familiarity. Similarly, four of the five information measures are related to support for citizen participation in Shizuoka. Overall, then, the impact of knowledge on the direction of policy orientations seems greater in Shizuoka than in Spokane. Moreover, the particular policy orientation affected by knowledge is different in Japan than in the United States.

Table 6.6 shows the variation accounted for in the four environmental policy preferences when employing three separate sets of predictive variables: 1) only education and participation; 2) only the five measures of knowledge; and 3) education, participation and the five knowledge measures considered simultaneously. In almost every case the inclusion of policy-relevant knowledge results in a substantial increase in the variation explained in environmental attitudes over and above that accounted for by education and participation.

While it appears that policy-relevant knowledge makes a contribution to the *direction* of environmental attitudes, several caveats are in order. First, the conclusion must be tempered with realism as to the *amount* of total explained variation. The percentage of explained variation is relatively low in each specific attitude area. There is ample opportunity for influences other than knowledge to account for these particular environmental policy preferences.

A second reservation concerns assumptions of causal direction. The working hypothesis is that knowledge would somehow *lead to* particular policy attitudes. Indeed, an assumption underlying

Table 6.5

Correlation (Gamma) of Policy-Relevant Knowledge Measures and Environmental Policy Attitudes in Shizuoka Prefecture and Spokane County

	Environmental Policy Attitudes							
	Preservationist Identification		Priority Ranking of Preservation		Attitude Toward Citizen Participation		Herbicide as Pollution	
Policy-Relevant Knowledge Index [a]	Japan	U.S.	Japan	U.S.	Japan	U.S.	Japan	U.S.
Term Familiarity	-.01	.07	-.06	-.09	.22	.24	.27	.14
Local Affairs	.01	-.17	-.08	.02	.24	-.05	.16	-.05
Ecology Science	-.04	.13	-.15	.02	.09	.04	.17	-.07
Problem Identification	.08	.20	-.03	-.11	.19	.22	.15	.18
Self-Assessment	.10	-.14	-.04	.03	.15	.07	.13	-.03

[a]Using trichotomized indices.

Table 6.6

Association (R^2) Between Education, Knowledge and Policy Process Participation and Direction of Environmental Policy Attitudes in Shizuoka Prefecture and Spokane County[a]

Environmental Policy Attitudes

Variables Explaining Variation	Preservationist Identification		Policy Ranking of Preservation		Attitude Toward Citizen Participation		Herbicide as Pollution	
	Japan	U.S.	Japan	U.S.	Japan	U.S.	Japan	U.S.
Education and Participation	.01	.01	.00	.01	.04*	.03*	.02*	.00
Five Knowledge Measures[b]	.02	.10*	.02	.08	.07*	.09	.06*	.12*
Education, Participation and Five Knowledge Measures	.03	.12*	.04	.10	.08*	.10	.06*	.12*

* $p \leq .05$

[a]The entry in each cell is the amount of variation explained (R^2) in each environmental policy attitude by the variable sets listed in the left column of the table.

[b]Term familiarity, local knowledge, scientific facts, problem identification and self-assessment.

contending arguments over the public's capacity for active involvement in policymaking is that information will make opinions different. It is possible, of course, that the causal chain works in the other direction. That is, it may be that the environmental policy preference is the source of motivation to acquire information. Individuals who are preservationist, support policy priorities emphasizing the preservation use of natural resources, support citizen participation, and view herbicides as pollutants may be more highly motivated to acquire information.

What is the consequence of additional information on the degree to which citizens appear to group their environmental attitudes consistently? Greater knowledge levels could be expected to enhance an individual's understanding of the common elements shared among the different attitude objects of a given policy arena. An essential question in this regard, of course, is the relative impact of policy-relevant knowledge compared to that of education and participation. Education may provide the individual with the training and cognitive skills for assessing the mutual implications of different attitude objects in the same policy domain (Hanson, 1979). However, research on the impact of education on belief system organization is mixed (Converse, 1975; Pierce and Lovrich, 1980). Participation can similarly be expected to enhance belief system constraint. Experience in the policy process may forge a consistency born of the necessity to simplify a complex reality for the sake of effective participation (Lovrich and Abe, 1984). The average correlations among the four environmental beliefs within three levels of policy-relevant knowledge, three levels of education, and three levels of participation are shown in Table 6.7. As in previous analyses, the specific measure of policy-relevant knowledge employed in this table is that of technical term familiarity.

Rather distinctive nation-specific patterns appear in Table 6.7. In Spokane, knowledge clearly has the biggest impact on the level of consistency obtaining among environmental policy beliefs. While the highest level of knowledge has a mean correlation (.33) only a little greater than that of the highest levels of education (.27) and participation (.30), very low levels of knowledge severely depress constraint. A very different pattern is present in Shizuoka. Among the Japanese the impact of policy-relevant knowledge and education is much less than that of participation. The question arises, then, as to why knowledge would tie together environmental beliefs in Spokane, while in Shizuoka participation would occupy that role.

The greater impact of participation in Japan may result from the distinctive character of Japanese environmental politics. Japanese environmental politics is citizen movement politics (McKean, 1981).

Table 6.7

Mean Correlation (Gamma) Among Environmental Policy
Attitudes, Controlling for Policy-Relevant Knowledge,
Education and Participation: Shizuoka Prefecture and
Spokane County

Policy-Relevant Knowledge[a]	Shizuoka Prefecture	Spokane County
Low	$.10^b$	.13
Medium	.19	.25
High	<u>.15</u>	<u>.33</u>
Difference	+.05	+.20
Education		
Low	.14	.22
Medium	.14	.25
High	<u>.15</u>	<u>.27</u>
Difference	+.01	+.05
Participation		
Low	.10	.19
Medium	.09	.17
High	<u>.27</u>	<u>.30</u>
Difference	+.17	+.11

[a]Technical term familiarity.

[b]The mean is based on six correlations.

Environmental activism thus is part of political activism more generally. Politics in Japan tends to be local in focus, and political mobilization is primarily local in focus. Environmental activists often are recruited into the environmental movement even though lacking many of the expected accompanying beliefs (Pierce et al., 1986b). Many Japanese environmental activists are involved in the environmental movement in a secondary way, as a consequence of their local political allegiances. Consequently, the belief system consistency that would come from knowledge could be replaced by that from being told how things go together.

Attitudinal Sources of Environmental Beliefs

One important reason for studying knowledge is its potential for heightening the citizen's sensitivity to the self-interest implications of policy alternatives. Pluralistic democratic politics rests on the assumption that those individuals who share a self-interest will come to similar policy preferences on those questions that have direct implications for that shared interest (Truman, 1951; Easton, 1965). The expectation guiding this section is that individuals with greater knowledge will be more aware of their self-interest. That awareness will surface in the tendency to exhibit more consistent patterns of association between specific policy area beliefs and more general political and social orientations.

In this context we are interested in determining the degree to which the four policy attitudes are related to two sets of more general political/social orientations. We label these general orientations traditional and postindustrial. These more general orientations are used here as the surrogate for the citizen's definition of self-interest. This allows an analysis of whether citizens link their policy stands to traditional political standards or to more contemporary social/political dimensions.

The impact of the postindustrial orientations on the four environmental attitudes is shown in Table 6.8. In each case the set of postindustrial attitude dimensions has a significant ($p \leq .05$) relationship to the environmental attitudes. Nonetheless, the amount of explained variation in the individual attitude dimension never surpasses ten percent. Generally, the impact of the postindustrial orientations is greater in Spokane than in Shizuoka. The greatest difference surfaces on the relative ranking of preservation as a policy priority. In this case ten percent of the variation is explained in Spokane, but only two percent in Shizuoka. The New Environmental Paradigm (NEP) exhibits the strongest impact on environmental policy

Table 6.8

Multiple Regression for Environmental Policy Attitudes with New Environmental Paradigm, Postmaterialist Values and Support for Science and Technology

Environmental Policy Attitudes

	Preservationist Identification		Priority Ranking of Preservation		Support for Citizen Participation		Herbicide as Pollution	
	Japan	U.S.	Japan	U.S.	Japan	U.S.	Japan	U.S.
R	.24	.31	.15	.31	.27	.25	.24	.28
R^2	.06	.10	.02	.10	.08	.06	.06	.08
F	10.4	12.6	4.13	12.1	13.9	7.9	10.1	9.7
FSig	.000	.000	.007	.000	.000	.000	.000	.000
New Environmental Paradigm[a]	.11**	.25***	--	-.26***	.20***	.16**	.14**	.19***
Postmaterialist Values	--	--	-.13*	-.14**	.15***	.16**	.15***	.18***
Faith in Science and Technology	-.18***	-.13*	--	--	--	--	--	--

[a]Standardized Regression Coefficients

* $p \leq .05$ ** $p \leq .01$ *** $p \leq .001$

attitudes (see the standardized regression coefficients). Not only does the NEP index appear in seven of the eight potential cases, it also has the largest coefficients. At the same time, postmaterial values are related to all of the environmental policy attitudes except for preservationist identification; significantly, though, it is similar in its impact in both the Japanese and American settings.

Perhaps the most impressive element in Table 6.8 is the overall similarity in results for the Japanese and American cases. There is near perfect similarity in the direction of connections made between the general orientations and the environmental attitudes. We now look to see if the patterns are reproduced for the traditional orientations.

Table 6.9 repeats the analysis, substituting the traditional political orientations of partisanship, ideological identification (liberal/ conservative) and class identification (working/middle) for the postindustrial orientations. Again, the overall impact of the three variables is relatively weak in both countries. In both settings party identification is related to preservationist identification and to the perception of herbicides as a pollutant. Ideological identification is related to preservationist identification. It is also related to the rank of preservation as a policy priority in Spokane and to support for citizen participation in Shizuoka. In no case is class identification related to environmental attitudes, suggesting that the environment has indeed become a cross-strata policy domain (Van Liere and Dunlap, 1980). Most important, perhaps, is the fact that the traditional political variables are less powerful predictors of environmental attitudes than are the postindustrial variables.

The greater relative influence of the postindustrial variables is underscored by the results displayed in Table 6.10. That table contains regression results when all six of the general orientations are employed simultaneously to predict the policy attitudes. The NEP and values measures dominate the table. In Spokane the NEP is related ($p \leq .05$ or better) to each of the four environmental policy attitudes, even when controlling for all of the other variables at the same time. Moreover, it is related to two environmental beliefs in Shizuoka. Postmaterialist values are related to environmental attitudes in five of the possible eight instances, three in Shizuoka and two in Spokane. Thus, the NEP is the more pervasive orientation in Spokane, and postmaterialist values are the more compelling in Japan.

Even with the broad impact of the postindustrial political orientations, though, the effects of party identification and ideological identification do not disappear. In Spokane, party identification is related to preservationist identification and to the perception of

Table 6.9

Multiple Regression for Environmental Policy Attitudes with Party, Class and Ideology

Environmental Policy Attitudes

	Preservationist Identification		Priority Ranking of Preservation		Support for Citizen Participation		Herbicide as Pollution	
	Japan	U.S.	Japan	U.S.	Japan	U.S.	Japan	U.S.
R	.15	.28	.13	.19	.20	.06	.19	.22
R^2	.02	.08	.02	.04	.04	.00	.03	.05
F	3.65	11.12	2.66	4.8	7.04	.41	6.07	6.5
FSig	.013	.000	.047	.003	.0001	.745	.001	.0003
Party[a]	.13*	-.12*	--	--	--	--	.14**	-.21***
Ideology	--	-.21**	--	.17**	-.18***	--	--	--
Class	--	--	--	--	--	--	--	--

[a]Standardized Regression Coefficients

* p ≤ .05   ** p ≤ .01   *** p ≤ .001

Table 6.10

Multiple Regression for Environmental Policy Attitudes with Traditional Orientations and Postindustrial Orientations

Environmental Policy Attitudes

	Preservationist Identification		Priority Ranking of Preservation		Support for Citizen Participation		Herbicide as Pollution	
	Japan	U.S.	Japan	U.S.	Japan	U.S.	Japan	U.S.
R	.26	.40	.19	.36	.34	.24	.25	.33
R^2	.07	.16	.04	.13	.12	.06	.06	.11
F	5.11	10.18	2.65	7.8	9.72	3.24	5.03	6.53
FSig	.000	.000	.015	.000	.000	.004	.0001	.000
Party[a]	--	-.11*	--	--	--	--	-.12*	-.18**
Ideology	--	-.22***	--	.14*	-.12*	--	--	--
Class	--	--	--	--	--	--	--	--
New Environmental Paradigm	.10*	.17**	--	-.24**	.24***	.14*	--	.15**
Postmaterialist Values	--	--	-.13*	--	.12*	.15**	.12*	.16**
Faith in Science and Technology	-.17***	-.12*	--	--	--	--	--	--

^{a}Standardized Regression Coefficients *p $\leq$ .05 **p $\leq$ .01 ***p $\leq$ .001

herbicides as pollutants. In Shizuoka, party is also related to the perception of the polluting nature of herbicides. Similarly, in Spokane ideological self-classification is connected with preservationist identification and with the ranking of preservation as a policy priority. In Japan ideology is linked to support for citizen participation.

The central issue of this chapter is the impact of knowledge on relationships obtaining between general orientations and environmental policy attitudes. Technical term familiarity is used here as the knowledge measure once again. The first stage in this analysis is the examination of the effect of controlling for knowledge when assessing the association between the postindustrial variables and the environmental attitudes in question.

Controlling for knowledge produces quite different results in Spokane than occur in Shizuoka. In Spokane (see Table 6.11), on three of the four attitudes there is a substantial increase in explained variation with increased knowledge. Only in predicting the policy priority of preservation does knowledge fail to have the expected effect. In Shizuoka, in contrast, there is no consistent increase in explained variation with increased knowledge; in some cases, knowledge even suppresses the impact of the postindustrial beliefs.

It is clear that knowledge affects the impact of postindustrial dimensions on policy-relevant beliefs, particularly among the American respondents. It is possible, of course, that knowledge will not have the same impact on the linkage between traditional political orientations and environmental attitudes. By definition, the "traditional" political orientations will not be as new to the citizen. Long experience in using those orientations may make knowledge less useful in assessing the relationship among the political orientations and environmental attitudes. A multiple regression analysis again was performed.

Once more, knowledge fails to affect the association between political orientations and environmental attitudes in the Shizuoka case; no increase in explained variation occurs across information levels. In Spokane, in contrast, on three of the four environmental attitudes there is a slight increase in explained variation with greater knowledge. As in the Japanese case, the predominant political orientation at the highest knowledge level is ideological identification (see Table 6.12).

Combining the traditional and the postindustrial orientations in the same statistical model serves to heighten the effect of knowledge. As Table 6.13 shows, in the Spokane high knowledge group the six variables explain thirty-five percent of the variation in preservationist identification. This compares to 20 percent and 15 percent in the lower two groups. Similarly, the variation explained in support for citizen participation increases from five percent to nineteen percent. In

Table 6.11

Multiple Regression for Environmental Policy Attitudes, Controlling for Technical Term Familiarity: Spokane County and Shizuoka Prefecture

	Preservationist Identification		Priority Ranking for Preservation		Support for Citizen Participation		Herbicide as a Pollutant	
	Japan	U.S.	Japan	U.S.	Japan	U.S.	Japan	U.S.
Low Information								
R	.23	.30	.21	.28	.31	.23	.41	.24
R^2	.05	.09	.04	.08	.10	.05	.17	.06
F	1.42	4.3	1.16	3.6	2.6	2.2	5.03	2.6
Sig	.24	.007	.33	.02	.058	.09	.003	.055
Postmaterialist Values	x	x	x	x	x	.19[a]	x	.24[b]
New Environmental Paradigm	x	.19[c]	x	-.20[a]	.26[a]	x	.40[b]	x
Faith in Science and Technology	x	-.20[c]	x	x	x	x	x	x
Medium Information								
R	.35	.27	.16	.37	.31	.18	.25	.41
R^2	.12	.07	.02	.14	.10	.03	.06	.17
F	11.6	3.2	2.09	6.7	8.8	1.48	5.35	8.33
Sig	.000	.02	.10	.00	.000	.22	.001	.000
Postmaterialist Values	x	x	x	x	x	.15[a]	.20	x
New Environmental Paradigm	.18[c]	.20[c]	x	-.34[c]	.22[c]	x	x	.39[c]
Faith in Science and Technology	-.24[c]	x	x	x	-.12[a]	x	x	x
High Information								
R	.21	.52	.23	.29	.17	.45	.17	.39
R^2	.05	.27	.05	.08	.03	.20	.03	.15
F	2.9	8.5	3.4	2.07	1.9	5.79	1.9	4.14
Sig	.03	.0001	.02	.11	.13	.001	.13	.00
Postmaterialist Values	x	.23[a]	x	x	x	x	x	.35
New Environmental Paradigm	x	.38[c]	x	x	x	x	.42[c]	x
Faith in Science and Technology	.21	x	x	x	x	x	x	x

[a] $p \leq .05$ [b] $p \leq .01$ [c] $p \leq .001$

Table 6.12

Multiple Regression for Environmental Policy Attitudes with Traditional Orientations, Controlling for Policy-Relevant Knowledge

	Preservationist Identification		Priority Ranking of Preservation		Support for Citizen Participation		Herbicide as a Pollutant	
	Japan	U.S.	Japan	U.S.	Japan	U.S.	Japan	U.S.
	Low Knowledge							
R	.17	.26	.16	.20	.20	.07	.34	.15
R^2	.03	.07	.02	.04	.04	.01	.11	.02
F	.71	3.4	.59	1.86	.96	.256	3.01	1.07
F Sig	.54	.02	.62	.138	.42	.86	.036	.36
Ideology	--	--	--	.20*	--	--	--	--
Party	--	--	--	--	--	--	.36**	--
Class	--	--	--	--	--	--	--	--
	Middle Knowledge							
R	.16	.35	.06	.25	.20	.14	.14	.32
R^2	.02	.12	.00	.06	.04	.02	.02	.10
F	2.05	6.48	.25	2.99	3.53	.95	1.66	5.14
F Sig	.11	.000	.86	.03	.016	.42	.177	.002
Ideology	--	-.26**	--	--	-.15*	--	--	--
Party	.14*	--	--	--	--	--	--	.28***
Class	--	--	--	--	--	--	--	--
	High Knowledge							
R	.15	.37	.23	.29	.21	.20	.26	.35
R^2	.02	.14	.05	.09	.05	.04	.07	.12
F	1.37	4.11	3.26	2.35	2.82	1.09	4.37	3.58
F Sig	.25	-.29*	.023	.078	.04	.36	.005	.017
Ideology	--	--	--	.25*	-.20*	--	-.20*	--
Party	--	--	--	--	--	--	--	-.29*
Class	--	--	--	--	--	--	--	--

*p ≤ .05   **p ≤ .01   ***p ≤ .001

Shizuoka, in sharp contrast, the reverse pattern occurs--the amount of explained variation in environmental attitudes actually *decreases* with increased knowledge.

The final task is to assess the impact of knowledge compared to education and participation. Because education and political participation are strong predictors of policy-relevant information holding, it is possible that the apparent influence of information holding on policy-relevant attitudes simply reflects the intervening effects of education and participation. Table 6.14 summarizes the impact of controlling serially for knowledge, education and participation. That table provides the proportion of the variation in each environmental attitude explained by the six independent variables at three (low, medium and high) levels of information, education and political participation, respectively.

The relative impact of knowledge, education and participation varies from one environmental policy attitude to the next, and depends on the national setting. Knowledge and education both enhance the impact of political orientations on preservationist identification in Spokane. In Shizuoka, though, only education makes an appreciable difference. In Spokane, the ranking of preservation as a policy priority is enhanced only by increased education levels. On the support for citizen participation measure, only knowledge enhances the explained variation in Spokane. In Shizuoka the greatest explanatory power actually is present among those with the least information, lowest education, and lowest participation.

In summary, then, in the Spokane case knowledge enhances the association between environmental policy attitudes and **both** traditional and postindustrial political attitudes. For Spokane area citizens the impact of knowledge clearly compares favorably to or exceeds that of education and participation. In the Shizuoka setting, in sharp contrast, knowledge has no such impact. Indeed, for Shizuoka Prefecture residents in most cases the ability to predict environmental attitudes actually decreases as the level of policy-relevant knowledge increases.

Table 6.13

Multiple Regression for Environmental Policy Attitudes with Traditional and Postindustrial Orientations, Controlling for Level of Knowledge of Policy-Relevant Technical Terminology: Shizuoka Prefecture and Spokane County*

Environmental Attitudes

	Preservationist Identification		Support for Citizen Participation		Preservation Ranking		Herbicide as Pollution	
	Japan	U.S.	Japan	U.S.	Japan	U.S.	Japan	U.S.
Low Knowledge								
R	.31	.39	.43	.22	.31	.36	.50	.25
R^2	.10	.15	.18	.05	.10	.13	.25	.06
F	.95	3.33	2.00	.91	.95	2.69	3.07	1.19
FSig	.46	.005	.08	.49	.47	.017	.01	.314
Postmaterialist Values	--	--	--	--	--	--	--	.21[a]
New Environmental Paradigm	--	--	.42[b]	--	--	-.19[a]	.39[b]	--
Faith in Science and Technology	--	-.23[a]	--	--	--	--	--	--
Party	--	--	--	--	--	--	--	--
Ideology	--	--	--	--	--	--	--	--
Class	--	--	--	--	--	--	--	--

*Only standardized regression coefficients with a p ≤ .05 are included in the table.

[a] p ≤ .05   [b] p ≤ .01   [c] p ≤ .001

(continues)

Table 6.13 (continued)

Environmental Attitudes

	Preservationist Identification		Support for Citizen Participation		Preservation Ranking		Herbicide as Pollution	
	Japan	U.S.	Japan	U.S.	Japan	U.S.	Japan	U.S.
Medium Knowledge								
R	.33	.44	.36	.25	.18	.50	.24	.47
R^2	.11	.20	.13	.06	.03	.25	.06	.22
F	4.37	4.51	5.23	1.21	1.22	6.18	2.23	5.26
FSig	.001	.000	.000	.308	.30	.000	.042	.000
Postmaterialist Values	--	--	--	--	--	--	--	--
New Environmental Paradigm	.18[b]	.18[a]	.25[c]	--	--	-.37[c]	--	.34[c]
Faith in Science and Technology	.21[b]	--	--	--	--	--	-.14[a]	--
Party	--	--	--	--	--	--	--	-.20
Ideology	--	-.23[a]	--	--	--	--	--	--
Class	--	--	--	--	--	--	--	--

*Only standardized regression coefficients with a p ≤ .05 are included in the table.
[a] p ≤ .05   [b] p ≤ .01   [c] p ≤ .001

(continues)

Table 6.13 (continued)

Environmental Attitudes

	Preservationist Identification		Support for Citizen Participation		Preservation Ranking		Herbicide as Pollution	
	Japan	U.S.	Japan	U.S.	Japan	U.S.	Japan	U.S.
High Knowledge								
R	.25	.59	.29	.44	.24	.35	.32	.53
R^2	.06	.35	.08	.19	.06	.12	.10	.28
F	1.78	5.37	2.40	2.37	1.67	1.37	3.08	3.90
FSig	.11	.000	.03	.04	.13	.24	.007	.002
Postmaterialist Values	--	--	--	--	--	--	--	--
New Environmental Paradigm	--	.35[b]	.16[a]	.33[b]	--	--	--	--
Faith in Science and Technology	.20[a]	--	--	--	--	--	--	--
Party	--	--	--	--	--	--	--	-.35[b]
Ideology	--	--	--	--	--	--	-.20[a]	--
Class	--	--	--	--	--	--	--	--

*Only standardized regression coefficients with a p ≤ .05 are included in the table.
[a] p ≤ .05   [b] p ≤ .01   [c] p ≤ .001

Table 6.14

Summary of Explained Variance (R^2) When Predicting Environmental Policy Attitudes from Postindustrial and Traditional Orientations Under Controls for Knowledge, Education and Participation*

	Preservationist Identification		Priority Ranking of Preservation		Support for Citizen Participation		Herbicide as Pollution	
	Japan	U.S.	Japan	U.S.	Japan	U.S.	Japan	U.S.
Policy-Relevant Knowledge Level*								
Low	.10	.15	.10	.13	.18	.05	.25	.06
Medium	.11	.20	.03	.25	.13	.06	.06	.22
High	.06	.35	.06	.12	.08	.19	.10	.28
R^2 Change	-.05	+.20	-.04	-.01	-.10	+.14	-.15	+.22
Education Level								
Low	.16	.07	.07	.10	.26	.10	.09	.13
Medium	.04	.19	.06	.22	.13	.08	.04	.11
High	.30	.33	.05	.22	.20	.11	.14	.25
R^2 Change	+.14	+.26	-.02	+.12	-.06	+.01	+.05	+.12
Participation								
Low	.07	.16	.10	.15	.29	.08	.12	.04
Medium	.06	.17	.04	.12	.08	.03	.08	.13
High	.11	.26	.09	.19	.19	.11	.08	.18
R^2 Change	+.04	+.10	-.01	+.04	-.10	+.03	-.04	+.14

*Term familiarity is the measure of policy-relevant information used here.

Conclusion

Environmental policy attitudes are more consistent in Spokane than in Shizuoka. Knowledge has a greater impact on the *direction* of environmental attitudes in Shizuoka than in Spokane. In contrast, knowledge is more important in belief *consistency* in Spokane than in Shizuoka. Personal involvement in the policy process is more important in attitude consistency in Shizuoka than in Spokane. While postindustrial orientations are similarly intertwined with environmental policy attitudes in the two locations, the magnitude of the linkage is greater in Spokane. In both study sites, traditional political orientations (party, class and ideology) are relatively weak predictors of environmental attitudes. Postindustrial dimensions (NEP, Postmaterialist Values and Faith in Science and Technology) are more important than the traditional orientations.

Knowledge holding increases the impact of postindustrial dimensions on environmental attitudes in Spokane, but does not do so in Shizuoka. In Spokane, when all six independent variables are considered simultaneously, knowledge enhances the explained variation in policy attitudes. In sharp contrast, in Shizuoka there is actually a *decrease* in the variation explained in environmental attitudes at higher levels of knowledge.

Knowledge also has a major impact on environmental attitudes in Shizuoka and Spokane. However, the character of that impact is very different in the two national settings. In Shizuoka, knowledge influences the *direction* of environmental attitudes, while in Spokane knowledge increases *consistency* among attitudes, and between those attitudes and the more general political orientations. In Shizuoka, in contrast, consistency among attitudes is more a product of participation than knowledge holding.

Once again, then, the results of this chapter reveal a major role for knowledge in linking the postindustrial citizen to significant policy questions. The role of knowledge in this linkage remains consistent with the dominant characteristics of the politics, the culture and the environmental policy processes of the two nations. Knowledge is more important where mobilization into environmental politics appears to be more motivation-based (the American case). Participation levels appear to be more important where patterns of general and traditional political activism seem to be a primary and sometimes inadvertent mobilizer of environmentalism. Finally, knowledge accentuates the impact of postindustrial orientations on environmental beliefs in the more postindustrial society.

7

Knowledge and Power

Introduction

The three preceding chapters suggest that the possession of policy relevant knowledge likely influences individuals' evaluations of information sources, their views of the future, and the content and structure of their beliefs. Earlier chapters demonstrated that the acquisition of knowledge is very likely as much motivational in origin as it is a product of immutable social and demographic attributes.

Despite all of this progress toward understanding the consequences of knowledge holding, however, the analysis still falls short of addressing the book's central political question: What is the impact of knowledge on the distribution of *power*? The proof is in the pudding, as the cliche goes, and power is the postindustrial pudding.

Power and Postindustrial Politics

Issues of power--its distribution and acquisition--in democratic politics generally concern the conditions that structure the influence of mass publics. Indeed, we have argued throughout this work that the character of postindustrial politics makes the power position of democratic publics particularly problematic.

The nature of political issues that dominate postindustrial politics poses several problems for the exercise of power by democratic citizenries. First, many issues (e.g., acid rain, nuclear waste disposal, in vitro fertilization) are novel and unfamiliar. Citizens frequently have few familiar guides in the determination of their own self-interested position. Traditional partisan attachments and ideological reference points can even provide conflicting and often confusing directions to the wayward postindustrial traveler.

Second, postindustrial politics disrupts conventional patterns of mass mobilization and political linkage. In the United States in particular, public loyalties to the major parties have become greatly attenuated (Nie et al., 1976). The national and state level party organizations are much less effective as vehicles for the organization and exercise of power than they once were (Fiorina, 1980). The traditional mix of economic interest groups has been replaced by a plethora of single-interest groups (Tatalovich and Daynes, 1984), public interest groups (McFarland, 1976), business and labor Political Action Committees (Olson, 1982: 75-117) and human rights or quality of life groups (e.g., womens rights, ethnic rights, environmental organizations) (Naisbitt, 1982: 159-188). Elections in the United States have suffered a decline in mass participation and a loss of legitimacy in the public's mind (Gilmour and Lamb, 1975). In sum, the traditional political channels for connecting mass publics to public policy have been greatly weakened.

Third, the complex, technical and/or scientific character of many public policy issues presents a bewildering smorgasboard of concern to the attentive citizen. As Robert Dahl has written with regard to the issue of controlling nuclear weapons:

> Numerous crucial technical questions about nuclear weapons and strategy are all outside the realm of ordinary experience. They require specialized knowledge, some of it both intricate and secret, that ordinary citizens not only do not possess, but cannot reasonably be expected to possess (1985: 14).

It is difficult for the individual to monitor, scrutinize and constrain the behavior of elected public officials. The task of the involved individual is made even more arduous by the frequently competing claims of many "experts" representing different political positions, all of whom seem to present equally legitimate credentials to the public (Benveniste, 1972).

This discussion requires a distinction between the *perception* of power and the *exercise* of power. The concepts of "political efficacy" (Campbell et al., 1960) or "subjective competence" (Almond and Verba, 1965) deal precisely with citizen perceptions of the responsiveness of government to "persons like themselves." The sense of political efficacy grows out of such traits as education and occupational status; the more well-educated and the occupationally more well-placed are more likely than less fortunate citizens to feel politically efficacious. Moreover, political efficacy is also associated with political participation, especially in the electoral process.

Knowledge is linked to some of the same personal traits as political efficacy. Education and participation are common covariates of both efficacy and knowledge. Might knowledge be related only to *perceptions* of power as opposed to the exercise of actual influence? If knowledge produces perceptions of power but not the power itself then its acquisition has a placebo effect as opposed to an empowerment effect.

It would be quite another matter, of course, if knowledge fails to produce *feelings* of political influence even while it leads to higher levels of *actual* influence. Knowledge need not lead to a desire to exercise influence over public affairs. In some circumstances, the stimulus to acquire information could be the sentiment that one *lacks* influence over elites. It also is possible that poorly informed citizens falsely believe that they have considerable influence, or at least that incumbent political elites respond to people such as themselves. Such a sentiment would account for low motivation to acquire knowledge. Finally, there is substantial symbolic content to the general belief that citizens influence government in democratic societies. This belief is often taught as an important part of the socialization process, the content of which is handed down between generations (Roelofs, 1976). Indeed, the importance of knowledge in understanding democratic postindustrial societies may be strengthened if knowledge produces power, but not political efficacy.

The Meaning of Power

As a preface to the empirical analysis, it is important to make more precise our meaning of power. In the tradition of Verba and Nie's work *Participation in America* (1972), *concurrence* will be used as the operational indicator of power. Of course, concurrence is not the only important indicator of how much political power and influence an individual or a group may have. However, concurrence is both applicable to our concerns with knowledge and is amenable to measurement by the survey evidence at our disposal.

Concurrence is the extent to which the policy preferences of an individual (or aggregation of individuals) are proportionally present among political elites (Weissberg, 1978). One definition of political power is the ability to see one's goals and interests reflected in the authoritative allocation of values in a society. As Verba and Nie note:

> We can consider our concurrence measure to be an indicator of how much an individual or group gets from the government (1972: 337).

The higher the percentage of elites preferring a particular policy relative to the proportional presence of that preference in the population, the greater is the power of individuals with that preference.

Power is thus viewed as preference representation. Our expectation is that individuals with greater knowledge will be more effective in choosing elites with concurring policy preferences, and that they will be more effective in influencing existing elites to adopt their view. Individuals with greater knowledge should be better able to understand differing policy positions and their implications. They also should be in a more advantageous political position because knowledge will make them better armed when competing with others for influence over elites.

There are, of course, some significant limitations to the use of preference representation as a measure of individual and group power. What political elites say they believe and what they produce as actual public policy may be quite different (Nimmo, 1978: passim). Actual public policy and its implementation may differ from that preferred by the public, and even from that preferred by political activists and elites (Dye, 1976). Concurrence is simply one form of representation--of which others may be preferred under certain circumstances when trying to assess power (Pitkin, 1967).

Power often is defined by the social/demographic characteristics of those who hold significant political positions. When important positions are occupied by white males, for example, it is concluded that as a group white males are more powerful than either women or minority males. As an alternative to the representational approach, some scholars focus on the formal involvement of particular segments of society in the choice of political leaders. Within this context power reflects the extent to which access to the processes of leader choice are available to particular types of individuals and groups of individuals. The ways in which electoral boundaries are drawn, the nature of voting restrictions, and differential rates of participation all are important in this context.

This chapter examines the impact of knowledge on the extent to which the policy preferences held by individuals are shared by political activists and elites. This focus upon power as policy preference concurrence grows out of the challenges to democratic governance posed by postindustrial politics. Indeed, one author has argued that democracy *is* "the extent to which public opinion influences public policy. In other words, democracy is the correlation between what the people ask for and what they get from the political process" (Monroe, 1975: 6). Since postindustrial society is said to have changed both what people ask for and what they are liable to get from the political process

164

(Hancock, 1972), it remains crucial to identify the role of knowledge in their influence over that process.

Other Considerations

As in earlier chapters, we assess the relative importance of knowledge vis-a-vis competing sources of influence--namely, education and participation. Any impact of knowledge on power might simply be a function of its covariation with education and participation. Moreover, education and participation themselves structure political power. Verba and Nie have shown that the highly participant citizens have high concurrence scores (our measure of political power). Their studies also indicate, however, that among the highly participant, upper social status individuals have greater influence than middle and lower social status citizens (Verba and Nie, 1972: 337). Education, of course, is a primary element of social status. As in the previous analyses, then, it will again be necessary to demonstrate the independent effect of knowledge--independent of the effects of education and participation.

Finally, there is the question of why different patterns may appear in Shizuoka than in Spokane. First, while similar policy questions have emerged in the two countries, the processes to deal with them have taken somewhat different forms. Much of American environmentalism, for instance, is preservationist while Japanese environmentalism focuses on pollution treatment and victim compensation. Participation in American environmental politics is primarily value based, founded most commonly upon the individual's commitment to preservationist goals and principles. In sharp contrast, participation in Japanese environmental politics results from a mixture of motives. Japanese citizen involvement often arises in the context of localized pollution-produced victimization or anticipated industrial development. Participation may occur as a by-product of allegiance to a traditional political organization the leaders of which have taken on an environmental issue.

These differences suggest that variations in knowledge may have consequences for political power different in the United States than in Japan. Involvement in environmental policy processes tends to be more value-based and self-initiated in the United States than in Japan. We thus might expect participation levels to be more important in producing concurrence in the U.S. than in Japan.

In this analysis both activists and policymaking elites are examined as objects of public influence. The environmental activists are members of voluntary political organizations that compete for policy influence. Activists are included along with the policymaking elites as objects of citizen influence for several reasons. First, activists often claim to (and frequently do) represent the public in its interaction with governmental and technical policymakers. Second, in some policy settings activists are coopted by the policymaking and technical elites with which they interact. There is some evidence of this cooptation in both Spokane and Shizuoka (Lovrich and Abe, 1984). Finally, activists are often viewed both by the public and by decisionmakers as representative of public demands on government.

Measuring Political Power

The measure of political power employed here is straightforward. The greater the *relative* proportional representation of a citizen's policy preferences among the activist and elite groups, the greater the power of that citizen. The most powerful citizens are those whose policy preferences are disproportionately *over*-represented among the activists and elites. Conversely, the least powerful are those who are disproportionately *under*-represented among the activists and elites.

A range of beliefs and attitudes is employed to assess the impact of knowledge on individual power:

1. Postmaterialist value orientations.
2. Support for the New Environmental Paradigm.
3. Support for science and technology.
4. Preservationist identification.
5. Ranking of preservation as a policy priority.
6. Perception of herbicides as pollutants.
7. Support for citizen participation in environmental policy formation.

Two approaches to the measurement of concurrence are employed here, one aggregate and the other individual. Most of the subsequent analysis relies on the individual measure. The aggregate measure compares *distributions* of preferences within levels of knowledge; the individual measure, in contrast, identifies preferences for *individuals* first, then examines variations in preference representation across knowledge levels.

The aggregate and individual concurrence measures reflect two substantially different perspectives. The individual measure shows whether information helps some individuals become more powerful than other individuals. The aggregate measure focuses on equivalence in distributions of preferences of elites and activists on the one hand,

and knowledge-differentiated groups of citizens on the other. Indeed, if knowledge is as crucial in postindustrial policy as some suggest (Miller et al., 1980), the distribution of policy preferences of the most knowledgeable should closely match those of the activist and elite elements of society.

The aggregate measure of concurrence used here is the Gini Coefficient of Inequality (Alker, 1965). With precisely identical distributions of preferences in two (e.g., public and elite) sets of responses, the Gini Coefficient is zero. Where complete dissimilarity in the distributions obtains, the Gini score reaches unity (1.0). In an absolute sense there is no clear-cut standard for evaluating the meaning of any particular level of inequality, although Meier (1975) has suggested .25 as a cutoff point for equality. Within both the Japanese and American public samples respondents are classified into low, medium and high levels of knowledge on the basis of the technical term familiarity measure. The distribution of individual policy preferences within each of those three categories is compared to the distribution for both the activists and the elites across the seven selected attitudinal measures. Table 7.1 shows how distributions of attributes produce Gini Coefficients of differing relative sizes.

Table 7.1 shows how the distribution of postindustrial value preferences among Shizuoka activists and elites matches the distributions found at different levels of public knowledge. The mix of value orientations among the highly informed more closely matches the activist and expert distributions than do the low and middle knowledge distributions. The low knowledge group has a Gini index of .31 with the activists and .34 with the elites. In contrast, the high knowledge group Gini scores are only .05 and .04, respectively. Those in power thus reflect more closely the postmaterialist value orientations of the most knowledgeable.

The individual measure of power also is based in the proportion of activists or elite respondents holding a particular view. In this method, the higher the relative proportion of activists at a policy position compared to that of the public, the greater the relative power of any individual holding that position. The greater the relative representation of any particular position, the greater the power for those who share that position. Table 7.2 provides an example, using the ranking of preservation as a policy priority. Individuals at rank two (2) are the most powerful among the Spokane area public. At that rank, substantially greater percentages of the activists and elite (ratios of 1.78 and 1.67) hold that opinion than do citizens generally. In contrast, the least powerful citizens reside at position six with ratios of .62 and .73.

Table 7.1

The Postmaterialist Value Distributions of the Shizuoka Prefecture Public (by Policy-Relevant Knowledge Level), Activists and Elites: Percentage Distributions and Associated Coefficients of Inequality (Gini Coefficients)

	Shizuoka Prefecture Public			Shizuoka Prefecture Elite Strata	
					Govt.
				Policy	& Related
Political	Low	Medium	High	Area	Elite
Values	Knowledge	Knowledge	Knowledge	Activists	Actors
Materialist	50%	39%	33%	30%	29%
Mixed	42%	48%	49%	49%	47%
Postmaterialist	8%	13%	18%	21%	25%
Total	100%	100%	100%	100%	101%

Gini Coefficients of Inequality

	Low Knowledge	Medium Knowledge	High Knowledge
Activists	.31	.15	.05
Elite	.34	.18	.04

Table 7.2

Example of Calculation of Individual Power Scores: Ranking of Preservation as a Priority Among Spokane Area Respondents

Preservation Rank	(1) Spokane Public	(2) Spokane Activists	(3) Spokane Elite	Powact[a] (2)/(1)	Powlit[b] (3)/(1)
1	4%	6%	5%	1.5	1.25
2	9%	16%	15%	1.78	1.67
3	10%	13%	11%	1.3	1.1
4	18%	19%	16%	1.06	.89
5	24%	23%	23%	.96	.96
6	26%	16%	19%	.62	.73
7	10%	7%	12%	.70	1.2

[a]Power score for members of the public at each position of the ranking of preservation with respect to the activists.

[b]Power score for members of the public at each position of the ranking of preservation with respect to the elite.

The use of the individual level measure means each respondent has fourteen individual power scores--seven each for their relationship to the activists, and then to the elites. It is possible that the multiple measurement of power will prove redundant--i.e., that the measures will be highly intercorrelated. Table 7.3 presents the correlations (r) among the fourteen power measures in Shizuoka and Spokane. Only the statistically significant correlations ($p \leq .05$) are shown.

First, there are high correlations among the measures of citizen power in terms of activists and elites, largely because of the similarity in the distributions of the activist and elite samples on the seven measures. Second, other than the strong relationships among activist and elite measures on the same attitudinal variables, the remainder of the correlations are not particularly large. While a number of the relationships are statistically significant, their absolute values are not very sizable. Thus, power is only minimally concentrated across policy measures. (Later this chapter addresses the question of whether knowledge levels are associated with the concentration of power). A summary index was constructed which aggregates power scores across the seven policy area attitudes, first for the activists and then for the elites. It is possible that while knowledge might have a relatively small impact on individual policy power measures, such an effect could accumulate across attitudes.

Knowledge and Aggregate Distributions of Power

The aggregate concurrence measure (the Gini Coefficient of Inequality) assesses the extent to which there are comparable distributions in two separate samples. Our interest here is whether inequalities separating activists and elites from the public diminish at the higher ranges of public knowledge.

Table 7.4 displays the Gini index scores for respondents on low, medium and high knowledge scores. The patterns are more clear and more uniform in Shizuoka than in Spokane. In comparison both to activists and to elites, in Shizuoka there is a substantial decline in the Gini index as one moves from the low knowledge to the high knowledge categories. In some cases the major drop is between the low and medium groups, while in others it is between the medium and high knowledge categories, and in still others it is uniform across groups. It is clear, though, that in Shizuoka knowledge makes a major impact on the distribution of power. Inequalities among the least knowledgeable are erased among the most knowledgeable. The impact of knowledge on power is greater for elite concurrence than for activist

Table 7.3

Correlation (r) Matrix Among Individual Influence Measures (p ≤ .05 Significance Only) for Policy Area Activists (A) and Elite Actors (E)[a]

Shizuoka Prefecture (columns/row group A) · _Spokane Area_ (row group E)

	A_1	A_2	A_3	A_4	A_5	A_6	A_7	E_1	E_2	E_3	E_4	E_5	E_6	E_7
A^1	x	*	*	*	*	.15	-.09	.72	*	*	*	*	.16	*
A^2	*	x	*	.17	*	*	*	*	.98	*	*	*	.16	*
A^3	.22	.16	x	*	*	*	.12	.15	*	.82	*	.17	*	*
A^4	.16	.17	.11	x	*	*	*	*	*	*	.86	.10	*	.13
A^5	.18	.13	.18	.12	x	*	*	*	.15	*	*	.98	*	*
A^6	*	*	*	*	*	x	*	*	*	*	*	*	.99	.13
A^7	*	.22	.10	.15	.14	*	x	.19	.09	*	.10	.15	*	.77
Spokane Area														
E^1	-.26	*	*	*	-.11	*	*	x	*	.15	*	-.09	.14	*
E^2	.10	.63	.15	.16	.15	*	.09	*	x	.08	*	.20	.14	.14
E^3	.16	.14	.82	*	*	-.09	*	.15	.08	x	*	.07	*	*
E^4	.11	.11	*	.86	*	*	.10	*	*	*	x	.11	*	.10
E^5	.17	.13	.17	.10	.98	*	.15	-.09	.20	.07	.11	x	*	.17
E^6	-.16	*	*	*	-.08	.99	*	.14	.14	*	*	*	x	*
E^7	*	.14	*	*	.16	.13	.77	*	.14	*	.10	.17	*	x

[a] The following is the key to the attitudes.

1. Preservationist identification.
2. Postmaterial values.
3. Rank of preservation.
4. Perception of herbicides as a pollutant.
5. New Environmental Paradigm.
6. Support for Science and Technology.
7. Support for Citizen Participation.

Table 7.4

Patterns of Aggregate Concurrence (Gini Coefficients) for Postindustrial Orientations, Controlling for Technical Term Familiarity*

ACTIVISTS

Knowledge	Shizuoka Prefecture				Spokane Area			
	Low	Medium	High	(D)**	Low	Medium	High	(D)
Postmaterial Values	.31	.15	.05	(.26)	.34	.23	.30	(.04)
New Environmental Paradigm	.31	.01	.09	(.22)	.33	.10	.11	(.22)
Faith in Science and Technology	.32	.19	.03	(.29)	.03	.13	.22	(-.19)
Mean	.31	.18	.06		.23	.15	.21	

ELITE

Knowledge	Shizuoka Prefecture				Spokane Area			
	Low	Medium	High	(D)**	Low	Medium	High	(D)
Postmaterial Values	.34	.18	.04	(.30)	.15	.02	.08	(.07)
New Environmental Paradigm	.44	.05	.07	(.37)	.31	.11	.08	(.23)
Faith in Science and Technology	.38	.22	.04	(.34)	.13	.05	.09	(.04)
Mean	.39	.15	.05		.20	.06	.08	

*The entry in each cell is the Gini Coefficient of Inequality, based on the comparison of the citizens with a particular knowledge level to either the activists or the elites.

**D is the difference in the Gini scores for the low and high knowledge groups.

concurrence. In each case, inequality is greater at the low knowledge group for the elites than for the activists.

The impact of knowledge in erasing inequality in Shizuoka is not present in Spokane. In Spokane the patterns are mixed, and results differ between activists and elites. For postmaterial values, the activist-based Gini inequalities are high at all levels of knowledge, but in the elite comparison they are relatively low at all knowledge levels. In both cases the impact of knowledge is relatively small, but the differences in the absolute values are rather large between elites and activists. Only on the NEP measure does knowledge have the kind of inequality-reducing impact in Spokane that is present in Shizuoka.

The effect of knowledge on concurrence with respect to the more specific attitudinal orientations is shown in Table 7.5. The results in Table 7.5 are not as clear as they were for the general value orientations displayed in Table 7.4. In Shizuoka knowledge makes little difference in the distribution of power on preservationist identification and on the ranking of preservation as a policy priority. On the other hand, knowledge does affect the elite based Gini scores in the perception of herbicides as pollutants and support for citizen participation.

In Spokane, knowledge reduces somewhat the inequality between citizens and the activists. When citizens are compared to the elites, only for herbicides and citizen participation does knowledge change the Gini scores. In most comparisons--even among the high knowledge respondents--the inequality scores remain relatively high. In six of the eight cases these scores are higher in Spokane than in Shizuoka.

In summary, then, these aggregate patterns suggest that knowledge affects the distribution of power among citizens in Shizuoka and Spokane. While some variations occur, the general effect of knowledge is to create more proportional or "equal" distributions of power.

Knowledge and the Individual Measure of Power

The individual measure of power gives each respondent an influence score based upon comparisons with both the activists and elites for each of the seven orientations. That influence score is the ratio of the percentage of the activists (for example) to the percentage of the general public with that individual's policy position. Thus, individuals who hold an opinion shared by a percentage of the public smaller than the percentage of the elites are more powerful than individuals who hold opinions shared by larger percentages in the public than in the elite sample. Two summary measures of influence

Table 7.5
Patterns of Aggregate Concurrence for Environmental Attitudes, Controlling for Technical Term Familiarity[a]

ACTIVISTS	Knowledge:	*Shizuoka Prefecture*				*Spokane Area*			
		Low	*Medium*	*High*	(D)[b]	*Low*	*Medium*	*High*	(D)[b]
Preservationist Identification		.10	.03	.04	(.06)	.30	.30	.13	(.17)
Priority Ranking of Preservation		.16	.10	.13	(.03)	.28	.17	.21	(.08)
Herbicides as a Form of Pollution		.30	.15	.03	(.27)	.30	.15	.13	(.17)
Support for Citizen Participation		.29	.15	.07	(.22)	.45	.29	.29	(.16)
Mean		.21	.11	.07		.33	.23	.19	
ELITE									
Preservationist Identification		.14	.06	.05	(.09)	.11	.08	.06	(.05)
Priority Ranking of Preservation		.20	.16	.04	(.16)	.23	.11	.22	(.01)
Herbicides as a Form of Pollution		.26	.08	.13	(.13)	.32	.15	.12	(.20)
Support for Citizen Participation		.45	.13	.21	(.26)	.55	.36	.34	(.21)
Mean		.26	.11	.11		.30	.18	.19	

[a]The measure of concurrence is the Gini index of inequality, calculated on the basis of a comparison of distributions of each knowledge group with the appropriate reference group--activist or elite. The higher the Gini index the less the similarity in the two distributions.

[b]D refers to the difference between the low and high knowledge levels.

Table 7.6

Correlation (r) of Knowledge Measures and Summary Measures of Power: Shizuoka Prefecture and the Spokane Area

Knowledge Measure	Shizuoka Prefecture		Spokane Area	
	Activist Influence	Elite Influence	Activist Influence	Elite Influence
Technical Term Familiarity	.30	.32	.22	.30
Knowledge of Local Factors	.09	.06	-.03	.06
Knowledge of Ecology Science	.20	.27	.02	.02
Identification of Policy Area Problems	.19	.23	.24	.26
Self-Assessed Level of Knowledge	.12	.12	.04	.10
Summary Index of Policy-Relevant Knowledge	.24	.25	.02	.10

are available as well. These summary measures are created by adding up the influence scores on the seven attitude and value dimensions, first with respect to the activists and then with respect to the elites.

Table 7.6 presents the correlations (r) between the two summary influence measures for activists and for elites, and the knowledge measures developed in this study. Two of those knowledge measures are related to the summary influence measures in both Shizuoka and Spokane. Those two measures are technical term familiarity and articulation of policy area problems. In Spokane those two measures alone have an impact on power, while in Shizuoka four of the six knowledge measures are related to influence. At the individual level, then, knowledge is related to policy influence. This impact is more broadly based in Shizuoka than in Spokane.

The summary measures of influence are related to variations in individual knowledge. Two questions remain. Does knowledge make a bigger difference in certain kinds of attitudes than it does on others? and, Do such differences appear in both the American and Japanese settings? It is important, moreover, whether the impact of knowledge is different from that exhibited by participation and education. The results of these comparisons are shown in Tables 7.7a-c. Those tables contain the average individual influence scores within the three levels of knowledge (7.7a), participation (7.7b) and education (7.7c).

Knowledge (technical term familiarity) again is somewhat more important in Shizuoka than in Spokane. This pattern is particularly striking with regard to the more general orientations of postmaterial values, support for the New Environmental Paradigm, and support for science and technology. Only on the NEP measure (among the general orientations) does knowledge have a significant impact in Spokane. In contrast, in Shizuoka knowledge has a statistically significant effect on all three general orientations. The impact of knowledge on power with regard to herbicides and citizen participation is similar in both countries. Knowledge has little effect on the influence citizens have with regard to what we frequently have hypothesized to be the central dimension in environmental politics--namely, the ranking of preservation as a policy priority and preservationist identification.

Knowledge seems more important in generating policy-relevant influence in Shizuoka than in Spokane. Quite the reverse is true for the impact of participation levels (see Table 7.7b). On only two of the fourteen influence measures does participation make a difference in Shizuoka. In contrast, in Spokane, participation has a significant impact in ten of the fourteen cases, and in six of the seven activist measures. Thus, while knowledge is more important in Shizuoka than in Spokane, the reverse is true for the effect of participation.

Table 7.7a

Analysis of Variance of the Effects of Knowledge on Individual Concurrence Scores: Shizuoka Prefecture and the Spokane Area[a]

Citizen to Activist Power	Shizuoka Prefecture				Spokane Area			
	Low Knowledge	Medium Knowledge	High Knowledge	P	Low Knowledge	Medium Knowledge	High Knowledge	P
Postmaterial Values	.95	1.00	1.04	≤.02	.98	.97	1.07	*
New Environmental Paradigm	.96	1.01	1.01	≤.02	.93	1.05	1.11	≤.001
Faith in Science & Technology	.91	.97	1.04	≤.001	1.03	1.01	.99	*
Preservationist Identification	.99	1.01	1.02	*	.98	.97	1.07	*
Priority Rank of Preservation	1.03	1.04	1.04	*	.97	1.01	1.06	*
Herbicide as a Pollutant	.94	.98	1.07	≤.001	.91	1.03	1.10	≤.002
Support for Citizen Participation	1.05	1.00	1.03	*	.90	1.06	1.10	≤.026

Citizen to Elite Power	Shizuoka Prefecture				Spokane Area			
	Low Knowledge	Medium Knowledge	High Knowledge	P	Low Knowledge	Medium Knowledge	High Knowledge	P
Postmaterial Values	.95	1.00	1.06	≤.03	.97	.97	1.01	*
New Environmental Paradigm	.86	1.02	1.05	≤.001	.001	1.04	1.04	≤.001
Faith in Science & Technology	.91	.97	1.04	≤.001	1.03	1.01	.99	*
Preservationist Identification	.97	1.02	1.03	*	1.00	1.02	1.03	*
Priority Rank of Preservation	1.03	.99	1.05	*	1.00	1.01	1.04	*
Herbicide as a Pollutant	.98	1.01	1.04	≤.05	.89	1.06	1.10	≤.001
Support for Citizen Participation	.95	1.06	1.04	≤.05	.85	1.07	1.19	≤.001

[a]The entry in each cell is the mean influence score of individuals in that knowledge category for that particular policy-relevant belief. Technical term familiarity is the indicator of policy-relevant knowledge employed here. (* = not statistically significant.)

Table 7.7b
Analysis of Variance of the Effects of Participation on Individual Concurrence Scores: Shizuoka Prefecture and the Spokane Area[a]

Citizen to Activist Power	Shizuoka Prefecture				Spokane Area			
	Low	Medium Participation	High	P	Low	Medium Participation	High	P
Postmaterial Values	1.01	1.00	1.01	*	.89	1.04	1.00	≤.05
New Environmental Paradigm	1.00	1.00	1.01	*	.93	1.03	1.07	≤.001
Faith in Science & Technology	.97	.98	1.02	*	1.05	1.01	1.00	≤.05
Preservationist Identification	1.01	1.02	.97	≤.05	.91	1.04	1.04	≤.01
Priority Rank of Preservation	1.00	1.05	1.04	*	.95	1.00	1.04	*
Herbicide as a Pollutant	1.00	1.00	1.03	*	.92	1.06	1.03	≤.05
Support for Citizen Participation	1.01	1.01	1.03	*	.81	1.04	1.15	≤.001
Citizen to Elite Power								
Postmaterial Values	1.03	1.01	1.03	*	.95	1.01	1.01	≤.01
New Environmental Paradigm	1.02	.98	1.03	*	.93	1.02	1.07	≤.001
Faith in Science & Technology	.98	.99	1.03	*	1.02	1.00	1.03	*
Preservationist Identification	1.02	1.03	.99	*	1.01	.99	1.04	≤.01
Priority Rank of Preservation	1.04	1.00	1.04	*	.98	1.02	1.01	*
Herbicide as a Pollutant	.99	1.01	1.05	≤.05	.94	1.02	1.03	*
Support for Citizen Participation	1.04	1.03	1.05	*	.83	.99	1.17	≤.001

[a]The entry in each cell is the mean influence score of individuals in that participation category for that particular policy belief.
(* = not statistically significant.)

Table 7.7c

Analysis of Variance of the Effects of Education on Individual Concurrence Scores: Shizuoka Prefecture and the Spokane Area[a]

	Shizuoka Prefecture				Spokane Area			
Citizen to Activist Power	Low Education	Medium Education	High Education	P	Education	Low Education	Medium Education	High P
Postmaterial Values	.97	1.00	1.07	≤.01	.97	.97	1.01	*
New Environmental Paradigm	.98	1.00	1.01	*	.94	1.03	1.05	≤.01
Faith in Science & Technology	.92	1.01	1.01	≤.01	1.03	1.03	.99	≤.05
Preservationist Identification	1.02	1.01	1.01	*	1.00	.94	1.06	≤.05
Priority Rank of Preservation	1.06	1.03	1.04	*	.98	1.01	1.01	*
Herbicide as a Pollutant	1.00	1.00	1.03	*	.99	.97	1.05	*
Support for Citizen Participation	1.03	1.01	1.02	*	.97	1.02	1.02	*
Citizen to Elite Power								
Postmaterial Values	.96	1.02	1.01	*	.99	1.01	1.02	*
New Environmental Paradigm	.94	1.00	1.06	≤.01	.93	1.02	1.04	≤.01
Faith in Science & Technology	.91	1.02	1.02	≤.01	1.00	1.00	1.04	*
Preservationist Identification	1.02	1.02	1.01	*	.99	1.01	1.02	*
Priority Rank of Preservation	.99	1.02	1.03	*	1.00	1.02	1.00	*
Herbicide as a Pollutant	.99	1.02	1.03	*	.97	.96	1.06	*
Support for Citizen Participation	1.06	1.02	1.05	*	.90	.98	1.09	≤.05

[a]The entry in each cell is the mean influence score of individuals in that participation category for that particular policy belief.
(* = not statistically significant.)

The effect of education on the individual influence scores is shown in Table 7.7c. No consistent pattern emerges across the two study sites. Controlling for education in Shizuoka does affect citizen influence on activist postmaterialist values, faith in science and technology, and preservationist identification. Education enhances the influence of Spokane area citizens over elite support for the NEP and for citizen involvement in the environmental policy process. Given the interrelatedness of education, policy-relevant knowledge and policy process involvement it would have been most surprising had education not manifested at least some impact on the individual influence scores. The impact of education, on balance, is of lesser magnitude than those of participation and knowledge, and is confined to the more general value orientations.

Two *general influence* scores were also generated. Table 7.8 shows the effect of knowledge, participation and education on the general influence of Shizuoka and Spokane citizens. Statistically significant differences in power appear across knowledge, participation and education levels in both Shizuoka and Spokane. The largest difference is the effect of knowledge on elite influence (D=1.20) in Shizuoka. The effect of knowledge on public influence with elites is also the largest in Spokane (D=.99). In both locations the smallest difference is the impact of education on citizen-to-activist influence scores (D=.54 and D=.50). The effects of participation generally lie somewhere between those of knowledge and education. Again, then, in both locations knowledge appears to have the greatest impact on citizen influence.

The next question is the extent to which the effect of knowledge on influence is mitigated by controls for participation and education. The mean influence scores within combined categories of knowledge and participation, and within knowledge and education, are shown in Table 7.9a and 7.9b. Even when controlling for participation, in both countries knowledge retains its independent impact on power. When elite- directed influence is examined, the impact of knowledge is much greater in Shizuoka than in Spokane.

Table 7.9 shows results when controlling for education and knowledge. Knowledge and education are both significant in Shizuoka, but only knowledge has a significant impact in Spokane. There is an interesting cross-national contrast in citizen influence on activists in the low education groups. For the low education Spokane area residents, knowledge makes almost no difference in influence; in Shizuoka, however, knowledge has a sizeable impact.

In any case, when examining knowledge along with participation or education, knowledge retains its effect on power. The effect of the

180

Table 7.8

Mean Summary Power Scores with Levels of Knowledge, Participation and Education: Shizuoka Prefecture and Spokane Area Citizens

		Knowledge				
		Low	Medium	High	D*	P**
Elite	Shizuoka	5.77	6.80	7.07	(+1.20)	≤.001
	Spokane	6.12	6.80	7.11	(+ .99)	≤.001
Activist	Shizuoka	6.02	6.73	6.99	(+ .77)	≤.001
	Spokane	6.16	6.73	7.06	(+ .90)	≤.001

		Participation				
		Low	Medium	High	D*	P**
Elite	Shizuoka	6.21	6.78	6.91	(+ .70)	≤.001
	Spokane	5.96	6.85	6.82	(+ .86)	≤.001
Activist	Shizuoka	6.21	6.76	6.99	(+ .78)	≤.001
	Spokane	6.14	6.75	6.83	(+ .59)	≤.001

		Education				
		Low	Medium	High	D*	P**
Elite	Shizuoka	6.26	6.75	6.98	(+ .72)	≤.001
	Spokane	6.21	6.50	6.85	(+ .64)	≤.001
Activist	Shizuoka	6.35	6.73	6.89	(+ .54)	≤.001
	Spokane	6.26	6.57	6.76	(+ .50)	≤.05

*D is the difference between the mean of the high and low categories.
**Probability of differences produced by one-way analysis of variance.

Table 7.9a

Mean Power Scores Within Combinations of Policy-Relevant Knowledge and Policy Process Participation: Shizuoka Prefecture and Spokane Area Public Samples*

Activists		**Knowledge**			
Participation		Low	Medium	High	Difference
Low	Shizuoka	5.46	6.52	6.57	1.11
	Spokane	5.66	6.35	6.23	.57
Medium	Shizuoka	6.37	6.76	7.00	.63
	Spokane	6.65	6.81	7.53	.88
High	Shizuoka	6.38	6.83	7.20	.82
	Spokane	6.15	6.95	7.06	.91
Difference	Shizuoka	.92	.31	.63	
Difference	Spokane	.49	.60	.83	
Elites		**Knowledge**			
Participation		Low	Medium	High	Difference
Low	Shizuoka	5.29	6.60	6.71	1.42
	Spokane	5.76	6.49	6.09	.33
Medium	Shizuoka	6.01	6.81	7.03	1.02
	Spokane	6.58	6.86	6.93	.35
High	Shizuoka	6.19	6.95	7.30	1.11
	Spokane	6.73	7.22	7.17	.44
Difference	Shizuoka	.90	.35	.59	
Difference	Spokane	.97	.73	1.08	

*Knowledge and participation effects are both significant ($p \leq .001$) when subjected to two-way analysis of variance. Interaction effects are insignificant.

Table 7.9b

Mean Individual Power Scores Within Combinations of Policy-Relevant Knowledge and Education: Shizuoka Prefecture and Spokane Area*

Activists Education		Low	Medium	High	Difference
		Policy-Relevant Knowledge			
Low	Shizuoka	5.45	6.65	6.74	1.29
	Spokane	6.18	6.75	6.43	.25
Medium	Shizuoka	6.23	6.73	7.03	.80
	Spokane	5.98	6.74	7.52	1.54
High	Shizuoka	6.39	6.86	7.05	.66
	Spokane	6.51	6.79	6.99	.48
Difference	Shizuoka	.94	.21	.31	
Difference	Spokane	.33	.04	.56	

Elites Education		Low	Medium	High	Difference
		Policy-Relevant Knowledge			
Low	Shizuoka	5.14	6.66	6.68	1.54
	Spokane	6.05	6.83	6.76	.71
Medium	Shizuoka	5.96	6.81	7.13	1.17
	Spokane	6.02	6.74	7.35	1.33
High	Shizuoka	6.31	6.98	7.18	.87
	Spokane	6.58	6.90	7.07	.49
Difference	Shizuoka	1.17	.32	.50	
Difference	Spokane	.53	.07	.31	

*When subjected to two-way analysis of variance, among the Shizuoka Prefecture respondents both knowledge and education effects are significant ($p \leq .001$; $p \leq .001$; $p \leq .002$). Among Spokane area respondents, knowledge effects are significant ($p \leq .001$; $p \leq .001$) while education effects are non-significant.

Table 7.10

Multiple Regression of Summary Influence Measures with Education, Policy Process Participation and Policy-Relevant Knowledge[a]

	Shizuoka Prefecture		Spokane Area	
	Activist Measure	Elite Measure	Activist Measure	Elite Measure
R	.37	.38	.26	.33
R^2	.13	.14	.07	.11
F	33.99	36.17	11.11	17.71
Level of Education	.13***	.14***	ns	ns
Policy Process Participation	.19***	.16***	.15**	.11*
Policy-Relevant Knowledge	.24***	.27***	.16**	.23***

*$p \leq .05$; **$p \leq .01$; ***$p \leq .001$

[a]Technical term familiarity is the policy-relevant knowledge measure used in this analysis.

three independent variables--knowledge, participation and education considered simultaneously is shown in Table 7.10. That table presents the results of a multiple regression analysis. Two clear patterns emerge. First, education has no independent effect on policy-relevant influence in the American setting. But, significantly, such is not the case in Shizuoka. Even when controlling for participation and knowledge, the more highly educated Japanese are more likely to have their policy preferences shared by political activists and political elites.

Second, in both Shizuoka and Spokane knowledge retains its independent effect on policy influence. Indeed, in both places the impact of knowledge is as great or greater than that of the other two variables. The relative superiority of knowledge in producing influence is greater when the object of that influence is the elite sample than when it is the activist sample.

Knowledge does produce power, at least as that concept is operationalized here. Knowledge is associated with beliefs that are disproportionately shared by political elites. The rationale is that knowledge leads to influence on the selection of elites with shared values, and on the character of the policy positions taken by elites once they are in positions of influence. Nonetheless, an alternative interpretation is admissible. It might be argued, for example, that the causal process works in precisely the opposite direction. That is, citizens with greater knowledge levels are better able to identify the policy positions of activists and elites, and therefore they can more accurately take cues from the relevant elites as to what the policy ought to be. Consequently, policy-relevant knowledge would promote a dependence on political activists and elites rather than foster independence from them.

Consistent with the central concern of this book and its analytical structure, our position is that knowledge does indeed enhance policy-relevant influence for citizens in postindustrial polities. To be sure, actual involvement in the policy process is also related to a correspondence between citizen preferences and those of elites; but even when taking into account the level of participation, knowledge adds to influence over and above the impact of activism.

Knowledge and the Perception of Power

It is significant that knowledge has an independent impact on the citizen's policy influence. At the same time, however, it is also crucial to determine the extent to which knowledge is related to the individual's *perception* of influence. Are individuals with greater knowledge more likely to feel they are heard by policymakers?

This section examines this question of whether more knowledgeable citizens are more likely to perceive themselves as having influence. The perception of influence is measured through the following set of questions (Spokane form).

> According to what you have read, heard of, or know from your own experience, how much opportunity does each level of government listed below provide citizens like you to express their views on natural resource and environmental issues?

	Great Deal	Some	A Little	None at All
Federal	1	2	3	4
State	1	2	3	4
County	1	2	3	4
City	1	2	3	4

A nearly comparable question was used in Japan, with the exception that no county form of government exists in the Japanese setting. Consequently, the analysis presented below is based on perceptions of influence in national, state (prefectural) and city governments in Shizuoka and Spokane. A summary measure also was constructed by adding scores across the three levels of government.

Table 7.11 shows the correlation (r) between each of the knowledge measures and the four perceived power measures (the three individual items and the summary index). The impact of knowledge on perceived power is unimpressive. In Shizuoka those citizens with more local knowledge are a little more likely to see government as listening to them. In Spokane individuals with more science knowledge are more likely to see responsiveness at the state level and overall.

While knowledge may not be a particularly important predictor of perceived power, the actual level of power may affect how people see their own influence. Table 7.12 shows the correlation of the two summary power measures and the individual's perception of citizen influence at national, state and local levels. Only one correlation reaches statistical significance.

The perception of political influence--of being listened to--is close kin to the feeling of political efficacy. Political efficacy is closely linked to political participation and to education level. Table 7.13 includes participation and education along with knowledge and power in predicting perceptions of influence. In most cases (except for Shizuoka at the national level) the five independent variables combine to produce a statistically significant impact upon perceptions of influence.

Table 7.11

Correlations (r) of Policy-Relevant Knowledge and Perceived Influence: Shizuoka Prefecture and the Spokane Area*

Knowledge Measure	Shizuoka Prefecture				Spokane Area			
	National	Prefecture	Local	Summary	Federal	State	Local	Summary
Technical Term Familiarity	-.02	-.03	-.03	-.01	-.04	-.09	-.02	-.07
Knowledge of Local Factors	-.11	-.12	-.12	-.15	-.05	.07	.07	.04
Knowledge of Ecology Factors	-.04	.05	.00	.01	-.11	-.20	-.07	-.16
Articulation of Policy Problems	-.02	-.02	-.03	.00	.01	.00	-.01	.01
Self-Assessed Knowledge	-.08	-.02	-.06	-.05	-.05	-.03	.00	-.04
Summary Index	-.05	.00	-.09	-.06	-.03	.06	.14	.06

*Negative sign means high knowledge linked to high perceived influence.

Table 7.12

**Correlation of Power Measures and Perceived Influence at
National, State and Local Levels**

	Shizuoka Prefecture		Spokane Area	
	Powact	Powlit	Powact	Powlit
National	.03	.04	.04	-.06
State	.02	.06	.02	-.05
Local	-.01	.04	-.05	-.15*

*p ≤ .001

NOTE: Negative sign means that as actual influence increases, so does perception of influence.

Table 7.13

Multiple Regression of Perceived Influence with Policy-Relevant Knowledge, Policy Process Participation, Educational Attainment and Actual Influence Measures[a]

	National/Federal		State/Prefectural		Local/City		Summary Measure	
	Japan	U.S.	Japan	U.S.	Japan	U.S.	Japan	U.S.
R	.09	.16	.17	.17	.23	.23	.21	.18
R^2	.01	.03	.03	.03	.05	.05	.04	.03
F	1.05	2.32	3.83	2.39	6.49	4.55	5.49	2.99
F Sig	.38	.04	.002	.037	.001	.0005	.001	.01
Policy Process Participation	--	--	-.14**	--	-.19	--	-.15***	--
Level of Education	--	--	--	--	--	-.15**	--	-.11*
Policy-Relevant Knowledge	--	--	--	--	--	--	--	--
Power/Activist	--	-.24**	--	--	--	-.18*	--	-.20*
Power/Elite	--	-.23**	-.16*	--	--	-.28***	-.17**	-.21**

[a]Entries are standardized regression coefficients.

NOTE: Negative direction of influence perceived, whereby 1 is 'high' and '4' is low.

*p ≤ .05; **p ≤ .01; ***p ≤ .001

Table 7.14

Multiple Regression Predicting Perception of Power (Summary Measure) Controlling for Policy-Relevant Knowledge[a]

	Shizuoka			Spokane		
	Low	Medium	High	Low	Medium	High
		Knowledge			Knowledge	
R	.23	.22	.29	.22	.17	.14
R^2	.05	.05	.08	.05	.03	.02
F	1.53	3.61	4.83	2.12	1.13	.42
Fsig	.20	.006	.001	.08	.34	.79
Participation	--	-.18**	-.25**	--	--	--
Education	--	--	--	--	--	--
Power/ Activists	--	--	--	-.25*	--	--
Power/Elites	-.41***	--	--	-.25*	--	--

[a]Entries are standardized regression coefficients.

*p ≤ .05; **p ≤ .01; ***p ≤ .001

At the same time, though, the amount of variation explained is small (no greater than five percent). Once again knowledge plays no significant role in individuals' perceptions of their political influence. Education's impact is limited to the perception of influence at the local level, and to the summary measure in Spokane. In contrast, the influence of participation is confined to Shizuoka.

It is clear that knowledge has no significant effect on public perceptions of influence. It is possible, however, that knowledge might heighten the relationship between actual power and perceived power. More knowledgeable individuals may have a better sense of their own impact on government. Table 7.14 shows the impact of participation, education and actual power on perceived power within three levels of knowledge. In Shizuoka, participation remains important as a predictor of felt influence for the medium and high knowledge levels. Among the least knowledgeable, however, actual power is the strongest predictor of perceived influence. Thus, less policy-relevant knowledge leads to a more realistic perception of one's influence. This finding is mirrored in Spokane, where the only significant relationships are between actual power and perceived influence--and only among the least knowledgeable.

These findings raise the question of why greater knowledge depresses the relationship between actual power and perceived power. Why do the least informed have the most accurate view of their own influence? The answer might be found in differing perceptions of what constitutes the opportunity to express views--the measure of perceived power used in this study. The least knowledgeable citizens may see correspondence between their views and those of elites and activists (the measure of actual power used here) as the important indicator of their views being heard. On the other hand, the most knowledgeable may see actual responsiveness in terms of behavior, policy outcomes, or contact with policymakers as the true meaning of influence. The more knowledgeable may have a more expansive and perhaps more realistic view of what power is and their perceptions of it may be less fully rooted in the correspondence between their beliefs and those of elites.

Conclusion

This chapter has examined the impact of knowledge on political power. Power has been measured by the extent to which citizens' policy preferences are represented among political activists and political elites. Only the most general findings will be reviewed here. First, the general effect of knowledge is to create more equal distributions of power, although this is more striking in Shizuoka than in Spokane. Second, knowledge has a direct impact on individual variations in influence. Third, knowledge is more important in producing influence in Shizuoka than in Spokane. Fourth, the greater influence of knowledge in Shizuoka is most evident on general orientations--postmaterialist values, NEP and support for science and technology. Fifth, knowledge has no influence on measures of power reflecting support for preservation--what might well be thought to be the central dimension of the natural resource/environment policy area. Sixth, participation is more important in predicting influence in Spokane than in Shizuoka, at least on the individual policy measures. Seventh, knowledge retains its effect on influence when controlling for participation and education in both the Japanese and the American settings. Participation is important in both countries also, but education contributes independently to influence of elites more fully than to influence of activists, while participation is marginally more important vis-a-vis activists. Finally, knowledge has little discernable impact on citizens' perceptions of their power, but knowledge does depress the impact of actual power on perceived power levels.

The analysis has put knowledge holding through a major test. Knowledge is important not only because of the normative arguments about its centrality to preparation for democratic citizenship, but also because it contributes to the influence of the citizens possessing it. Knowledge helps the individual obtain more from the political system. Better informed citizens are more likely than others to have their views shared by activists and elites. Knowledge appears to be a potential corrective to influence deficits produced by disadvantaged social locations or by lack of access to the policy process through extended participation.

8

Knowledge and the Possibility
of Democracy

Our central concern throughout has been how differences in levels of citizen knowledge affect democratic governance in postindustrial societies. Complex scientific and technical policy issues give rise to concerns about the ability of citizens to recognize and act on their self-interest. We have focused on environmental policy as a prototypical postindustrial issue. Environmental policy questions involve fundamental value choices, and they pose difficult and technically complicated policy alternatives for citizens and elites alike. The cross-national context of this study has provided an opportunity to assess the effects of both convergent postindustrial forces and divergent cultural and political forces.

Japan and the United States share postindustrial status, democratic political institutions, highly salient environmental policy arenas, and a recent history of extensive citizen involvement in environmental politics. At the same time, however, the two nations differ in actual patterns of political influence and mobilization, in cultural values and social norms, in response to postindustrial change, in character of environmental activism, and in the prevailing views of the relationship of humans and nature. These contrasts have served as the primary sources of contextual understanding of our empirical findings. This final chapter summarizes these findings, and speculates about the consequences of knowledge for the identification and promotion of self-interest. The conclusion then ponders the future--considering the prospects for and problems facing the exercise of citizen influence in postindustrial democratic nations.

192

Summary

The overall *distribution* of knowledge is remarkably similar in Japan and the United States. In both Spokane and Shizuoka, the publics are less well informed than are the elites and activists. Moreover, the *structure* of knowledge--i.e., the relationships among the separate measures of knowledge--is similar in Shizuoka and Spokane. In addition, in both sites there is considerable *variation* in knowledge among both mass and elite respondents, confirming the need to identify the sources and consequences of that variation.

In both Japan and the United States, a range of social and demographic factors exercise a significant impact on the individual's knowledge. However, the specific social forces at work tend to differ somewhat between the two countries. For example, the level of education is more important in Spokane than in Shizuoka, while occupational status and level of income have a relatively greater impact in Japan. Similarly, generational cohort is more important in Japan, while gender exercises more influence over knowledge in the United States. In both locations motivational factors have a significant impact on knowledge, even when controlling for background attributes. Participation in environmental politics has a greater impact on knowledge in Spokane than in the Japanese setting. The perceived effectiveness of political involvement is a more significant factor for respondents in Shizuoka than in Spokane. Taken together, the background and motivational variables account for more variation in knowledge in Spokane than in Shizuoka, a finding we attribute to the differential patterns of citizen and activist mobilization characteristic of the two cultural settings.

American respondents are slightly more postmaterialist, while the Japanese exhibit greater support for the New Environmental Paradigm (NEP). Ideological orientation is linked to the NEP more strongly in Japan than in the United States, but is more highly correlated with postmaterial values among the Americans. A factor analysis of political orientations reveals similar structures among the general publics of the two countries. The underlying dimensions are similar in the two study settings, although they differ in their relative importance. Knowledge has a major impact on those factor structures. In both countries, knowledge integrates postmaterial value orientations into traditional partisan and ideological dimensions. NEP items in both the American and Japanese settings also cluster differently at different levels of knowledge.

194

Knowledge has a greater impact on the direction of environmental policy attitudes among Japanese respondents than among American subjects. However, the particular attitude affected by knowledge is again different in Spokane (preservationist identification) than in Shizuoka (support for citizen participation). Postindustrial beliefs have a significant impact on specific environmental policy preferences in both countries. Knowledge enhances the linkage between postindustrial beliefs and environmental policy preferences more fully in Spokane than in Shizuoka. On the other hand, participation has the same effect for Japanese but not for Americans. Knowledge enhances citizen power when measured as the representation of citizen beliefs by activists and elites. In both Spokane and Shizuoka, knowledge retains its effect on power even after controlling for education and participation. Knowledge is more important in producing power in Shizuoka than in Spokane, but participation is more important in Spokane than in Shizuoka.

Implications

Throughout we have attempted to assess the implications of the empirical findings with respect to the major research questions raised at the very beginning of the volume. In particular, we have been concerned with how knowledge affects the identification of self-interest and the exercise of political influence, and with the role of political culture in structuring those effects of knowledge. Attention here will be limited to four major concerns--the role of political culture, the contribution of knowledge to political power, the contribution of knowledge to the perception of self-interest, and the educability of the postindustrial citizenry.

Political Culture

A number of our findings are common to both Japanese and American citizens. That commonality underscores the signal importance of knowledge in the structuring of citizen values, beliefs and attitudes in postindustrial societies. At the same time, one reason for comparing similar problems in similar locations in Japan and the United States is that these two countries differ in some very significant social and political respects. In every chapter there is evidence of the impact of political culture on cross-national differences. These cross-national differences are consistent with what is known about differences in Japanese and American political cultures (Richardson, 1974), environmental movements (McKean, 1981), patterns of political involvement (Matsushita, 1975), and responses to postindustrial change (Ike, 1973 and Flanagan, 1979).

Chapter Three examined the impact of several important social and demographic attributes on knowledge. Taken collectively, the conventional social and demographic variables investigated have about the same impact among the Japanese and Americans. However, there are significant differences in the relative importance of specific background factors. Education and gender are more important in predicting information levels in the United States than in Japan, while occupational status, family income and generational cohort are more important in Japan.

The greater impact of gender on knowledge in the United States than in Japan may be a consequence of a strong American women's movement. The less restrictive American social system may provide relatively greater opportunity for the development of gender-based differences in views of social and political issues than occurs in Japan (Lebra, 1984). Similarly, the greater role of education in knowledge in the United States seems a natural outgrowth of the distinctiveness of the educational systems in the two nations. Generally, the Japanese educational system focuses attention on the fundamentals of language arts, mathematics and natural science. The American educational system is inclined to be less rigid and to devote far greater attention to the development of individualism and problem solving skills (Nakamura, 1964; Ozawa, 1974).

The greater importance of family income, occupational status and generational cohort in Japan also may derive from different patterns of social stratification in the two nations. The Japanese social structure is commonly considered to be more rigid than that which exists in America. Social structural distinctions also are widely thought to have greater political meaning in Japan than in the United States. It is thus likely that the resources necessary for the exercise of political power-- such as knowledge--also will be more consistently attached to those background attributes (Nakane, 1970; Vogel, 1979).

Cross-national differences also appear in the impact of motivation on knowledge. Participation is important in Spokane while *attitudes* about citizen participation are important in Shizuoka. Citizen participation has been central to environmental movements in both countries, but, it is clear that localized citizen movements have had a relatively greater impact in Japan than in the United States (Krauss and Simcock, 1980). Indeed, in Japan the citizen's movement and the concept of citizen participation are directly tied to the environmental movement. Support for environmental change in Japan has been directly linked to participation in the citizen's movement and its ties to local political organizations (Lewis, 1980). Since there are relatively *few* citizen movements in contemporary Japanese politics (McKean, 1981), attitudes about citizen participation are quite likely tied to the same motivational roots as those that feed the consumption of policy-relevant information. In contrast, in the United States citizen movements are relatively plentiful. Moreover, participation in environmental policy processes is generally not directly tied to citizen movement politics at the mass level (Downs, 1972; VanLiere and Dunlap, 1980). Indeed, in the United States the environmental movement often has been accused of elitism in its social composition and in its goals (Milbrath, 1984).

The greater impact of participation in Spokane also meshes with the characteristics of environmental politics in the two locations. Environmental politics in Japan tends to be citizen movement politics, most often occurring in the context of locale-specific, victim-oriented political goals. Japanese participants in the environmental movement often are serendipitously involved as a consequence of their intersecting social connection with local political organizations and those organizations' involvements with citizen movements (Pierce et al., 1986a). Thus, the foundation for political involvement among the Japanese is likely to be less motivational and more structural than in the United States. In the United States, participation in the environmental movement is typically tied into no other local political structure (with the occasional exception of some general "good government" organizations, such as the League of Women Voters). For Americans, concern with the policy area itself--and often in a broad, more general and less locale-specific form--constitutes the primary drive to participate. This policy-based motivation also would fuel the desire for the acquisition, consumption, and use of policy-relevant information (Lovrich and Pierce, 1984).

Background and motivational attributes collectively explain a greater proportion of variation in knowledge in Spokane than in Shizuoka. This, too, reflects the character of environmental politics in the two locations. At the time of our surveys, the respective histories of environmental conflict differed somewhat in the two settings. The period of public arousal over environmental issues was substantially longer in Shizuoka than in Spokane. Consequently, there was greater opportunity for knowledge to become broadly diffused throughout the population, spanning motivational and background attributes that would otherwise lead to variable levels of knowledge. In Shizuoka, then, a "knowledge ceiling" may obtain for those with the characteristics normally leading to information gathering. A knowledge ceiling can occur for a variety of reasons (Ettema and Kline,

1977).   One reason is that after a certain period the most knowledgeable individuals reach a level beyond which they acquire little additional information while the least knowledgeable individuals begin to close the information gap.   The result is that factors which might differentiate among individuals early in the history of an environmental conflict tend to lose their differentiating power with the passage of time. If the Spokane conflict is sustained over a similar two-decade period of time at a rather elevated level of intensity and public salience, one may find that the collective predictive power of the motivational and background variables will be much less than is presently the case.

The Japanese and Americans differ in some important ways in their beliefs about the future--their postmaterial values, their support for the New Environmental Paradigm, and their support for Science and Technology.   Perhaps the most striking finding is the greater coherence found among the NEP beliefs for the *least* knowledgeable Japanese and for the *most* knowledgeable Americans.   This pattern may reflect a difference in the stage of postindustrial development separating Japan and the United States, and the extent to which beliefs composing the NEP reflect either traditional or "new" ways of thinking about the proper relationship between humans and nature.

More specifically, major socio-economic and political changes associated with postindustrialism can be unsettling to established and consensual belief systems.   Citizens must integrate new environmental realities and pressures from political values which are quite divergent from those to which they are accustomed.   Until widely accepted and traditional belief systems are by-and-large displaced by new consensual social paradigms, it is likely that there will be an uneven response to postindustrialism on the part of citizens (Catton and Dunlap, 1980).   It seems to us that the nature of belief system adaptation to postindustrial change will depend on three factors: 1) the extent to which citizens "engage" the relevant environmental changes; 2) the amount of change exhibited in the environment; and 3) the extent to which the resulting "new" paradigm is distinct from the "old" one. Since knowledge is one form of engagement with the environment, at the individual level more knowledgeable individuals will respond more rapidly to the belief system implications of postindustrial change.   The greater the amount of postindustrial change, the more extensive will be change in their belief system.   Finally, the more the new paradigm differs from the old, the greater will be the change in belief systems.

The American electorate exhibits greater value response to postindustrialism than does the Japanese citizenry--at least in these two study sites.   The new belief system paradigm produced by postindustrialism in Japan also seems a much less radical departure from the traditional Japanese environmental belief system than is the case in the American setting. The traditional view of the human to nature relationship in western nations has been human *domination* over nature, while the traditional Japanese view has been one of a natural unity of humans living in harmony with nature (Murota, 1985).

The four groups--Americans and Japanese with high and low knowledge--differ in significant ways, thereby affecting the organization of beliefs composing the New Environmental Paradigm. The Spokane high knowledge group exhibits NEP belief system consistency because that group has high engagement with the environment (knowledge), is in the system further along the developmental path (U.S.), and clearly understands the implications of postindustrial change for old and new views of the world. The Spokane low knowledge group has low consistency among NEP beliefs because, while it is in the more postindustrial country, persons in this group are without the knowledge required to make systematic and shared connections among the different parts of the "new" paradigm. The low knowledge group in Shizuoka, in contrast, has higher consistency among NEP beliefs because: 1) the "new" environmental paradigm is in fact similar to the traditional Japanese view of nature; 2) they do not possess the knowledge to see the conflicts between the new and the old; and 3) postindustrial development has not progressed to the point where those conflicts are apparent to the less knowledgeable. The high knowledge Shizuoka group is less consistent in its organization of NEP beliefs because it has the knowledge to see the conflicts between old and new views of the world. Moreover, Japanese postindustrial development has not proceeded to the point where even the highly informed have sorted out the relationships among the several NEP beliefs.

Another major difference between the Japanese and the Americans studied is the relative impact of knowledge on the relationship between postindustrial attitudes and environmental policy preferences. Knowledge heightens the impact of postindustrial attitudes to a greater extent in Spokane than in Shizuoka. Among Japanese citizens, participation elevates the relationship between postindustrial and environmental beliefs. These patterns, we have suggested, are consistent with the dominant characteristics of political mobilization in the two countries. Knowledge plays a larger role in the location (Spokane area) where mobilization is based in large part on a commitment to a particular view of the state of the environment, organized along the preservationist-developmentalist continuum.

Participation in the policy process, in contrast, has a greater effect in the locale (Shizuoka Prefecture) where political mobilization is primarily a consequence of one's integration into local political structures. In Shizuoka, much of the political debate in the past two decades has focused upon the role of citizen participation in public policy formation.

A different pattern emerges in the comparison of the Japanese and American respondents with respect to the role of knowledge in producing political power. Knowledge is more important in predicting power (understood as policy preference concurrence with incumbent decision makers) among the Japanese respondents than among their American counterparts. On the other hand, participation has a greater effect on power in Spokane. Even so, in both countries knowledge retains an independent impact on power, even under controls for education and participation.

These findings suggest that cross-national perspectives are central to understanding the role of citizens in promoting their self-interest and achieving political representation in postindustrial democracies (Enloe, 1975). While the forces of postindustrial change clearly constitute a powerful and common influence on contemporary democratic politics, there is nevertheless much political behavior which remains interpretable only in terms of nation-specific politics.

Political Power

One reason for studying knowledge relates to the need to understand the extent to which the enhanced dissemination of information affects the distribution of power in postindustrial societies. The preceding chapters suggest that knowledge does lead to political power--a finding of special relevance in postindustrial societies where complex scientific and technical issues appear on the political agenda. To be sure, disagreement exists as to the extent to which citizen preferences *should* be a central concern in public policy. Some commentators on postindustrial society advocate the empowerment of political guardians with both the knowledge of policy and the right to determine the public good (Moore, 1979). For those who advocate public influence on the policy process, two beliefs are cardinal: 1) that policy-relevant knowledge can be elevated (if found wanting) in the short-run; and 2) that elevated policy-relevant knowledge will promote rational citizen involvement and the formulation of appropriate policy outcomes (Barber, 1984).

The findings in Chapter 7 suggest that knowledge does indeed enhance citizen influence over public policy. To be sure, our measure of political power has its limitations. The fact that proportionally more elites agree with citizen A rather than citizen B obviously fails to prove that citizen A is the more powerful. The distribution of elite attitudes itself does not translate directly into a comparable probability of a particular policy outcome. Elite position in the policy process, the command of significant political resources, the degree to which the policy environment admits to change--these all intervene between elite preferences and the content of policy outcomes. These qualifications aside, however, citizens whose policy preferences *are* shared by greater proportions of elites would clearly be at an advantage in the public policymaking process.

Knowledge has an independent effect on power even while controlling for education and political participation; however, knowledge tends to share that influence with education and participation. Knowledge may provide a "leg up" in the power struggle, but it surely will take participation to complete the jump to political power. Individuals with higher levels of formal education and policy-relevant knowledge who participate in attempts to influence policy surely possess a powerful combination of resources giving them an advantage over those lacking such capabilities.

In this case, the impact of education on power probably is different than that exercised independently by knowledge. Education can represent a particular social status *and* it can reflect a package of general knowledge and insight. Since knowledge, education and participation frequently coincide, the lower status individual of any particular knowledge level may remain at some disadvantage. At the same time, persons lacking the requisite social status need not be relegated to the realm of the ineffectual. When knowledge and participation combine, persons of lower and middle social status possess a clear potential for the exercise of political power.

Democratic politics requires *both* the availability of knowledge and access to channels of political participation. However, neither the widespread dissemination of information nor the extensive exercise of rights to political participation occur in a political vacuum. The political environment in which the policy process unfolds must admit to both acumen and activity. The self-interested citizen is unable to become informed if the relevant knowledge is withheld by elites. Similarly, for the informed individual who wishes to influence policy, frustration and alienation inevitably follow the absence of a conduit for action. The democratic polity requires *both* that information be freely available to those who wish it, and that participatory paths to the policy process be open and clear to those who would follow them.

Self-Interest and Knowledge

If knowledge leads to power, the important question then arises as to "power to what end?" The answer throughout this work has been power for the purpose of achieving policy goals. Those goals are defined either in terms of individual self-interest, or in terms of personal or shared conceptions of the public interest (Held, 1970). To what extent, then, are preferences formed, ordered and applied in a way that suggests citizen understanding of their implications for their own interest (Hollis, 1979)? The empirical question is whether knowledge enhances self-interest among citizens in the complex public policies typical of postindustrial democracies.

Our evidence suggests that knowledge contributes to the citizen's ability to think about politics in ways that enhance their subjective self-interest. Subjective self-interest is reflected in the individual's own statements of their fundamental values and public policy goals. Our findings indicate that knowledge is associated with the consistent evaluation of policy alternatives. That is, such evaluations tend to be consistent with the individual's preferred values and policy goals. The most knowledgeable members of the public are most likely to hold consistent sets of policy orientations.

To be sure, all respondents tend to relate policy preferences to their general value orientations. However, the informed public is more likely to engage in such behavior systematically. Chapter Five showed that only for the high knowledge respondents--in both Japan and the United States--do the traditional political orientations of party identification and ideological inclination coexist on the same dimension as post-material value preferences. The informed citizens are particularly consistent in lining up their fundamental political goals-- their political values--with the major long-standing vehicles for policy implementation and political conflict (Lovrich and Pierce, 1986).

Public Educability

The possibility of democracy in the postindustrial age may, in the end, turn primarily on the question of the educability of the public. To be sure, some conceptions of "democracy" do not require highly involved, well-informed mass citizenries (Schumpeter, 1942). Even so, in postindustrial society knowledge would seem to be a particularly critical democratic resource. In novel and complex policy areas the public will begin in a knowledge-deficient state. The educability of the public thus takes center stage in discussions as to how best to proceed *politically* in generating public policy (Olien et al., 1983; Lovrich and Pierce, 1984).

If the public has some capacity to assimilate complex information, if knowledge "makes a positive difference" on the ability of citizens to perceive and act upon their self-interest, and if one is normatively committed to democratic processes, the political task becomes two-fold. First, the opportunity for genuine public involvement must be broadened to facilitate participation by the general public (Dahl, 1970). Second, the information relevant to the policy in question must be made available and must be made relatively inexpensive to acquire by the general public (Nelkin, 1979).

Our evidence on public educability suggests considerable elasticity in public knowledge. Recall, in particular, the distinction between transsituational and situation-specific correlates of knowledge holding. Transsituational variables reflect individuals' relatively unchangeable social and demographic characteristics. Those characteristics both would be carried across policy areas and would impose severe limits on the ability of some people to increase their knowledge. Situation-specific attributes vary across policy areas, and are elastic for the individual over time. This study found that both transsituational and situation-specific attributes have an independent impact on knowledge in both Shizuoka and Spokane.

In both locales a wide range of motivational attributes affect knowledge, even when controlling for the impact of an individual's background. The perceived seriousness of the policy area, perceptions of the value of citizen participation, level of policy area participation, and extremity of policy preference are all related to possession of knowledge. These results suggest that knowledge in the public might be altered by a focus on the citizen's motivational engagement of the policy domain. Highlighting the seriousness of policy area problems, emphasizing a belief in the importance of citizen involvement, facilitating active involvement for those with strong preferences--these will likely increase the public's knowledge. Such an increase will occur even for those who are characterized by background attributes limiting knowledge acquisition (e.g., Bowes et al., 1978; Goodfield, 1982).

While these data suggest the educability of the public, one ought not assume that individuals will be motivated to acquire information without some pressing reasons. In the absence of the public concern necessary for knowledge growth, what then is the appropriate strategy for enhancing public knowledge? One answer seems to be that the flow of information should come after communications about the significance of the policy area. A second response is to increase opportunities for citizen involvement, both opening up channels of influence and providing the incentives essential to stimulate information seeking.

In the area of environmental policy, there may be greater opportunity for public educability in the United States than in Japan. Motivation explains a greater proportion of the variance in knowledge among Americans than Japanese. Several explanations are possible. One possibility is that the Japanese social structure is more rigid than the American. Norms and mores attached to particular social locations in Japan would likely suppress the contribution of motivation to information gathering. A second possibility is that the coastal cities of Mishima, Numazu and Fuji in Shizuoka Prefecture have been flooded with information about environmental pollution. That flooding would mean that even individuals of relatively weak motivation levels have absorbed policy-relevant information. A third possibility is that the nature of much environmental participation in Japan may account for the somewhat lesser impact of motivation. For many Japanese, involvement in environmental politics is a by-product of attachment to local political organizations formed around traditional allegiances unrelated to concern about the environment.

Our conclusion, then, is that there exists substantial evidence that the public is educable. Relatively unchangeable socio-economic and demographic attributes do not impose rigid ceilings on knowledge among the mass public. Knowledge affects the exercise of political power. Knowledge also contributes to the perception of self-interest in political alternatives. Finally, motivational sources affect information acquisition. These findings provide considerable justification for the belief that public knowledge can be improved in a way that will enhance democratic government. It goes without saying, of course, that knowledge does not reside in a political vacuum. The potential for democratic government depends as clearly on the attributes of political institutions as it does on the qualities of the citizens (Sennett and Cobb, 1972; McWilliams, 1973; Kariel, 1977).

Knowledge and the Possibility of Democracy

The extent to which citizens are able to convert knowledge into self-interested and effective political behavior depends in large part on the nature of the political system. Three elements of the political environment seem particularly relevant in this respect. First, there must be a free flow of information available to the general public. Second, formal structures and elite attitudes must facilitate the public's use of such knowledge to influence public policy. Third, public policy issues must be framed in a manner that informs citizens of their stake in policy outcomes.

204

Information Flow

The public's ability to acquire information, to use that information to identify and expand on its self-interest, and to act on that knowledge in exercising political influence all depend on the availability of information. If knowledge is power for the public, it clearly is power for elites as well. Since elites develop their own definitions of the public interest (Latham, 1952; McConnell, 1966), they may feel compelled to restrict the flow of critical information to the public (Schattschneider, 1960: 97-142).

That the exercise of control over information is a political tool is neither an unusual nor recent observation (Galbraith, 1967: 291-303). It does, however, raise some significant questions about the implications of our findings for democratic publics. For example, under what conditions can one expect elites to expand rather than narrow the scope of the policy-relevant information made available to the public? One condition would be when a more informed public might be expected to contribute to the maintenance of elite power. Some elite groups may believe that an informed public would be unfailingly supportive of their own particular policy position (Zurcher, 1970). A second condition would be when one or more elite groups somehow believed that "better policy" would result from a more well-informed citizenry (Redford, 1969; Cantril and Cantril, 1974). The feeling that honest communication with the public will in the long run serve society well is a widespread article of faith in at least some democratic nations (Straussman, 1978). A third condition under which elites might disseminate information would be when they are required to make their knowledge public. Freedom of information and open-meeting laws, legislative and administrative requirements for citizen involvement, and the existence of a tradition of investigative reporting can all generate substantial pressure on elites to inform the general public of its interests in ongoing public policy matters (Gardner, 1961; 1964).

Public Knowledge and the Political Process

Individuals may have access to information, and the general public may be able to employ that knowledge in its thinking. Nonetheless, there remains no guarantee that the political system--formal structures and elite attitudes--will facilitate the public's attempt to influence policy. The public's application of knowledge to the political arena is problematic for several reasons.

First, important public policy decisions may be hidden from public view for various reasons of state--or for reasons of convenience.

Specific policy decisions that involve the implementation of general goals and guidelines may occur in the remote recesses of the bureaucracy, in locations largely unavailable even to the informed general public or inquisitive press (Nadel, 1971). Similarly, public policy outcomes may hinge upon critical legal decisions made by courts purposely removed from the push and pull of normal political life (Jacqueney, 1973). When the public has no policy impact, or believes it has no impact, the utility of acquiring information must be questioned. It is thus ironic that the public is criticized frequently for failing to have the requisite knowledge for becoming involved in policy areas far removed from its view or influence. That condition itself markedly diminishes the incentive to acquire information for all but the most intensely motivated citizens (Braybrooke and Lindblom, 1970: 169-173).

Second, even if citizens have access to the policy process, the alternatives may be framed in a way that knowledge will fail to contribute to the formation of individual preferences. In the electoral process, for example, ambiguity in issue positions may obscure the relevance of candidate positions. In other cases, the way the "real" policy decision is made may be irrelevant to public knowledge and beliefs. For example, the siting of nuclear waste depositories may be decided as much on the basis of national political forces as on the efficacy of geologic structures of specific sites (Rydell, 1984).

Changing political processes to create more access for informed citizens will have little impact unless information of the sort commanded by the public is a central element of the decision. For there to be public influence, the political process must be open to the information relevant to the citizen's policy preferences. We know that knowledge makes a difference in what people believe, how they put those beliefs together, how they apply those beliefs to the interpretation of incoming information and the exercise of political influence (Sheldon and Lovrich, 1982; Tichenor et at., 1970). We know that background attributes *and* motivations have independent impacts on public knowledge levels. We know too that the sources of knowledge and the consequences of knowledge are remarkably similar in two postindustrial countries possessed of distinct cultures, social traditions and political institutions.

We do *not* know, however, what particular political mechanisms might be best for both informing citizens of their choices for collective action and providing for their informed preferences to be translated into effective and responsive public policy. Should contemporary postindustrial democracies rely primarily on improving the informational content of the electoral process? Is the institutionalized, pluralistic group contest for power the best mechanism for more broadly disseminating the policy-relevant knowledge underlying contemporary political conflict? Should we perhaps seek refuge in a high-tech future of computer-linked households and instantaneous voting via two-way exchanges between citizens and government (Porat, 1977)? Or perhaps we should pay heed to those who warn of the false idols of science and technology, and seek comfort in a return to the wisdom of the ages and a re-establishment of smaller-scale, less complex forms of technical and social life (Mishan, 1967; Schumacher, 1973; Hirsch, 1976).

The form and content of public education will greatly affect the nature of the consequences of citizen involvement for the shaping of public policy. A system of public education may emphasize the rightful role of citizen involvement and develop talents for participation in democratic undertakings. Such a system will certainly occasion a higher level of motivation to acquire information among citizens than one which does not have these goals. Inevitably, however, one comes to the question of 'knowledge for what ends'. The education accorded postindustrial societies' elites must avoid the twin dangers of preparing 'technocrats' and 'technocretins' (Cook, 1985)--neither of whom has sufficient regard for a public voice in public policy to guarantee the sanctity of democratic forms. For the technocrats, the public can never be as qualified as they themselves--the "best and brightest"--to make decisions in the public interest. For the technocretins, the uninformed public's interference in the neat and orderly administration of public affairs can only serve to endanger the quality of governance. "Democratic leadership" obligates elites to both include and educate the public (Waldo, 1971). Finding the appropriate link between the citizen and the democratic, postindustrial polity is a difficult task. This task, though difficult, is at the very core of the challenge of postindustrial democratic politics.

References

Alford, Robert. (1963) *Party and Society*. New York: Rand McNally.

Alker, Hayward R., Jr. (1965) *Mathematics and Politics*. New York: Macmillan.

Almond, Gabriel A. and Sidney Verba. (1965) *The Civic Culture: Political Attitudes in Five Nations*. Boston: Little, Brown and Company.

Arnstein, Sherry. (1969) "A Ladder of Citizen Participation." *Journal of the American Institute of Planners* 35:216-228.

Barber, Benjamin. (1984) *Strong Democracy: Participatory Politics for a New Age*. Berkeley: University of California Press.

Barnes, Samuel and Max Kaase (eds). (1979) *Political Actions: Mass Participation in Five Western Democracies*. Beverly Hills, Calif: Sage Publications.

Bazelon, David T. (1967) *Power in America: The Politics of the New Class*. New York: McGraw-Hill Book Co.

Bell, Daniel. (1962) *The End of Ideology*. Glencoe, IL: The Free Press.

Bell, Daniel. (1973) *The Coming of Postindustrial Society*. New York: Basic Books.

Benjamin, Roger and Kan Ori. (1981) *Tradition and Change in Postindustrial Japan*. New York: Praeger Publishers.

Benveniste, Guy. (1972) *The Politics of Expertise*. Berkeley: Glendessary Press.

Berger, Peter L. (1979) "The Worldview of the New Class: Secularity and Its Discontents." In B. Bruce-Briggs (ed.), *The New Class? America's Educated Elite*. New York: McGraw-Hill Book Co.

Bowes, J.E., Stramm, K.R. and J. Moore. (1978) *Communication of Technical Information to Lay Audiences*. Seattle: School of Communications, University of Washington.

Braybrooke, David and Charles E. Lindblom. (1970) *A Strategy of Decision: Policy Evaluation as a Social Process*. New York: The Free Press.

Buchanan, James M. and Richard E. Wagner. (1978) *Fiscal Responsibility in Constitutional Democracy*. Hingham, MA: Kluwer Boston, Inc.

Burnham, Walter Dean. (1975) "The End of American Party Politics.: In Peter Woll (ed.), *American Government: Readings and Cases*, 5th Edition. Boston: Little, Brown and Company.

Campbell, Angus, Converse, Philip E., Miller, Warren E. and Donald E. Stokes. (1969) *The American Voter*. New York: John Wiley and Sons.

Cantril, Albert H. and Susan D. Cantril. (1974) *The Report of the Findings of the League Self-Study*. Washington, D.C.: League of Women Voters.

Catton, William R. and Riley E. Dunlap. (1978) "Environmental Sociology: A New Paradigm." *American Sociologist* 13:41-49.

Catton, William R. and Riley E. Dunlap. (1980) "A New Ecological Paradigm for Post-Exuberant Sociology." *American Behavioral Scientist* 24:15-47.

Chafee, S. and J. McLeod. (1973) "Individual Versus Social Predictors of Information Seeking." *Journalism Quarterly* 50:237-245.

Cirino, Robert. (1971) *Don't Blame the People: How the News Media Use Bias, Distortion and Censorship to Manipulate Public Opinion.* New York: Random House.

Cobb, Roger W. and Charles D. Elder. (1972) *Participation in American Politics: The Dynamics of Agenda-Building.* Boston: Allyn and Bacon, Inc.

Continental Group. (1982) *Toward Responsible Growth: Economic and Environmental Concern in the Balance.* Stamford, CT: The Continental Group, Inc.

Converse, Philip E. (1964) "The Nature of Belief Systems in Mass Publics." In David Apter (ed.), *Ideology and Discontent.* New York: The Free Press.

Converse, Philip E. (1975) "Public Opinion and Voting Behavior." In F. Greenstein and N. Polsby (eds.), *Handbook of Political Science, Vol. 4.* Reading, MA: Addison-Wesley.

Cook, Terrence. (1985) "Commentary on the Blacksburg Manifesto: A Polemic in Defense of Administrative Elitism in American Government." Paper presented at the Annual Meeting of the American Society for Public Administration (Region IX), Spokane, Washington.

Dahl, Robert A. (1970) *After the Revolution? Authority in a Good Society.* New Haven: Yale University Press.

Dahl, Robert A. (1985) *Controlling Nuclear Weapons: Democracy Versus Guardianship.* Syracuse: Syracuse University Press.

Dalton, Russell J., Beck, Paul Allen and Scott C. Flanagan. (1984) "Electoral Change in Advanced Industrial Democracies." In Russell J. Dalton, Scott C. Flanagan and Paul Allen Beck (eds.), *Electoral Change in Advanced Industrial Democracies.* Princeton: Princeton University Press.

Davies, J. Clarence. (1985) "Coping with Toxic Substances." *Issues in Science and Technology* 1:71-79.

DeSario, Jack and Stuart Langton. (1984) "Citizen Participation and Technology." *Policy Studies Review* 3:223-233.

Devine, Donald J. (1970) *The Attentive Public: Polyarchical Democracy.* Chicago: Rand McNally.

Dillman, Don A. (1978) *Mail and Telephone Surveys: The Total Design Method.* New York: John Wiley and Sons.

Donohue, G.A., Tichenor, P.S. and C.N. Olien. (1975) "Mass Media and the Knowledge Gap: A Hypothesis Reconsidered." *Communication Research* 2:3-23.

Douglas, Mary and Aaron Wildavsky. (1982) *Risk and Culture: An Essay on the Selection of Technical and Environmental Dangers.* Berkeley: University of California Press.

Downs, Anthony. (1957) *An Economic Theory of Democracy.* New York: Harper & Row.

Downs, Anthony. (1972) "Up and Down with Ecology--the 'Issue Attention Cycle.'" *Public Interest* 29:38-50.

Dunlap, Riley and Kent D. Van Liere. (1978) "The 'New Environmental Paradigm': A Proposed Measuring Instrument and Preliminary Results." *Journal of Environmental Education* 9:10-19.

Dunwoody, Sharon. (1980) "The Science Writing Inner Club: A Communication Link Between Science and the Lay Public." *Science, Technology and Human Values* 5:14-22.

Dutton, Diana. (1984) "The Impact of Public Participation in Biomedical Policy: Evidence from Four Case Studies." In James C. Petersen (ed.), *Citizen Participation in Science Policy.* Amherst: The University of Massachusetts Press.

Dye, Thomas R. (1976) *Policy Analysis: What Governments Do, Why They Do It, and What Difference It Makes.* University, AL: University of Alabama Press.

Easton, David. (1965) *A Systems Analysis of Political Life.* New York: John Wiley & Sons.

Edelman, Murray. (1964) *The Symbolic Uses of Politics.* Urbana: University of Illinois Press.

Enloe, Cynthia. (1975) *The Politics of Pollution in a Comparative Perspective.* New York: David McKay.

Environment Agency of Japan. (1982) *Public Opinion Poll on Environmental Pollution.* Tokyo: Government Printing Office.

Ettema, J.S. and F.G. Kline. (1977) "Deficits, Differences and Ceilings: Contingent Conditions for Understanding the Knowledge Gap." *Communication Research* 4:179-202.

Fiorina, Morris. (1980) "The Decline of Collective Responsibility in American Politics." *Daedalus* 109:25-46.

Flanagan, Scott C. (1979) "Value Change and Partisan Change in Japan." *Comparative Politics* 11:253-278.

Flanagan, Scott C. (1980) "Value Cleavages, Economic Cleavages and the Japanese Voter." *American Journal of Political Science* 24:177-206.

Flanagan, Scott C. (1982) "Changing Values in Advanced Industrial Societies." *Comparative Political Studies* 14:403-444.

Freudenburg, William R. and Eugene A. Rosa (eds.). (1984) *Public Reactions to Nuclear Power: Are There Critical Masses?* Boulder: Westview.

Fukutake, Tadashi. (1967) *Japanese Rural Society.* Ithaca: Cornell University Press.

Galbraith, John K. (1967) *The New Industrial State.* Boston: Houghton Mifflin.

Gans, Herbert J. (1973) *More Equality.* New York: Pantheon Books.

Gappert, Gary (1979) *Post-Affluent America: The Social Economy of the Future.* New York: Franklin Watts.

Gardner, John W. (1961) *Excellence.* New York: Harper & Row.

Gardner, John W. (1964) *Self-Renewal.* New York: Harper & Row.

Genova, B.K. and B.S. Greenberg. (1979) "Interest in the News and the Knowledge Gap." *Public Opinion Quarterly* 43:79-91.

Gibney, Frank. (1979) *Japan: The Fragile Super Power.* New York: Meridian Books.

Gilmour, Robert S. and Robert B. Lamb. (1975) *Political Alienation in Contemporary America.* New York: St. Martin's Press.

Godschalk, David R. and Bruce Stiftel. (1981) "Making Waves: Public Participation in State Water Planning." *Journal of Applied Behavioral Science* 17:597-614.

Goodfield, J. (1982) *Reflections of Science and the Media: Some Examples, Conclusions, and Constraints.* Washington, D.C.: American Association for the Advancement of Science.

Goodman, Paul and Percival Goodman. (1960) *Communitas: Means of Livelihood and Ways of Life.* New York: Vintage Books.

Gresser, Julian, Fujijura, Koichito and Akio Morishima. (1981) *Environmental Law in Japan.* Cambridge, MA: The MIT Press.

Groves, D.L. and B.J. Thompson. (1982) "Natural Resource Planning: The Complex Web of Special Interests." *International Journal of Environmental Studies* 19:17-24.

Gulowsen, Jon. (1976) "From Technological to Ecological Dominance." *Acta Sociologica* 19:357-374.

Hagner, Paul R. and John C. Pierce. (1982) "Correlative Characteristics of Levels of Conceptualization in the American Public." *Journal of Politics* 44:779-807.

Hagner, Paul R. and John C. Pierce. (1984) "Political Conceptualization and the Holding of Political Information." Paper presented at the Annual Meeting of the Midwest Political Science Association.

Hancock, M. Donald. (1972) "Post-Welfare Modernization in Sweden: The Quest for Cumulative Rationality and Equality." In M. Donald Hancock and Gideon Sjoberg (eds.), *Politics in the Post-Welfare State: Responses to the New Individualism.* New York: Columbia University Press.

Hanson, Donald W. (1979) "The Education of Citizens: Reflections on the State of Political Science." *Polity* 11:457-477.

Hardin, Garrett. (1968) "The Tragedy of the Commons." *Science* 162:1243-1248.

Heidenheimer, Arnold J., Heclo, Hugh and Carolyn Teich Adams. (1975) *Comparative Public Policy: The Politics of Social Choice in Europe and America.* New York: St. Martin's Press.

Heisler, Martin O. (ed.). (1974) *Politics in Europe: Structures and Processes in Some Postindustrial Democracies.* New York: McKay.

Held, Virginia. (1970) *The Public Interest and Individual Interests.* New York: Basic Books.

Hirsch, Fred. (1976) *The Social Limits to Growth.* Cambridge, MA: Harvard University Press.

Hofstede, Geert. (1979) "Value Systems in Forty Countries." In C.J. Lammers and D.J. Hickson (eds.), *Organizations Alike and Unalike: International and Inter-Institutional Studies in the Sociology of Organizations.* London: Routledge and Kegan Paul.

Hollis, Martin. (1979) "Rational Man and Social Science." In Rose Harrison (ed.), *Rational Action: Studies in Philosophy and Social Science.* London: Cambridge University Press [1-16].

Honadle, Beverly W. (1985) *Public Administration in Rural Areas and Small Jurisdictions: A Guide to the Literature.* New York: Garland Publishing.

Hottel, Althea K. (ed.). (1968) "Women Around the World" (Symposium issue title). *The Annals of the American Academy of Political and Social Science,* Vol. 375.

House, Verne W. (1981) *Shaping Public Policy: The Educator's Role.* Bozeman, MT: Westridge Publishing.

Huntington, Samuel P. (1974) "Postindustrial Politics: How Benign Will It Be?" *Comparative Politics* 6:163-191.

Ike, Nabutake. (1973) "Economic Growth and Intergenerational Change in Japan." *American Political Science Review* 67:1194-1203.

Inglehart, Ronald E. (1971) "The Silent Revolution in Europe: Intergenerational Change in Postindustrial Societies." *American Political Science Review* 65:991-1017.

Inglehart, Ronald E. (1977) *The Silent Revolution: Changing Values and Political Styles Among Western Publics.* Princeton: Princeton University Press.

Inglehart, Ronald E. (1979) "Value Priorities and Socioeconomic Change." In Samuel Barnes and Max Kaase (eds.), *Political Action: Mass Participation in Five Western Democracies.* Beverly Hills: Sage Publications.

Inglehart, Ronald E. (1981) "Postmaterialism in an Age of Insecurity." *American Political Science Review* 75:880-900.

Inglehart, Ronald E. (1982) "Changing Values in Japan and the West." *Comparative Political Studies* 14:445-479.

Inglehart, Ronald E. (1984) "The Changing Structure of Political Cleavages in Western Society." In Russell Dalton et al. (eds.), *Electoral Change: Realignment and Dealignment in Advanced Industrial Democracies.* Princeton, NJ: Princeton University Press.

Inglehart, Ronald E. (1985) "Aggregate Stability and Individual-Level Flux in Mass Belief Systems: The Level of Analysis Paradox." *American Political Science Review* 79:97-116.

Jacqueney, Theodore. (1973) "Nader Network Switches Focus to Legal Action, Congressional Lobbying." *National Journal* 5:840-849.

Jencks, Christopher. (1971) *Inequality: A Reassessment of the Effect of Family and Schooling in America.* New York: Harper Colophon books.

Jennings, M. Kent. (1981) "Comment on the Merelman-Jennings Exchange." *American Political Science Review* 75:155-156.

Jennings, M. Kent and Barbara G. Farah. (1980) "Ideology, Gender and Political Action: A Cross-National Survey." *British Journal of Political Science* 10:219-240.

Jennings, M. Kent and L. Harmon Zeigler. (1970) "The Salience of State Politics Among American Publics." In Edward C. Dreyer and Walter A. Rosenbaum (eds.), *Political Opinion and Behavior: Essays and Studies.* Belmont, CA: Wadsworth Publishing Company.

Kahn, Herman. (1972) *Things to Come.* New York: Macmillan.

Kariel, Henry S. (1977) *Beyond Liberalism, Where Relations Grow.* New York: Harper & Row.

Kessel, John. (1980) *Presidential Campaign Politics.* Homewood, IL: Dorsey Press.

Kimura, Shigeru. (1985) *Japan's Science Edge: How the Cult of Anti-Science Thought in America Limits U.S. Scientific and Technological Progress.* New York: University Press of America.

Krauss, E.S. and B.L. Simcock. (1980) "Citizens' Movements: The Growth and Impact of Environmental Protest in Japan." In Kurt Steiner, Ellis Krauss, and Scott Flanagan (eds.), *Political Opposition and Local Politics in Japan.* Princeton: Princeton University Press.

Kuklinski, John H., Metlay, Dennis S. and W.D. Kay. (1982) "Citizen Knowledge and Choices on the Complex Issue of Energy Policy." *American Journal of Political Science* 26:615-642.

Ladd, Everett Carl, with Charles D. Hadley. (1978) *Transformations of the American Party System,* 2nd Edition. New York: Norton.

Lafferty, William and O. Knutsen. (1985) "Postmaterialism in a Social Democratic State." *Comparative Political Studies* 17:411-430.

Lamb, Berton L. and Nicholas P. Lovrich. (1987) "Strategic Use of Technical Information in Urban Instream Flow Plans." *Water Resources Planning and Management.*

213

Lane, Robert. (1959) *Political Life: Why and How People Get Involved in Politics*. New York: The Free Press.

Lansing, Marjorie. (1974) "The American Woman, Voter and Activist." In J. Jacquette (ed.), *Women in Politics*. New York: John Wiley & Sons.

Lasch, Christopher. (1972) "Toward a Theory of Postindustrial Society." In M. Donald Hancock and Gideon Sjoberg (eds.), *Politics in the Post-Welfare State*. New York: Columbia University Press.

Latham, Earl. (1952) "The Group Basis of Politics: Notes for a Theory." *American Political Science Review* 46:376-397.

Lebra, S.T. (1984) *Japanese Women: Constraint and Fulfillment*. Honolulu: University of Hawaii Press.

Lewis, Jack G. (1975) *Hokaku Rengo: The Politics of Conservative-Progressive Cooperation in a Japanese City*. Ph.D. Dissertation, Stanford University.

Lewis, Jack G. (1980) "Civil Protest in Mishima: Citizens' Movements and the Politics of the Environment in Contemporary Japan." In Kurt Steiner, E.S. Krauss and Scott C. Flanagan (eds.), *Political Opposition and Local Politics in Japan*. Princeton: Princeton University Press [274-313].

Lipset, Seymour Martin and Stein Rokkan (eds.). (1967) *Party Systems and Voter Alignments: Cross-National Perspectives*. New York: The Free Press.

Lovrich, Nicholas P. and Takematsu Abe. (1984) "Citizen Participation in Scientific and Technical Policy Issues: A Japan-U.S. Comparative Study." Final Report to the Japan-U.S. Friendship Commission and the Institute of International Education for Japan-U.S. Faculty Pairing Program Grant, #I.I.E. 15822495.

Lovrich, Nicholas P. and John C. Pierce. (1984) "'Knowledge Gap' Phenomena: Effect of Situation-Specific and Transsituational Factors." *Communications Research* 11:415-434.

Lovrich, Nicholas P. and John C. Pierce. (1986) "The Good Guys and Bad Guys in Natural Resource Politics: Content and Structure of Perceptions of Interests Among General and Attentive Publics." *The Social Science Journal* 23:309-326.

Lovrich, Nicholas P., Pierce, John C., Tsurutani, Taketsugu and Takematsu Abe. (1985a) "Water Pollution Control in Democratic Societies: A Cross-National Analysis of Public Beliefs in Japan and the United States." *Policy Studies Review* 5:431-450.

Lovrich, Nicholas P., Pierce, John C., Tsurutani, Taketsugu and Takematsu Abe. (1985b) "Gender Differences in Policy Relevant Knowledge Holding: A Cross-National Analysis of Environmental Information Levels in the U.S. and Japan." In Glenna Spitze and Gwen Moore (eds.),

Women and Politics: Activism and Office-Holding. Greenwich, CT: JAI Press [147-170].

Lovrich, Nicholas P., Pierce, John C., Tsurutani, Taketsugu and Takematsu Abe. (1986) "Policy Relevant Information and Public Attitudes: Is Public Ignorance a Barrier to Nonpoint Pollution Management?" *Water Resources Bulletin* 22:229-236.

Maloney, Michael P., Ward, Michael P. and G. Nicholas Braught. (1975) "A Revised Scale for the Measurement of Ecological Attitudes and Knowledge." *American Psychologist* 30:787-792.

Marsh, Alan. (1978) "The 'Silent Revolution', Value Priorities, and the Quality of Life in Britain." *American Political Science Review* 69:21-30.

Marsh, Alan and Max Kaase. (1979) "Measuring Political Action." In Samuel Barnes and Max Kaase (eds.), *Political Action*. Beverly Hills: Sage Publications.

Maslow, Abraham H. (1970) *Motivation and Personality*, 2nd Edition. New York: Harper & Row.

Maslow, Abraham H. (1971) *The Farther Reaches of Human Nature*. New York: Viking Press.

Matsushita, Keiichi. (1975) "Politics of Citizen Participation." *Japan Interpreter* IX:451-465.

Mazmanian, Daniel A. and Jeanne Nienaber. (1976) "Prospects for Public Participation in Federal Agencies: The Case of the Army Corps of Engineers." In J.C. Pierce and H.R. Doerksen (eds.), *Water Politics and Public Involvement*. Ann Arbor: Ann Arbor Science.

Mazmanian, Daniel and Jeanne Nienaber. (1979) *Can Organizations Change?* Washington, D.C.: Brookings Institute.

Mazur, Allan. (1981) "Media Coverage and Public Opinion on Scientific Controversies." *Journal of Communication* 31:106-115.

McClosky, Herbert. (1964) "Consensus and Ideology in American Politics." *American Political Science Review* 58:361-382.

McClosky, Herbert. (1984) *The American Ethos: Public Attitudes Toward Capitalism and Democracy*. Cambridge, MA: Harvard University.

McConnell, Grant. (1966) *Private Power and American Democracy*. New York: Alfred A. Knopf.

McFarland, Andrew S. (1976) *Public Interest Lobbies: Decisions Making on Energy*. Washington, D.C.: American Enterprise Institute.

McKean, Margaret. (1974) *The Potential for Grass-Roots Democracy in Post-War Japan: The Anti-Pollution Movement as a Case Study in Political Activism*. Ph.D. Dissertation, University of California, Berkeley.

McKean, Margaret. (1981) *Environmental Protest and Citizen Politics in Japan*. Berkeley: University of California Press.

McWilliams, Wilson C. (1973) *The Idea of Fraternity in America*. Berkeley: University of California Press.

Meier, Kenneth J. (1975) "Representative Bureaucracy." *American Political Science Review* 69:526-547.

Milbrath, Lester. (1965) *Political Participation.* Chicago: Rand McNally and Company.

Milbrath, Lester W. (1984) *Environmentalists: Vanguard for a New Society.* Albany: State University of New York Press.

Miller, Jon. D., Suchner, R.W. and A.M. Voelker. (1980) *Citizenship in an Age of Science: Changing Attitudes Among Young Adults.* New York: Pergamon Press.

Miller, Warren E. and Teresa E. Levitin. (1976) *Leadership and Change.* Cambridge, MA: Winthrop Publishers.

Mishan, E.J. (1967) *The Costs of Economic Growth.* New York: Praeger Publishers.

Mitchell, Robert Cameron. (1980) *Public Opinion on Environmental Issues: Results of a National Opinion Survey.* Washington, D.C.: Resources for the Future.

Mitchell, Robert Cameron. (1984) "Rationality and Irrationality in the Public's Perception of Nuclear Power." In William R. Fraudenburg and Eugene A Rosa (eds.), *Public Reactions to Nuclear Power: Are There Critical Masses?* Boulder: Westview.

Monroe, Alan D. (1975) *Public Opinion in America.* New York: Dodd, Mead and Company.

Moore, Nancy. (1983) "A Sense of Limit." In A. Bruce Boenau and Katsuyuku Niro (eds.), *Post-Industrial Society.* New York: University Press of American.

Moore, S.W. (1979) "A Problem for the Future of 'Democracy': Complexity-Ignorance." *Futurics* 3:245-258.

Murota, Yasuhiro. (1985) "Culture and the Environment in Japan." *Environmental Management* 9:105-112.

Nadel, Mark V. (1971) *The Politics of Consumer Protection.* Indianapolis: Bobbs-Merrill.

Naisbitt, John. (1982) *Megatrends: Ten New Directions Transforming Our Lives.* New York: Warner Books.

Nakamura, Hajime. (1964) *Ways of Thinking of Eastern Peoples: India, China, Tibet and Japan.* Honolulu: East-West Center Press.

Nakane, Chie. (1970) *Japanese Society.* Berkeley: University of California Press.

Nelkin, Dorothy. (1979) "Scientific Knowledge, Public Policy, and Democracy: A Review Essay." *Knowledge: Creation, Diffusion, Utilization* 1:106-122.

Nelkin, Dorothy. (1984) "Science and Technology Policy and the Democratic Process." In James C. Petersen (ed.), *Citizen Participation in Science Policy.* Amherst, MA: University of Massachusetts Press.

216

Nie, Norman H., Verba, Sidney and John R. Petrocik. (1976) *The Changing American Voter*. Cambridge, MA: Harvard University Press.

Nimmo, Dan. (1978) *Political Communication and Public Opinion in America*. Santa Monica, CA: Goodyear Publishing Company.

Olien, C.N., Donohue, G.A. and P.J. Tichenor. (1983) "Structure, Communication and Social Power: Evolution of the Knowledge Gap Hypothesis." In E. Wartella and D.C. Whitney (eds.), *Mass Communication Review Yearbook*, Vol. 4. Beverly Hills: Sage Publications.

Olson, Mancur. (1982) *The Rise and Decline of Nations: Economic Growth, Stagflation, and Social Rigidities*. New Haven: Yale University Press.

Ozawa, T. (1974) *Japan's Technological Challenge to the West, 1950-1974: Motivation and Accomplishment*. Cambridge, MA: MIT Press.

Parenti, Michael. (1978) *Power and the Powerless*. New York: St. Martin's Press.

Pharr, Susan. (1981) *Political Women in Japan*. Berkeley: University of California Press.

Pierce, John C. (1977) "The Role of Preservationist Identification in the Belief Systems of Water Resource Group Leaders." *Polity* 9:538-550.

Pierce, John C., Beatty, Kathleen M. and Harvey R. Doerksen. (1976) "Rational Participation and Public Involvement in Water Resource Politics." In John C. Pierce and Harvey Doerksen (eds.), *Water Politics and Public Involvement*. Ann Arbor: Ann Arbor Science.

Pierce, John C. and Harvey R. Doerksen (eds.). (1976) *Water Politics and Public Involvement*. Ann Arbor: Ann Arbor Science Publishers.

Pierce, John C. and Nicholas P. Lovrich. (1980) "Belief Systems Concerning the Environment: The General Public, Attentive Publics, and State Legislators." *Political Behavior* 2:259-286.

Pierce, John C. and Nicholas P. Lovrich. (1982) "Survey Measurement of Political Participation: Selective Effects of Recall in Petition Signing." *Social Science Quarterly* 63:164-171.

Pierce, John C. and Nicholas P. Lovrich, (1986) *Water Resources, Democracy and the Technical Information Quandary*. Port Washington, NY: Associated Faculty Press.

Pierce, John C., Tsurutani, Taketsugu, Lovrich, Nicholas P. and Takematsu Abe. (1986a) "Vanguards and Rearguards in Environmental Politics: A Comparison of Activists in Japan and the United States." *Comparative Political Studies* 18:419-447.

Pierce, John C., Lovrich, Nicholas P. Tsurutani, Taketsugu and Takematsu Abe. (1986b) "Culture, Politics and Mass Publics: Traditional and Modern Supporters of the New Environmental Paradigm in Japan and the United States." *Journal of Politics* 48:43-63.

Pitkin, Hanna F. (1967) *The Concept of Representation*. Berkeley: University of California Press.

Porat, Marc. (1977) *Information Economy: Definition and Measurement*. Washington, D.C.: Office of Telecommunications, U.S. Department of Commerce.

Pranger, Robert J. (1968) *The Eclipse of Citizenship: Power and Participation in Contemporary Politics*. New York: Holt, Rinehart and Winston.

Rankin, William L. and Stanley M. Nealey. (1978) "Attitudes of the Public About Nuclear Wastes." *Nuclear News* 21:112-117.

Redford, Emmett S. (1969) *Democracy in the Administrative State*, Revised Edition. New York: St. Martin's Press.

Reich, Michael. (1983) "Environmental Policy and Japanese Society: Part I -- Successes and Failures." *International Journal of Environmental Studies* 20:191-198.

Reischauer, Edwin O. (1977) *The Japanese*. Cambridge, MA: Harvard University Press.

Richardson, B.M. (1974) *The Political Culture of Japan*. Berkeley: University of California Press.

Roelofs, H. Mark. (1976) *Ideology and Myth in American Politics: A Critique of a National Political Mind*. Boston: Little, Brown and Company.

Rokeach, Milton. (1968) *Beliefs, Attitudes and Values*. San Francisco: Jossey-Bass.

Rokeach, Milton. (1973) *The Nature of Human Values*. New York: The Free Press.

Rokeach, Milton. (1979) *Understanding Human Values: Individual and Societal*. New York: The Free Press.

Rosch, Eleanor. (1977) "Human Categorization." In N. Warren (ed.), *Studies in Cross-Cultural Psychology*, Vol. 1. London: Academic Press.

Rosenbaum, Nelson M. (1978) "The Origins of Citizen Involvement in Federal Programs." In C. Bezold and A. Toffler (eds.), *Anticipatory Democracy: People in the Politics of the Future*. New York: Vintage Books.

Rosenbaum, Walter A. (1973) *The Politics of Environmental Concern*. New York: Praeger Publishers.

Roszak, Theodore. (1972) *Where the Wasteland Ends: Politics and Transcendence in Postindustrial Society*. New York: Doubleday Press.

Rydell, Randy J. (1984) "Solving Political Problems of Nuclear Technology: The Role of Public Participation." In James C. Petersen (ed.), *Citizen Participation in Science Policy*. Amherst: University of Massachusetts Press.

Sartori, Giovanni. (1969) "Politics, Ideology and Belief Systems." *American Political Science Review* 63:398-441.

Schattschneider, E.E. (1960) *The Semisovereign People*. New York: Holt, Rinehart and Winston.

Schumacher, E.F. (1973) *Small is Beautiful: Economics as if People Mattered*. New York: Harper & Row.

Schumpeter, Joseph. (1942) *Capitalism, Socialism and Democracy*. New York: Harper & Row.

Segal, Howard P. (1985) *Technological Utopianiam in American Culture*. Chicago: The University of Chicago Press.

Sennett, Richard. (1978) *The Fall of Public Man: On the Social Psychology of Capitalism*. New York: Random House.

Sennett, Richard and Jonathan Cobb. (1972) *The Hidden Injuries of Class*. New York: Alfred A. Knopf.

Seward, Georgene H. and Robert C. Williamson (eds.). (1970) *Sex Roles in Changing Society*. New York: London House.

Sheldon, Charles H. and Nicholas P. Lovrich. (1982) "Judicial Accountability vs. Responsibility: Balancing the Views of Voters and Judges." *Judicature* 65:470-480.

Short, James F. (1984) "The Social Fabric at Risk: Toward the Social Transformation of Risk Analysis." *American Sociological Review* 49:711-725.

Sigel, Roberta S. and Marilyn B. Hoskin. (1981) *The Political Involvement of Adolescents*. New Brunswick: Rutgers University Press.

Simcock, B.L. (1973) "Citizens' Movements." *Japan Quarterly* 20:368-373.

Soden, Dennis L., Lovrich, Nicholas P. and John C. Pierce. (1985) "City-Suburb Perceptions of Groundwater Issues." *Proceedings of the American Water Resources Association Symposium on Groundwater Contamination and Reclamation (Tucson, Arizona)*.

Spokane County Engineers. (1982) "Synopsis of 208 Project." (Application for Award for Outstanding Local Projects for National Association of Counties). [Unpublished Manuscript].

Straussman, Jeffrey D. (1978) *The Limits of Technocratic Politics*. New Brunswick, NJ: Transaction Books.

Swanson, Thor and Nand Hart-Nabbrig. (1978) "Grass Roots in Washington." In Frank E. Mullen et al. (eds.), *The Government and Politics of Washington State*. Pullman, WA: Washington State University Press.

Tait, John, Wells, Betty L. and Ronald C. Powers. (1980) "An Evaluation of a Statewide Public Affairs Program: Land, Water and Energy in Century III." Technical Report PP61 of the Iowa State University Cooperative Extension Service. Ames, Iowa: I.S.U. Co-op Extension.

Takabatake, M. (1975) "Citizens' Movements: Organizing the Spontaneous." *Japan Interpreter* 9:315-323.

Tatalovich, Raymond and Byron W. Daynes. (1984) "Moral Controversies and the Policymaking Process: Lowi's Framework Applied to the Abortion Issue." *Policy Studies Review* 3:207-222.

Theobald, Robert. (1978) "The Deeper Implications of Citizen Participation." In C. Bezold and A. Toffler (eds.), *Anticipatory Democracy: People in the Politics of the Future*. New York: Vintage Books.

Thomas, Norman C. (1975) *Education in National Politics*. New York: McKay.

Tichenor, P.J., Donohue, G.A. and C.N. Olien. (1970) "Mass Media and Differential Growth in Knowledge." *Public Opinion Quarterly* 34:158-170.

Touraine, Alain. (1971) *The Post-Industrial Society: Tomorrow's Social History*. New York: Random House.

Truman, David B. (1951) *The Governmental Process: Political Interests and Public Opinion*. New York: Alfred A. Knopf.

Tsurutani, Taketsugu. (1977) *Political Change in Japan: Response to Postindustrial Challenge*. New York: McKay.

Van Deth, Jan W. (1983) "The Persistence of Materialist and Post-Materialist Value Orientations." *European Journal of Political Research* 11:63-79.

Van Liere, Kent D. and Riley E. Dunlap. (1980) "The Social Bases of Environmental Concern: A Review of Hypotheses, Explanations and Empirical Evidence." *Public Opinion Quarterly* 44:181-197.

Verba, Sidney and Norman H. Nie. (1972) *Participating in America: Political Democracy and Social Equality*. New York: Harper & Row.

Verba, Sidney, Nie, Norman H. and Jae-on Kim. (1978) *Participation and Political Equality*. London: Cambridge University Press.

Vickers, Geofrey. (1972) *Freedom in a Rocking Boat: Changing Values in an Unstable Society*. Middlesex, England: Penguin Books.

Waldo, Dwight. (1971) "Some Thoughts on Alternatives, Dilemmas, and Paradoxes in a Time of Turbulence." In D. Waldo (ed.), *Public Administration in a Time of Turbulence*. Scranton, PA: Chandler Publishing Company.

Wassenberg, Pinky S., Wolsborn, Kay G., Hagner, Paul R. and John C. Pierce. (1983) "Gender Differences in Political Conceptualization: 1956-1980." *American Politics Quarterly* 11:181-203.

Weissberg, Robert. (1978) "Collective vs. Dyadic Representation in Congress." *American Political Science Review* 72:535-547.

Welch, Susan and Patricia Secret. (1981) "Sex, Race and Political Participation." *Western Political Quarterly* 34:5-16.

Wenk, Edward, Jr. (1979) "Political Limits in Steering Technology: Pathologies of the Short Run." *Technology in Society* 1:27-36.

Wenner, Lettie McSpadden. (1982) *The Environmental Decade in Court*. Bloomington: Indiana University Press.

Wise, David. (1973) *The Politics of Lying: Government Deception, Secrecy and Power*. New York: Random House.

Yankelovich, Daniel. (1984) "Science and the Public Process: Why the Gap Must Close." *Issues in Science and Technology* 1:6-12.

Zimbardo, Philip and Ebbe B. Ebbesen. (1970) *Influencing Attitudes and Changing Behavior.* Menlo Park, CA: Addison-Wesley.

Zurcher, Louis A. (1970) "The Poverty Board: Some Consequences of 'Maximum Feasible Participation'." *Journal of Social Issues* 26:85-107.

About the Authors

John C. Pierce is Dean, Division of Humanities and Social Sciences, College of Sciences and Arts and Professor of Political Science at Washington State University. His research interests include the study of the structuring and content of individual political thinking, especially in the area of environmental politics. His work has been published in such journals as the *American Political Science Review*, *Social Science Quarterly*, *Journal of Politics*, *American Journal of Political Science*, and *Political Behavior*.

Nicholas P. Lovrich is Professor of Political Science and Director of the Division of Governmental Studies and Services at Washington State University. His research interests include the area of citizen participation in environmental policy processes, and his current writing on environmental politics in Japan and the United States stems from a grant from the Japan-U.S. Friendship Commission (administered by the Institute of International Education). His work has been published in such journals as *Comparative Political Studies*, *Journal of Politics*, *Political Behavior*, *Western Political Quarterly*, *Social Science Quarterly*, *Public Administration Review* and *Policy Studies Review*.

Taketsugu Tsurutani is Professor and Chairman, Department of Political Science at Washington State University. His current research interests are postindustrialism, Third World politics, and international security. His published work includes *Politics of National Development: Political Leadership in Transitional Societies*, *Political Change in Japan: Response to Postindustrial Challenge*, *Japanese Policy* and *East Asian Security* and articles in such journals as *Comparative Political Studies*, *Administration and Society*, *Asian Quarterly*, and the *Journal of Politics*.

Takematsu Abe is a Professor of Political Science in the College of International Relations at Nihon University. His research interests include comparative (Japan and the United States) environmental politics, American politics, and comparative regional and local government. His current writing is focused upon the areas of U.S. and Japanese environmental politics, reflecting his recent receipt of a grant from the Japan-U.S. Friendship Commission and the Ohta Foundation.

Author Index

Hadley, Charles D., 3, 4
Hagner, Paul R. 45n, 48
Hancock, M. Donald, 164
Hanson, Donald W., 144
Hardin, Garrett, 92
Hart-Nabbrig, Nand, 98
Heidenheimer, Arnold J., 9
Heisler, Martin O., 2
Held, Virginia, 201
Hirsch, Fred, 206
Hofstede, Geert, 97
Hollis, Martin, 201
Honadle, Beverly, 65
Hoskin, Marilyn B., 7, 62
Hottel, Althea, 60
House, Verne W., 73
Huntington, Samuel P., 2

Ike, Nabutake, 8, 9, 65, 71n, 96, 195
Inglehart, Ronald E., 2, 5, 6, 7, 8, 9, 10, 62, 79, 96, 97, 98, 99

Jacqueney, Theodore, 205
Jencks, Christopher, 49
Jennings, M. Kent, 48, 59, 60, 72
Johnson, Chalmers, 49

Kaase, Max, 10, 48
Kahn, Herman, 95
Kariel, Henry S., 203
Kessel, John, 35, 48
Kimura, Shigeru, 96
Kline, F.G., 12, 46, 47, 196
Knutsen, O., 8
Krauss, E.S., 16, 195
Kuklinski, John H., 22, 129
Kyogoku, Jun'ichi, 65, 71n

Ladd, Everett C., 3, 4
Lafferty, William, 8
Lamb, Berton L., 75, 161
Lane, Robert, 66

Langton, Stuart, 4
Lansing, Marjorie, 59
Lasch, Christopher, 2, 108
Latham, Earl, 204
Lebra, S.T., 60, 195
Levitin, Teresa E., 9, 108
Lewis, Jack C., 16, 62, 75, 89, 99, 133, 196
Lindblom, Charles E., 205
Lipset, Seymour Martin, 4
Lovrich, Nicholas P., 1, 12, 21n, 23, 28, 71n, 73, 74, 75, 86, 89, 95, 129, 131, 144, 165, 196, 201, 205

Maloney, Michael P., 23
Marsh, Alan, 8, 48
Maslow, Abraham, 6, 7, 97
Matsushita, Keiichi, 17, 96, 195
Mazmanian, Daniel, 10, 133
Mazur, Allan, 95
McClosky, Herbert, 4, 84
McConnell, Grant, 204
McFarland, Andrew S., 161
McKean, Margaret, 16, 63, 96, 133, 144, 194, 196
McLeod, J., 46
McWilliams, Wilson C., 203
Meier, Kenneth J., 166
Milbrath, Lester W., 2, 15, 17, 18, 73, 101, 128n, 196
Miller, Jon D., 35, 104, 166
Miller, Warren E., 9, 108
Mishan, E.J., 206
Mitchell, Robert Cameron, 96, 104
Monroe, Alan D., 163
Moore, Nancy, 96
Moore, S.W., 3, 129, 199
Murota, Yasuhiro, 104, 127, 198

Nadel, Mark V., 205
Naisbitt, John, 104, 161
Nakamura, Hajime, 195
Nakane, Chie, 49, 69, 195

Subject Index

Audubon Society, 35

Capitalism, 4
Citizen Knowledge, 10, 191
   and democracy, 203-206
   in Japan, 32, 35, 41, 44, 69, 71,
      77, 193-194
   and political power, 199-200
   and self interest, 201
   in Shizuoka, 60, 172, 175, 184,
      190-191, 194-195, 203
   in Spokane, 60, 172, 175, 184,
      190-191, 194-195, 202
   in United States, 35, 41, 44, 69,
      193-194
   see also Knowledge; Policy-
      Relevant Knowledge; Public
      Knowledge
Civil Rights, 5
Collectivism, 8
Council on Environmental Quality,
   104

DNA, 5

Environmental Activists, 14, 164-
   165
   see also Environmentalists
Environmental Agency of Japan,
   32
Environmental Beliefs,
   attitudinal sources of, 146-156
Environmental Policy, 2, 10, 17
Environmental Politics, 14
Environmental Pollution, 2, 79,
   135-140
   in Japan, 16, 203

Environmentalism 5, 9, 17-18, 104
   in Japan 91, 96, 164
   in United States, 17, 96, 164
Environmentalists, 19, 33, 35
   American, 17
   Japanese, 17
   see also Environmental
      Activists

Fuji City, Japan, 19, 20, 37, 45n,
   203

Great Britain, 49

Industrial Pollution
   in Japan, 16
"Information Generalists," 41
Information Holding, 49-56, 59
   see also Knowledge Holding;
      Public Knowledge
"Information Specialists," 41, 44
Italy, 49

Japan, 1 15-19, 24, 59, 65, 75, 81,
   123
   citizen knowledge in, 32, 35, 41,
      44, 69, 71, 77, 194-195
   and class identification, 56
   and collectivism, 81, 122
   education levels in, 50-52
   Environmental policy
      formation in, 133, 164-165
   income levels in, 49
   knowledge of environmental
      law in, 32-35
   nature of politics in, 146
   occupational structure in, 54

226

distribution of knowledge in,
39-44
environmental policy attitudes
in, 139, 141, 148, 159
policy-relevant knowledge in,
62, 144
political participation in, 116,
175, 196
postmaterialist values in, 99,
146, 148, 166
support for science and
technology in, 107, 127-128
Sierra Club, 35
Socialism, 4
Soil Pollution, 24, 26
Spokane, Washington, 18-20, 37,
41, 69, 84, 86, 118, 131, 134-
135, 151, 154, 164
citizen knowledge in, 60, 71,
121, 172, 175, 183, 189-190,
201
citizen power in, 169, 175
and class identification, 56, 59
concentration of knowledge in,
39-44
distribution of knowledge in,
22, 26, 28, 30
environmental policy attitudes
in, 139, 141, 148, 159
knowledge of environmental
conditions in, 32-35
policy-relevant knowledge in,
62, 144
political participation in, 116,
175, 195
postmaterialist values in, 98,
108, 146, 164
support for science and
technology in, 107, 127-128
Spokane County, Washington, 14,
18, 99
Star Wars, 6
Strategic Defense Initiative, 5

Technical Information Quandary, 1
Technocrats, 206
Tokyo, Japan, 60, 139

United States, 1, 15-18, 24, 26, 30,
59, 74
citizen knowledge in, 35, 41, 44,
69
and class identification, 56
concentration of knowledge in,
39, 44
education levels in, 50-52
educational systems in, 49
environmental policy formation
in, 133, 164-165
income levels in, 54
occupational structure in, 54
policy-relevant information in,
10
political behavior in, 66
political culture in, 193-198
political participation in, 84-86
political parties in, 161
postmaterialist values in, 113-
115
technical term familiarity in,
26-32

Washington, D.C., 17
West Germany, 49
Women's Rights, 5